D1545014

Colonial Kitchens,
Their Furnishings, and Their Gardens

THE FIRST DEFINITIVE
ACCOUNT BASED ON SETTLERS'
JOURNALS AND TRAVELERS'
DIARIES

Colonial Kitchens, Their Furnishings, and Their Gardens

BY FRANCES PHIPPS

DRAWINGS BY
KATHERINE HICKISH

A Helen Van Pelt Wilson Book

Hawthorn Books, Inc.
PUBLISHERS   NEW YORK

COLONIAL KITCHENS, THEIR FURNISHINGS, AND THEIR GARDENS

Copyright © 1972 by Frances Phipps. Copyright under International and Pan-American Copyright Conventions. All rights reserved, including the right to reproduce this book, or portions thereof, in any form, except for the inclusion of brief quotations in a review. All inquiries should be addressed to Hawthorn Books, Inc., 260 Madison Avenue, New York, New York 10016. This book was manufactured in the United States of America and published simultaneously in Canada by Prentice-Hall of Canada, Limited, 1870 Birchmount Road, Scarborough, Ontario.

Library of Congress Catalog Card Number: 78-158021.
ISBN: 0-8015-1434-7
3 4 5 6 7 8 9 10

TYPOGRAPHY BY HERBERT H. JOHNSON

For My Parents

FOREWORD
The Heart of the House

IN RECENT YEARS there has been increasing interest in the need to preserve those historic sites, especially old houses, still left to us. Throughout the country these buildings are being saved as never before through concerted work on federal, state, and local levels.

This interest is reflected in the growing number of local historical societies and state historical commissions, each organized to salvage and preserve tangible history through the acquisition of buildings and the collection of local and regional memorabilia of all types. Renewed concern is shown in the number of museum period rooms, either removed as a whole from ancient houses or reconstructed from antique materials and then furnished with the finest available examples of the decorative arts. A special—and too-often unremarked—contribution to the communities in which they live is also being made by innumerable private owners of old houses who enjoy the family avocation of restoring early homes for their own use.

All of this concern is commendable. However, as we continue, we are faced with the need to find adequate answers to fundamental questions: How exactly should each old house or room properly be interpreted and used? What will the restored house or period room say about the life-style of the original occupants? What will it reveal of the exigencies of the age in which it was built? Does it reflect the home of a wealthy or a poor man? Is it faithful to the craft standards of the colony in which its builder lived?

Too often, for want of time or adequate financing, or for lack of personnel trained in research, societies, committees, and individuals alike compromise and install what each would like to believe might have been used. In such cases the result is that the visitor to many an "historic house" or "period room" departs with distorted impressions. The visitor who had

[vii]

hoped to gain a sense of the immediacy of history instead may be confronted with a panorama of rare antiques, arranged by decorators in accordance with twentieth-century taste. The effect of such a setting is overwhelming; the visitor is awed by his ancestors' impeccable taste and sophisticated use of decorative themes. The other extreme, perhaps more common, is experienced by the visitor who is shown a hodge-podge of unrelated items thrown together with little knowledge of how they originally were used. Certainly it is discouraging to anyone who had hoped for assistance in planning the restoration of his own house.

Of course, we cannot know today exactly with which pieces each old house was furnished or where those furnishings were placed, but we can apply common sense to any restoration. Perhaps the first logical step is to refuse to allow our twentieth-century life to influence the choice of furnishings for a period house or room, that is, if we want the result to be true to history. Too often our likes and dislikes influence selection even of paint colors, floor coverings, and curtain fabrics. Often we "restore" by reaching the conclusion that surely "they" would have done thus and so or "they" would not have violated our preferences by, for example, combining what to us is a clash of colors and patterns.

Another widespread misconception—especially in later eighteenth-century restorations—is that each house or room must be furnished according to one period style. Today's planned obsolescence would have shocked the eighteenth-century family; in the colonial era it was not good sense to discard useful furnishings because new designs had appeared. The sensible colonist did not give away a Queen Anne high chest or Chippendale table or even his great-great-grandfather's Jacobean chair simply because the work of an Adam or a Hepplewhite disciple was being purchased by others. A functional piece of furniture was kept over the years and handed down from one generation to another.

Estate inventories, diaries, and account books make this obvious. The inventory of the estate of Mrs. Mary Lisle, taken at Philadelphia in 1763, included "3 Turkey workd chairs" and "1 Japand corner cupboard," an eclectic group of parlor furnishings that were more popular in the late seventeenth century and during the early years of the eighteenth century than when she died. Solomon Fussell, a furniture-maker of the same city, in 1714 charged a customer for an "ornament Ball for a Dressing Table," an appendage that suggests a William and Mary decoration being used in the Georgian period.

It is reasonable, therefore, that an early house or period room, especially one representing the later eighteenth century, should be furnished with a mixture of styles to give a true-to-life appearance, create a feeling of intimacy with the taste of the original owners, and sustain for us today

Seventeenth-century casement. Diamond-shaped panes are set in iron with three horizontal wood rods for extra support. Hempsted House, New London, Connecticut.

a more accurate sense of the past. Obviously, the only sources of information that can help us furnish period houses and rooms authentically are the contemporary manuscripts and printed records of the age itself; only from these bits and pieces can we extract the true flavor of the colonial era.

Of all the rooms of the colonial house, it was the kitchen that changed least architecturally over the years until the third quarter of the eighteenth century. Nevertheless, in today's restorations, it is the room that has suffered most from twentieth-century interpretation. Idealized conceptions have been substituted for knowledge of what this colonial room was like, what utensils were found therein, and what it now should reveal to us of the domestic activities performed there. The tendency has been to furnish the colonial kitchen with as many old utensils as possible, using these as fireplace decorations. Too often, many of the displayed items are of nineteenth century rather than colonial vintage.

The properly restored kitchen has relevance today because so many types of utensils used in the period still are needed. Though we now make them of plastic and new alloys, seldom of wood or iron, the twentieth-century chafing dish, mixing bowl, chopping knife, and mortar and pestle would be recognized by the colonial housewife, as would the modern skillet, griddle, colander, and saucepot.

Until now the dearth of accurate published information has hampered the development of the authentically restored colonial kitchen. With the appearance of *Colonial Kitchens, Their Furnishings, and Their Gardens* that void no longer exists—it has been filled admirably. In this pioneer work, facts have been culled from actual records of the period—from diaries and travel journals, inventories and manifests, broadsides and books—and then sensibly interpreted to illustrate how seventeenth- and eighteenth-century American kitchens evolved and were used and furnished. The author answers the questions that have perplexed amateur and professional restorationists alike in efforts to re-create what was once for so many families the most important room in the house.

The wealth of documented detail covers every facet of activity of the colonial kitchen in relation to its necessary adjunct, the garden. We follow generation by generation the way the room was constructed and the furniture and utensils with which it was furnished in each period. We can know for sure what herbs, vegetables, and "pleasure plants" were grown in the colonial garden and used in colonial cookery.

The three glossaries are the most complete ever offered to supplement a major text. Definitions are drawn from the dictionaries and encyclopedias that the colonists themselves used. The quotations come from books and newspapers read here in the seventeenth and eighteenth centuries.

Colonial Kitchens, Their Furnishings, and Their Gardens is an authoritative and highly readable book, consistently separating fact from fiction. Anecdotal concepts of the past are replaced by historically accurate, and so more fascinating, illustrations. Here is a significant contribution to our understanding of colonial life as it originally was reflected in the heart of the house.

ARTHUR W. LEIBUNDGUTH, Director
Antiquarian & Landmarks Society, Inc.

ACKNOWLEDGMENTS

THE AUTHOR ACKNOWLEDGES with gratitude the friendly cooperation and assistance of the staffs of the Antiquarian & Landmarks Society, Inc., of Connecticut, Arthur W. Leibundguth, director; the Missouri State Historical Society, Inc., George C. Mitchell, director; the New Hampshire State Historical Society, Inc., John F. Page, director; The Monmouth County (New Jersey) Historical Society, Inc., Edward Felton, director; the Society of Colonial Dames of America in the State of Connecticut, Susan C. Finlay, administrator, Wethersfield properties; the Charleston (South Carolina) Museum of Art, Molly Hartzog, assistant; Colonial Williamsburg, Inc.

For assistance in research the author thanks Mary Hickish, Carolyn P. Guptill, Joan Morris, Marni Wood, Ruth Middleton, and Elizabeth Forbes. And certainly not least, she salutes the patience shown and encouragement given by Helen Van Pelt Wilson, editor, Hawthorn Books.

F. P.

CONTENTS

[xv]

INTRODUCTION
The Promise and the Challenge

For us the winds do blow,
The earth resteth, heav'n moveth, fountains flow;
Nothing we see but means our good,
As our delight or as our treasure;
The whole is either our cupboard of food
Or cabinet of pleasure.

GEORGE HERBERT (1593–1633)

ON MARCH 25, 1584, Queen Elizabeth I granted a special charter to Sir Walter Raleigh, empowering him to "discover, search, finde out, and view such remote, heathen and barbarous lands, countries and territories . . . as to him shall seeme good. . . . [His company] shall goe or travaile thither to inhabite or remaine, there to build and fortifie . . . [and if] within six yeeres [they shall] make their dwellings [then] all and every of them . . . shall and may have all the privileges of free Denizens and persons native to England."

Elizabeth envisioned wealth from a New Indies with which to raise additional troops, to build up the island kingdom's small navy, and to challenge the burgeoning power of France and Spain. She dreamed of an outpost of empire she never expected to see.

Thousands of Englishmen, the majority of whom owned no land— nor could ever expect to under the old system of primogeniture, entailment, and royal and manorial holdings—dreamed of simpler, if more personally hazardous, goals. The royal promise had been made; if one worked six years to clear a patch in the wilderness, to fence, to build a house, then the fire-room, the paled garden, the land he had thus improved would be his own. He had only to risk his life.

Thus, the glorious adventure was begun. Elizabeth's empire now would stretch westward to new green lands; in time it might reach even to the far southern seas. New trade routes could be established—who knew what riches in mines and spices awaited discovery? At the least, these first adventurers would be able to cut timber, to build new ships in the harbors of Virginia, and to load them with a return cargo of lumber for an England in dire need of masts and building boards.

Other benefits were obvious: the cries of the poor in overcrowded London, Liverpool, and Bristol could be silenced if only people could be persuaded to take ship. When there was too much hesitation to exchange the known misery for the unknown, more stringent inducements were offered. Convicted petty thieves, footpads, trespassers, poachers; men, women, and children whose crimes were those of debtor, pauper, and orphan now were given a choice: jail or exile across the ocean.

For many there was the promise of fulfillment of ambitions impossible in seventeenth-century England: the second sons of barons and squires, prevented by the system of entailment from ever founding their own estates, the farmers and husbandmen whose families for generations had tilled leased strip-farms, now might themselves become landlords and indenture others.

Carpenters and wrights, turners, masons, smiths, tanners, fowlers, sawyers, tailors, potters, tylers, palmers, glovers, dyers, millers, reeves, weavers, barbers, fishers, lorimers, archers, even the Queen's own bowmen, hunters, and chamberlains, all suddenly knew the heady luxury of being needed: fortresses and new settlements could not be built and lived in without their skills. Even the towners of London—the chandlers and chapmen—and the middletowners—the shopkeepers of the small towns— envisioned a place in a new society that they themselves could build on the other side of the Atlantic.

The dream had an added dimension for those dissidents from the established church who bore such derisive nicknames as Puritan and Saint. The Old Testament verses of Samuel provided the text for Puritan sermons: "I will appoint a place for my people Israel, and will plant them, that they may dwell in a place of their own and move no more."

So they came, said William Bradford, with courage born of desperation: "They knew they were pilgrims." They sought new hope in a new land, not to retrieve fortune, for few had ever known it, but to achieve it for themselves and to ensure it for their descendants.

As would the great majority who followed, most had bought their passage by selling a portion of their lives, mortgaging one to seven or more years' work or profit. To them it seemed a fair exchange for the chance to know the kind of pride that eventually would redefine freedom in a Declaration of Independence and a Bill of Rights.

Though of diverse rural and urban backgrounds, education, and intellect, the majority had an ethnic bond: until the turn of the nineteenth century, as colony or new republic, America basically was of Anglo-Saxon heritage. In 1776 the seventh-generation colonists, spiritual descendants of the men who framed the Magna Charta, still would have agreed with Bradford: "Our fathers were Englishmen which came over this great ocean and were ready to perish in this wilderness."

Whether their reasons for leaving England were those of Saints or Strangers (the Puritans' name for those of other persuasions), whether they were driven by dreams of glory, gold, or God (the order of spurs given by Sir Francis Bacon), the voyagers on each arriving ship, their historians would note as had Bradford, once "brought safe to land, fell on their knees, and blessed the God of Heavens who had brought them over the vast and furious ocean."

Winter and summer, north and south, early emigrants landed on a terrifying "unknown coast . . . a wilderness full of wild beasts and wild men . . . of woods and thickets (with a desolate) and savage hiew." They were strangers in a physically alien land, alone in a sense few can know today. Here there were "no friends to wellcome them, nor inns to entertain or refresh their weatherbeaten bodys, no houses or much less townes to repair too, to seek for succore. . . . Their sowle was overwhelmed in them."

The more fortunate among those first arrivals found caves or dug pits, the tops of which could be covered by brush; others built "English wigwams" of hemlock boughs and salvaged canvas and blankets, huts of saplings and branches daubed with mud, in which they lived in each settlement for at least one year (and sometimes much longer) until finally the fire-room could be built and the harvest of a second spring "brought joyfull home."

So it was that much of what then was singularly British came here in memory and old patterns of living. Traditional British fare was brought over in seeds and roots to be planted where the familiar did not exist, just as that which was novel here was sent back home to become useful, if curious, additions to those older English gardens.

> *That which is far off . . . who can find it out?*
>
> ECCLESIASTES 7:24

For a generation that has searched the lunar landscape in anticipation of a journey to Mars, it is difficult to envision the wilderness desert out of which the seventeenth- and eighteenth-century farms were carved—lands that today are the sites of great industrial cities and crowded towns. For many born since 1900, it is physically impossible to return to a family home that ties them to a certain place and time. Some find that the buildings in which they were born and lived as children have been razed to make room for urban renewal projects. Outlying houses have disappeared as new highways and air terminals have been completed. Old farmsteads, once marked out against a background of woods, meadows, gardens, and marshes, now may be sites for shopping plazas and motels.

If we cannot give back to each individual his sense of identity with a family home, we can repair some of the displacement from our common past by restoring and preserving those solid antique structures that have escaped the bulldozer. Each is tangible evidence of the American's intent and ability to endure; each testifies that only so long ago as our own great-grandparents' time Americans were able to conquer the wilderness created by nature. Now, surely, we can learn to control the industrial wilderness assembled by man.

Today the few houses remaining of the first colonial period, and the many more of the eighteenth century, appear always to have been here—and so they have, in terms of our national history. We are so used to their time-blurred facades that it is difficult to imagine how different they looked when the nails were sharp, the clapboards and shingles bright from saw and frow. Few of even our smallest villages today are edged by woods. Most of the country roads "into the wilderness," once just wide enough for a team of oxen, have been doubled in width and covered with asphalt. It is only behind the fencelines of old pastures that wild flowers now can emerge each April, for diligent highway crews, spraying salt in winter and insecticides in summer, have killed all but the strongest roots. The wild berry bushes, the laden grapevines, the hickory, oak, and walnut trees, the alders, birches, and dogwoods that early travelers said lined colonial roads, have been stripped from the banks of twentieth-century superhighways.

As we have changed the landscape, we also have allowed the once-clear outlines of colonial patterns of living to blur, and so have lost much factual knowledge of early America. More than 350 years have passed since the first permanent settlements were established in Britannia in Virginia. This distance in time has helped to give a romantic aura to early American life that the colonists themselves surely would have found not only puzzling but hilarious.

Their lives still are reflected in microcosm, however, in the tangible assets of history: the utensils and furnishings that they brought with them, or adapted or created, and that we now call antiques and especially in the architectural character of the first room around which the early home was built. The kitchen was not only the center for cooking and preserving foods,

Daybook begun by John Hempsted in 1745 was used also for his records as New London, Connecticut, tax assessor in 1769. Left-hand page includes reminder that he lent a book to neighbor Saltonstall on June 10, 1751.

it reflected all other family activities. It served as workroom for carding, spinning, and weaving; sewing and quilting; dyeing and soapmaking; and for general repairs. It was schoolroom, office, dining hall, dispensary, distillery, and bedroom, as occasion required. Its hearth, shelf, cupboards, ells, and adjacent storerooms could, and often did, contain all of a family's lares and penates.

A generous Plato allowed the poet three removes from the truth. The historian, restorationist, or curious owner of an old house should attempt greater accuracy. The colonists left us the tools with which to retrieve knowledge, for our ancestors had a sense of history. They left records of their lives in their journals, diaries, shipping manifests, and shop accounts and in the daybooks of town clerks. It is time for us to go back to these original records and to learn from them how a society was created to which each member knew he had contributed, to consider the colonists' own descriptions of the way in which they built a new world.

With such assistance we can better restore, preserve, and enjoy those ancient homes and garden sites which have weathered two hundred and more years and which, because they were built to last, remain to challenge our ingenuity and perseverance today.

PART I

The Wilderness Rim

CHAPTER 1

The Fort at James's City

"To the Virginian Voyage"

In regions far
Such heroes bring ye forth
As those from whom we came
And plant our name
Under that star
Not known unto our north—
Virginia,
Earth's only paradise.
MICHAEL DRAYTON, 1607

ON DECEMBER 20, 1606, twenty-two years after that first charter had been awarded Sir Walter Raleigh, three tiny wooden-hulled ships sailed down the Thames bound on what was planned as a two months' voyage to Virginia. The *Susan Constant,* the *Godspeed,* and the *Discovery* carried as supercargo six councillors who would rule the new outpost and forty-eight gentlemen who along with the Virginia Company investors hoped to profit from efforts of the four carpenters, twenty laborers, four boys, and unnamed "divers others to the number of 100."[1]

They had set out expecting to arrive on the shores of Elizabeth's, and now James's, New Indies in early spring, gaining the advantage of a full season in which to explore, plant, and build. Instead, in Captain John Smith's terse phrase, "unprosperous winds" so delayed them, and fear and discouragement bred such near-mutiny, that it was not until April 26, 1607, that they anchored off Chesapeake Bay. From aboard ship they scanned the wilderness for a likely place of settlement; finally, they went ashore on May 14 to declare before God (and within earshot of curious natives watching from the woods) that thus was founded James's fort in Britannia in Virginia.

They gathered a scant cargo of roughly split clapboards, samples of what in London would turn out to be fool's gold, some sassafras, and a few furs for Captain Christopher Newport to take back to England as proof of the bounty of the new world.

The lengthy voyage to Virginia had so depleted the settlers' supplies that when Newport left on June 12 for England, the colonists faced their new wilderness life with little to sustain them. The ships gone, and "being left to our fortunes, within ten days scarce ten amongst us could either go [about work] or well stand, such extreme weakness and sickness oppressed us." And at that, Smith wrote, none would "marvel, if they consider the cause and reasons."[2]

So long as the ships had remained in port, the emigrants had been able to trade with the crew for ship's biscuit, pilfered from sea stores reserved for the voyage back to England. Those hard, dry crackers, Smith wrote bitterly, the seamen had been willing to

> sell, give or exchange with us for money, sassafras, furs, or love. But when they departed, there remained neither tavern, beer house, nor place of relief for us, but the common kettle.
>
> Had we been as free from all [other] sins as we thus [forcibly] were from gluttony and drunkenness, we would have been canonized for saints; our President, however, would never have been admitted [as a saint] for he took to his private [use all] oatmeal, sack, oil, aqua vitae, beef and eggs—all but the soup kettle; that indeed he allowed equally to be distributed, and in that was [only] half a pint of wheat with as much again of barley boiled with water for each man a day; this grain having fried some 26 weeks in the ship's hold, however, it contained as many worms as grains, so that we might truly call it so much bran than corn.
>
> Our drink was water.
>
> Our lodgings were castles in the air.
>
> With this kind of lodging and diet, our extreme toil in bearing and planting palisades so bruised and strained us, and our continual labor in the extremity of the heat so weakened us, [that we were miserable] and eventually unable to work at all.[3]

Until September of that first year, those "who escaped death, lived only upon sturgeion and sea crabs. Fifty men in this time we buried.

"Then just when all our provision [was] spent, the sturgeion gone, all helps abandoned, each hour expecting the fury of the savages, God, the patron of all good endeavours in our desperate extremity so changed the hearts of the savages, that they brought to us such plenty of their fruits, and provision that no man wanted."[4]

Unhappily, this friendly truce was not to last. Nothing had been planted by the company, for they had "lost the time and season." Close again to madness from fear and near-starvation after the Indians' gift of supplies had run out, the settlers decided to march on "the natives' houses" where they saw "great heaps of corn." Smith attempted to restrain the raiders from the "taking of it, expecting the savages would assault them . . . as they did, with a most hideous noise.

"Being well-armed with clubs, shields, bows and arrows, they charged the English, who received them with loaded muskets. Down fell the [Indian] god, and divers natives lay sprawling on the ground; the rest fled to the woods, and ere long sent one of their [warriors] back to offer peace and to redeem their *Okee* [idol]."[5]

Smith told them "if only six would come unarmed and load his boat with food, he would not only be their friend, but would restore their *Okee* and give them beads, copper, and hatchets besides: which on both their sides was to their contents performed; the natives brought venison, turkeys, wild fowl, and bread [and there was] singing and dancing in sign of friendship till they departed."

Though the colonists still lived with only scraps of canvas to shelter them, their spirits were revived temporarily by the food gifts of the Indians and the autumn arrival of "swans, geese, ducks and cranes." They "could feast on these and Virginia peas, pumpkins and putchamins [persimmons], fish, fowl and divers sorts of wild beasts as fat as we could eat them. As a result none of our tuftaffety humorists desired to go [back] to England,"[6] at least at that time, Smith said.

Throughout the first winter the now-haggard settlers continued to live in "the open woods under the lee of a hill where all the ground was covered with snow and hard frozen." To keep warm, Smith wrote, "the snow were digged away and we made a great fire in the place; when the ground thus was well-dried, we shovelled away the fire; and covering the [heated earth] with a mat, there we lay very warm.

"To keep us from the wind, we made a shade of another mat; as the wind turned we turned our shade; and when the ground grew cold we removed the fire to another [place and repeated the process]. And thus many a cold winter night we lay in this miserable manner."[7]

Although they were strengthened by the arrival of two supply ships in 1608, little actually was accomplished during the balance of the second year of settlement. Part of the reason for the lack of advancement was pointed out by Smith when he listed each ship's arrival and its preponderantly nonworking supercargo. The *Phoenix*, he noted carefully, brought to the colony an additional councillor, thirty-three gentlemen, twenty-one laborers, two apothecaries, six tailors, a jeweler, two refiners, a goldsmith, a gunsmith, a perfumer, a surgeon, a cooper, a tobacco pipe maker, a blacksmith, "and divers others to the number of 120." The second supply brought three more councillors, twenty-five gentlemen, plus the wife of one, "mistress Forrest," and her maid, Ann Burras; twenty-six laborers, two boys, and "8 Dutchmen and Poles, with some others to the number of 70 persons."[8]

Between February and April 1609, Smith and the company scriveners recorded, work finally began in earnest. For the first time, "a well of excellent sweet water" was dug. "We so quietly followed our business that we made three or four lasts of tar, pitch and soap ashes" and even, through the efforts of the Polish and Dutch workers, "produced a trial of glass."[9] Some twenty cabins were built, probably of mud and wattle.

Even so, there was little permanent sense of satisfaction among the colonists. Some decamped, disappearing into the woods on their own; others joined the Indians and, to "stop disorders of our [own] disorderly thieves" as well as those "of the savages, we built a blockhouse in the neck of our isle. No one was allowed to pass or re-pass, savage nor Christian, without the President's permission."[10]

Spring brought a renewal of determination, enough so that some thirty acres were plowed and planted. "Our three sows [had by now] increased to 60 and odd pigs. And near 500 chickens brought up themselves without having any meat given them."[11] The men made "clapboard and wainscot"[12] to be sent back to England. The calm of those early spring weeks disappeared, however, when "searching our casked corn [purchased from the Indians] we found it half rotten, and the rest so consumed by many thousands of rats that increased so fast—their original was from the ships—as we knew not how to keep what little we had. This did drive us all to our wits' end, for there once again was nothing [to eat] but what nature afforded."[13]

In desperation, they attempted to save themselves by dividing the colony into small groups and sending out search parties for food. "60 or 80 with Ensign Laxon were sent down the river to live upon oysters; and 20 with Lieutenant Percy went fishing at Point Comfort. . . . Master West with as many went up to the falls; nothing could be found there but a few acorns; of that every man had equal proportion."[14]

They lived thus on a diet of acorns and sturgeon; as a matter of fact, Smith reported, "we had more sturgeion than could be devoured by dog and man." Some gathered tuckahoe roots and "on those wild fruits and what we caught we lived very well—[if one likes] such a diet. But the want of corn [to make pudding and bread] occasioned the end of all our works, it being work sufficient to provide victuall." During this starving time, Smith wrote, "for one basket of corn they would have sold their souls."[15]

It would not be until after the arrival of Governor Thomas Dale and a group of skilled men two years later, the eventual reorganization of the Virginia Company, and the reversion of the colony to the Crown that those first hopeful attempts, begun so bravely in 1606, could be said to have resulted in the establishment of a truly permanent settlement.

The names of the first planters, who landed in Virginia on May 14, 1607, were listed by Smith and his company clerks as

Members of the Council: Master Edward Maria Wingfield, Captain Bartholomew Gosnold, Captain John Smith, Captain John Ratcliffe, Captain John Martin, Captain George Kendall.

Gentlemen: Master Robert Hunt, Preacher; Master George Percy, Anthony Gosnoll, George Flower, Captain Gabriel Archer, Robert Fenton, Robert Ford, William Brewster, Edward Harrington, Dru Pickhouse, Thomas Jacob, John Brookes, Ellis Kingston, Thomas Sands, Benjamin Best, Jehu Robinson, Thomas Mouton, Eustace Clovill, Stephen Halthorp, Kellam Throgmorton, Edward Morish, Nathaniel Powell, Edward Browne, Robert Beheathland, John Pennington, Jeremy Allcock, George Walker, Thomas Studley, Richard Crofts, Nicholas Houlgrave, Thomas Webbe, John Waller, John Short, William Tankard, William Smethes, Francis Snarsbrough, Richard Simons, Edward Brookes, Richard Dixon, John Martin, Roger Cooke, Thomas Wotton, Surgeon; John Stevenson, Thomas Gore, Henry Adling, Francis Midwinter, Richard Frith.

Carpenters: William Laxon, Edward Pising, Thomas Emry, Robert Small.

Laborers: John Laydon, William Cassen, George Cassen, Thomas Cassen, William Rodes, William White, Old Edward, Henry Tavin, George Goulding, John Dods, William Johnson, William Unger, James Read, Blacksmith; Jonas Profit, Sailor; Thomas Cowper, Barber; William Garret, Bricklayer; Edward Brinto, Mason; William Love, Tailor; Nicholas Scott, Drummer; William Wilkinson, Surgeon; Samuel Collier, boy; Nathaniel Pecock, boy; James Brumfield, boy; Richard Mutton, boy, with divers others to the number of 100.

CHAPTER 2

The Settlement at Plymouth

*Let us single out some remarkables and
glorify our God!* COTTON MATHER[16]

W HEN THE 104 MEN, women, and children who made up the
Mayflower passenger list sailed westward September 6, 1620,
to a new land of new hope, they took for shipboard sustenance hardtack, "salt horse"[17] dried fish, cheese, beer, and
"strong waters."

Three centuries of pleasant legend to the contrary, the forty-one
Saints, forty Strangers, five Hired Hands, and eighteen Servants—for so
the supercargo was styled—would have been the first to acknowledge (some
would have insisted you know) that when they left Southampton they had
little in common save one certain belief: All could be better off only somewhere other than in England, or indeed than anywhere in Europe.

The outnumbered Saints, of course, were those whom we later were
to call Pilgrims, and who in England were known as Brownists and Separatists.[18] Hounded for their open disapproval of "Papish anticks" of the
Anglican church, they had first exiled themselves to Holland, from whence
eleven years later they set out on the heroic adventure to free themselves
forever of European society and the rituals required by any established
church.

In most other ways their outlook differed little if at all from that of
other late Elizabethans. They were radicals in religious theory only; they
enjoyed good food when they could and they drank the suspect water only
when reduced to it, preferring beers and "strong waters"—the popular
euphemism for gin or brandy. Their search for individual religious freedom
was of necessity equally a quest for independence of government.

The Strangers on board the *Mayflower*, however, remained members
of the English church and generally resisted the Saints' attempts at ship-

[8]

board conversion. The earthly salvation they looked forward to finding was purely economic: The one great common link all *Mayflower* passengers acknowledged was that all were of the poorer classes, with no aristocratic rights and privileges to leave behind.

Longfellow's nineteenth-century romanticism to the contrary,[19] to be counted among the Strangers were Priscilla Mullins, daughter of Master William Mullins, a Surrey shopkeeper, and Captain Myles Standish, an obdurate soldier of fortune whose bravery and common sense kept the company alive. One of the Hired Hands was a tall, sturdy twenty-year-old, John Alden, a cooper from Essex, whose fortunes would rise and fall with the years—he served as assistant governor and later treasurer of the colony, was arrested but acquitted for murder, and led persecutions of Quakers and Baptists, as well as marrying Priscilla. Alden was one of the first to leave the original settlement in order to build the new town of Duxbury. When he died, at the age of eighty-eight, he was the last of those who had signed the Mayflower Compact. Master (later Governor) William Bradford, "a commone blessing to them all," had been a Yorkshire fustian maker; he and Master William Brewster, onetime postmaster and tutor, were leaders among the Saints.[20]

Remarkably, most had survived the nine fearsome weeks of crossing the chill Atlantic, although the truly dangerous condition of the "sweet ship"—it had once been part of the Mediterranean wine trade—frankly terrified its passengers and wrought "greate distraction & difference of opinion" among the forty officers and near-mutinous crew.

"Not a little joyfull," Governor Bradford wrote later, they sighted the high dunes above Truro at dawn on November tenth. Running alongshore near what is now Chatham, the *Mayflower* "fell amongst dangerous shoulds & roaring breakers," and to "gett out of those dangers" they had to retrace their course along the coastline. They dropped anchor finally "in ye name of God, Amen, at Cap-Codd ye 11 of November" in what we now call Provincetown Harbor.

Eager to put ashore, they were forced to delay their landing because "discontents and murmurings . . . mutinous speeches & carriages" among "some of the Strangers" threatened to break up the company; they feared they would not be "freed from the government of any man." To bind all together before they left the ship, the Mayflower Compact was written, in which the signers "solemnly & mutually in ye presence of God and one of another, covenant and combine ourselves . . . for ye generall good of ye Colonie."[21] Not all signed, however. Subscribing their names according to station, those with the right to be called Mister signed first, including six Saints and six Strangers. Twenty-seven "goodmen" signed, as did four servants.

That Saturday and Sunday no work was accomplished, the Sabbath being spent in thanksgiving for "ye firme and stable earth." Monday, the women went ashore under guard to do the laundry, "as they had great need." While the women scrubbed, the carpenter's work gang repaired the shallop and youngsters played on the beach; others of the company searched the flats for the longed-for first supper of fresh food. That evening there was a great feast of soft-shell clams, quahogs, and also, unfortunately, enough mussels to cause many to "cast and scour."[22]

Self-banished, they had crossed terror-laden seas. Now, almost miraculously, they were ashore in an uncharted wilderness of dunes and far forests. Their patent had commanded them to head for Virginia, but as the colony's leaders later were to explain, they landed at New England due to a navigational error. There was some suspicion, too, that the Saints had agreed secretly to remain in New England, where there was no government and no established church representation. Had they continued on to Virginia, they would have had the advantage of earlier emigrants' experience. Instead, as Captain John Smith noted wryly, "their humorous ignorances" caused them for more than a year to endure a "wonderful deal of misery."[23]

On Wednesday, "with every man his musket, sword & corselet, under ye command of Captain Myles Standishe,"[24] exploratory parties began forays ashore, where they discovered Indian cornfields and mounds, some of which they correctly assumed were burial sites. "Though it would be odious . . . to ransack their sepulchres," this revulsion was overcome, and as much corn as could be carried was removed. The ears thus harvested were kept for the next spring's planting; indeed they were to provide the colony's only successful crop.

Onrushing cold and a genuine fear of starvation banished lingering scruples against further cemetery bedevilment: "it blowed & did snow . . . and froze withal." It was "God's good Providence . . . let his holy name have all ye praise," wrote Bradford, leaving no credit to the foresighted Indians, as foragers returned with a bag of beans, a bottle of oil, and more corn—in all, ten bushels.

Daring further on the Second Discovery, as the second major search for Indian stores was called, abandoned huts were found; from these broiled herring, venison, tobacco seed, pots, and vessels were commandeered.

A more precious commodity, time, had been squandered. Days had been lost as the company, still living aboard the *Mayflower*, squabbled over the proper site on which to build. Not until December 20 was it decided they would begin their colony farther west behind what is now Plymouth Rock, "where we may harbor our boats . . . and in this brooke [find] much good fishe . . . and much corne ground cleared" by the Indians.[25]

On Monday, December 25, the Saints prepared to erect the first "common house." They did not keep Christmas, for it was a "human invention," a survival of heathen custom. Some of the Strangers and the crew disagreed with the Saints' decision to build a common safe-house on what, in old England, was celebrated as a holiday. Of that first Christmas in New England, Bradford was to write later:

> I shall remember one passage more, rather of mirth then of waight. On the day called Chrismasday, the Govr caled them out to worke, (as was used) but the most of this new-company excused themselves and said it wente against their consciences to work on that day. So the Govr tould them that if they made it mater of conscience, he would spare them till they were better informed. So he led-away the rest and left them; but when they cam home at noone from their worke, he found them in the streete at play, openly; some pitching the barr and some at stoole-ball, and shuch like sports. So he went to them, and tooke awaye their implements, and tould them that was against his conscience, that they should play and others worke. If they made the keeping of it mater of devotion, let them kepe their houses, but ther should be no gameing or revelling in the streets. Since which time nothing hath been attempted that way, at least openly.[26]

New Plymouth had been founded. For many it was too late. During the weeks of winter terror and near-starvation that followed, the Greate Sickness killed half the company. Few thatched huts were completed. Many of the company continued to live aboard the *Mayflower*, anchored a mile and a half offshore, until April.

Fourteen of the eighteen mothers and wives who had survived the terrors of the crossing died that first winter; so did most of the aged and many of the children. Those who survived the daily struggle against fear, starvation, disease, and cold huddled in misery and waited for spring and for the *Fortune* to arrive with vitally needed supplies. Some hoped and prayed for a miracle.

All might easily have been lost had not what the Saints indeed considered a miracle occurred about March 16: a tall, powerful Indian strode into the forlorn settlement, astounding the colonists when he smiled, spoke to them in English, and asked for beer. His name, he said, was Samoset, and he too was a foreigner, having come originally from far up the Maine coast. He stayed the night, leaving the next day to return with a still more miraculous savage, Squanto.[27] Squanto, Samoset explained, had been in England and could speak better English.

Squanto had made two round trips to their English homeland by more hazardous routes than ever the Saints had envisioned: first taken to England by Captain Thomas Hunt in 1605 as a novelty, he was returned to America in 1614 with Captain Smith—only to be seized later that year by the renegade Captain Hunt and sold in the Malaga slave market. Rescued by local friars, Squanto escaped and managed to work his way back to London, where eventually he met another explorer, Captain Thomas Dermer. Dermer returned him in 1619 to the New England coast. At home, Squanto found his own family and tribe vanquished by plague and joined the Wampanoag tribe under Massasoit.

Happily for the colonists, once Squanto came to them he did not leave. He taught the mostly town-bred Saints how to grow the native corn, and he joined their church. He was "a speciall instrumente sent of God for their good beyond expectation."[28] Under Squanto's tutoring, the Saints harvested their first crop of twenty acres of native corn, though the wheat, barley, and peas, grown from seed brought from England, failed.

In Edward Johnson's words: "The Lord was pleased to provide for them great store of Fish in the spring time, and especially Alewives about the bignesse of a Herring, many thousands of these, they used to put under their Indian Corne, which they plant in Hills five foote asunder, and assuredly when the Lord created this Corne, hee had a special eye to supply these his peoples wants with it, for ordinarily five or six graines doth produce six hundred."[29]

The corn was enough to increase the weekly porridge ration on which each had subsisted for months; to the peck of familiar wheat meal brought from home there now could be added a peck of maize or cornmeal. With this for which to be thankful, a holiday was decreed. They had survived. And so, Edward Winslow wrote,

> Our harvest being gotten in, our governor sent four men on fowling, so that we might after a special manner rejoice together after we had gathered the fruit of our labors. The four in one day killed as much fowl, as with a little help besides, served the company almost a week. At which time amongst other recreations, we exercised our arms, many of the Indians coming amongst us, and among the rest their greatest king, Massasoit, with some 90 men, whom . . . we entertained and feasted; and they went out and killed five deer, which they brought to the plantation, and bestowed upon our governor, and the captain and others. And although it be not always so plentiful as it was at this time with us, yet by the goodness of God we are so far from want, that we often wish you partakers of our plenty.[30]

The holiday lasted three days, and to entertain their guests Captain Standish and the men gave a military review. Games were played—perhaps a form of the Indians' favorite football or stoole-ball—and they feasted.

The harvest thus gathered from the forests and marshes provided wild duck and goose, venison, cod, bass, eels, clams, and other shellfish and all sorts of "sallet herbes," including leeks and watercress. They had bread made from the Indian cornmeal and white bread from their meager store of English meal. Wild plums and dried berries provided a sweet. With it they enjoyed the colony's first wine, "very sweete & strong," made from wild white and red grapes.[31]

Though Bradford noted they had planted turnip, parsnip, cabbage, and other seeds brought with them from England, he did not list these in connection with the harvest feasts. They had not yet learned to make anything palatable of the cranberries that abounded in the bogs, or at least these first Thanksgiving reports make no mention of such accomplishment, and though Bradford had recorded wild turkeys flitting through the woods, they were not listed by him as part of the menu. Nor were the "pompions and squashes" mentioned, though these probably were cooked for that first Thanksgiving, stewed or baked in ashes.

"Ye Saincts, Strangers amongst Us, Hired Hands and Servants" who landed at Plymouth on November 11, 1620, included in the first category seventeen men, ten women, and fourteen children. They were:

Master Isaac Allerton, London tailor; Mrs. Allerton, who died in childbirth aboard the *Mayflower* in 1621; their children, Bartholomew (who returned to England), Mary, and Remember;

Master William Bradford, Yorkshire fustian maker, and Mrs. Dorothy Bradford, who drowned at Cape Cod in 1620;

Master William Brewster, Nottinghamshire postmaster and tutor, and Mrs. Mary Brewster; their children, Love and Wrestling;

John Carver, Yorkshire merchant, and Mrs. Catherine Carver, both of whom died in 1621; Francis Cooke, Nottinghamshire wool comber, and his son, John; John Crackston of Colchester and his son John; Moses Fletcher, Sandwich smith; Master Samuel Fuller, Norfolk say maker and "physician"; John Goodman, linen weaver, who died in 1621; Desire Minter, who returned to England; Degory Priest, London hatter, who died in 1621; Thomas Rogers, merchant, and his son John; Edward Tilley, London weaver, and Mrs. Anne Tilley, both of whom died in 1621; John Tilley, London weaver, and Mrs. Elizabeth Tilley, both of whom died in 1621; their daughter Elizabeth;

Thomas Tinker, London sawyer, Mrs. Tinker, and their son, all of whom died in 1621; John Turner, merchant, and his two young sons, all of whom died in 1621;

Master William White, wool carder who died in 1621, and Mrs. Susannah White, and their children, Resolved and Peregrine; and Master

"Mr. Hooker's Congregation Travelling through the Wilderness" to establish the Connecticut colony at Hartford, 1636, carried cooking pots and other family necessities with them. Contemporary accounts said only Mrs. Hooker, invalid wife of the minister, knew the luxury of a sedan. Illustration from Benjamin Trumbull's *A Complete History of Connecticut*, Hartford, 1797.

Edward Winslow, Worcestershire printer, and Mrs. Elizabeth Winslow, who died in 1621.

The Strangers, seventeen men, nine women, and fourteen children, included John Billington, Mrs. Ellen Billington, and their sons, Francis and John; Richard Britteridge, who died in 1620; Peter Browne; John Chilson, tailor, died 1620, Mrs. Chilson, died 1621, and their daughter, Mary; Richard Clark, died 1621; Humility Cooper, London orphan, who returned to England; Francis Eaton, Bristol carpenter, and Mrs. Sarah Eaton, who died in 1621, and their son, Samuel; Edward Fuller and Mrs. Ann Fuller, both of whom died in 1621, and their son, Samuel; Richard Gardiner, died 1621; Master Stephen Hopkins, Mrs. Elizabeth Hopkins, and his children, Giles and Constance, and their children, Damaris and Oceanus;

Edmund Margeson, died 1621; Master Christopher Martin, Mrs. Martin, and his stepson Solomon Prower, all of whom died in 1621; Master William Mullins, Surrey shopkeeper, and Mrs. Mullins, both of whom died in 1621; their son, John, who died in 1621, and his daughter, Priscilla; John Rigdale and Mrs. Alice Rigdale, both of whom died in 1621; Henry Samson, London orphan; Captain Myles Standish, Lancashire soldier, and Mrs. Rose Standish, who died in 1621; Master Richard Warren, London merchant; Thomas Williams, who died in 1621; and Gilbert Winslow, who returned to England.

The five Hired Hands were John Alden, Essex cooper; John Allerton, mariner, died 1621; a sailor named Ellis, who returned to England; Thomas English, a mariner, died 1621; and William Trevor, a sailor who returned to England.

The indentured servants—ten men, one woman, and six children—were William Button, assigned to the Fuller family, who died at sea in 1620; Robert Carter, Mullins family, died 1621; Edward Dotey, Hopkins family; William Holbeck, White family, died 1621; John Hook, Allerton family, died 1621; John Howland, Carver family; John Langemore, Martin family, died 1620; Edward Lester, Hopkins family; four orphans named More, including Ellen, Winslow family, died 1621; Jasper, Carver family, died 1620; Richard, Brewster family; and a brother, unnamed, assigned to the Brewster family, died 1621; Elias Storey, Winslow family, died 1621; George Soule, Winslow family; Edward Thompson, White family, died 1621; Roger Wilder, Carver family, died 1621; and an unnamed maid-servant, Carver family, who died in 1622.

By the end of 1621, seventeen Saints had died, as had nineteen Strangers, two hired hands, and eleven servants, mostly during the Great Sickness. The company was augmented by twelve Saints and twenty-three Strangers with the arrival of the *Fortune* in November 1621; two Strangers from the *Sparrow* in March 1622; thirty-two saints, fifty-eight Strangers, and six servants from aboard the *Anne* and *Little James* in August 1623; nine Saints and one Stranger from the second *Mayflower* in May 1629; thirty-five servants from the *Talbot*, July 1629; and sixty servants from the *Handmaid* in October 1630.

PART II

The Kitchen Common Room

CHAPTER 1

The First Abodes

Ye shall eat this year such as growest of itself, and the second year that which springest of the same; and in the third year sow ye, and reap, and plant vineyards, and eat the fruit thereof.

ISAIAH 55:2

INDEED IT WAS A WONDER that so many could survive the misery of those first years of primitive settlement, for it was truly a "Laborious Worke Planting This Wilderness," Edward Johnson declared in *Wonder Working Providence Of Sions Saviour*.[1] Once the settlement site had been decided, he wrote:

They burrow themselves in the Earth for their first shelter under some Hill-side, casting the Earth aloft upon Timber; they make a smoaky fire against the Earth at the highest side, and thus these poore servants of Christ provide shelter for themselves, their Wives and little ones, keeping off the short showers from their Lodgings, but the long raines penetrate through, to their great disturbance in the night season; yet in these poore *Wigwames* they sing Psalmes, pray and praise their God till they can provide them houses, which ordinarily was not wont to be with many till the Earth, by the Lords blessing, brought forth Bread to feed them, their Wives and little ones, which with sore labours they attaine every one that can lift a hawe to strike it into the Earth, standing stoutly to their labours, and teare up the Rootes and Bushes, which the first yeare beares them a very thin crop, till the soard of the Earth be rotten, and therefore they have been forced to cut their bread very thin for a long season.[2]

[19]

Dread of attack by unfriendly Indians

made them the more carefully to looke to them selves . . . they agreed to inclose their dwellings with a good strong pale, and make flankers in convenient places, with gates to shute, which were every night locked, and a watch kept and when neede required ther was also warding in the day time. And the company was by the Captaine and the Govr advise, deviding into 4 squadrons, and everyone had ther quarter apoynted them, unto which they were to repaire upon any suddane alarme. And if ther should be any crie of fire, a company were appointed for a gard, with muskets, whilst other quenchet the same, to prevent Indean treacher.

"This was accomplished very cherfully, and the towne impayled round by the begining of March, in which evry family had a pretty garden plote secured,"[3] was the way William Bradford recalled New Plymouth as it appeared in 1622.

By 1624 other ships had arrived, the first rude cottages had been completed, and Captain John Smith wrote of New Plymouth: "In this Plantation there is about an hundred and fourscore persons, some Cattell, but many Swine and Poultry; their Towne containes two and thirty houses, whereof seven were burnt, with the value of five or six hundred pounds in other goods, impailed about halfe a mile, within which there is a high Mount, a Fort, with a Watch-tower, well built of stone, lome, and wood."[4]

You must not thinke to goe to heaven on a feather-bed; if you will be Christ's disciples, you must take up his crosse, and it will make you sweat.
    THOMAS HOOKER, 1640[5]

Devout dissenter or land-hungry yeoman, those who had embarked on the grand adventure to conquer the wilderness found the Puritan leader's metaphor only too apt. Throughout the seventeenth and eighteenth centuries—indeed until there no longer was any frontier—it was taken for granted that at least four years' work, if not the six Elizabeth had allowed, was necessary before any but the rudest permanent shelter could be built.

Regulations under which new frontier communities were planned were similar in intention—if not always in the amount of land or the kind of charter involved—to those agreed to in 1673 by the handful of Connecticut families who left Farmington to begin a new plantation on Mattatuck Indian land some ten miles distant.[6] Explorers having reported the soil rich and worthy of improvement, settlers ready to journey to the colony's western edge signed articles which stipulated, "Every person that is accepted as an inhabitant shall have eight acres for a home lot; [and] every person that takes up an allotment, shall, within four years after the date hereof, build a good and fashionable dwelling house, 18 by 16, and 9 feet between joints, with a good chimney."

Before those "fashionable" one-common-room homes could be staked—whether in Virginia in 1616, Plymouth in the 1620's, or in any of the later settlements—underbrush had to be cut and burned and the stubborn hulks of large trees removed, so that a hurried acre of turnips might be planted, as many corn hills as possible set, and the first fruit trees started. The common lands had to be paled and at least one house fortified. Of necessity, each family's own garden lot was fenced. There was neither time nor energy to expend on building an attractive house; in each new community the first homes continued to be facsimiles of the original "miserable aboads," those thatch- and sedge-covered English wigwams or bark-shingled side-hill caves or cellars.

The orchard and garden were set out, if at all possible, to the south and west of the shelter. The cornfield, the turnip lot, and the onion or cabbage patch usually began no more than fifty feet, if indeed that far, from the door. The stumps of trees felled to make room for the house lot provided the settler with more than enough garden furniture. The stump nearest the house served as the block where kindling could be split at evening time; each spring and fall more than twenty cords of wood had to be cut and stacked nearby for use in the single hearth.

Little grass was allowed to grow near the house; when it did, it was scythed down two or three times during the summer. Often one tall tree was left standing when the lot was cleared so that it would provide shade for the kitchen-yard work area.[7] The trees in the new orchard were at best small saplings, usually started from seed and with seven years to grow before they would become wide-branched and bear fruit.

> *So we would have it . . . our riches shall not be in pompe, but in strength. A comonwele is readier to ebe then to flow when once fine houses and gay cloaths come up.* ROBERT CUSHMAN[8]

"The wealthy and principal men of New England, in the beginning of the colonies, commenced their first dwelling houses in this fashion," the colonial secretary at New Amsterdam reported to Holland in 1650, explaining:

Those in New Netherlands and in New England who have no means to build farmhouses at first according to their wishes [that is,

Thatched-roof cottage, one of the English "wig-wams" of the type built in the seventeenth and eighteenth centuries, was still in use in 1836 when John Warner Barber sketched it.

the kind they would like to have], dig a square pit in the ground, cellar fashion, 6 or 7 feet deep, as long and as broad as they think proper, case the earth inside with wood all round the wall, and line the wood with bark of trees or something else to prevent the caving in of the earth, floor this cellar with plank and wainscott it overhead for a ceiling, raise a roof of spars clear up and cover the spars with the bark or green sods, so that they can live dry and warm in these houses with their entire families, two, three or four years.[9]

The settlers who had chosen to dig a cellar home or to build out from the side of a hill had a natural advantage over neighbors who first had made do with wigwams or thatched cottages. Now their old "wainscoted" plank ceilings could be used as subflooring for the first permanent house; the new fashionable building automatically was provided with cellar storage space and a more solid chimney base.

CHAPTER 2

The Fire-Room

Wee have ordered that noe man shall build his chimney with wood nor cover his house with thatch, which was readily assented unto, for that divers houses have been burned since our arrival and some English wigwams have taken fire in the roofes with thatch or boughs.

THOMAS DUDLEY, 1631[10]

IN THOSE FEW AREAS where stone was plentiful and easily accessible, it was used to build chimney bases and flues at least as far as the loft floor and usually to the roof line. Those who could afford to purchase brick used this above the roof, often with a lime-base mortar. In such houses, when the kitchen cooking-fireplace was constructed, the oven usually was built into the back wall of the chimney.

In many settlements, however, particularly among each new generation of emigrants, numerous cabin or cottage owners made do with clay and straw flues, and some still continued throughout the eighteenth century to build equally hazardous chimneys out of wood chunks covered with clay. Where such materials were used, colonists often also repeated the early-seventeenth-century common frontier fashion of building outdoor ovens, a safety device usable save in the coldest winter weeks.

Peter Kalm reported in 1749 that he did not believe any of the new cottages then being built by the average emigrant in the middle colonies had an interior oven: "Since it has frequently happened that a disastrous fire has broken out because of having the oven in the cabin or dwelling house [they] have been abandoned entirely. So I have not seen an oven in a cottage anywhere."[11]

Though Kalm was writing more than 120 years after New England and Virginia had been settled, his description of that mid-eighteenth-

[23]

century middle-colony exterior oven could have served for its earlier prototype in either of the original plantations of the early 1600s: "It is built separately in the yard, a short distance from the house, and is generally covered by a little roof of boards, to protect it from rain, snow or storms. Usually it is elevated a few inches above the ground so that the chickens and other small animals can stand under it when it rains.

"The reason why some colonists still construct both fireplaces and ovens of nothing but clay is that in many places here it is impossible to find a stone as big as a fist, not to mention larger ones; that but little experience has been had in brick-making over a fire; and besides, a first settler who erects a house on a plantation cannot afford to buy brick."[12]

> *The houses stand at good distance each from the other, a field and garden between each house and so on both sides of the street for four miles or thereabouts.*
>
> SAMUEL MAVERICK[13]

Those who had survived the first harrowing years in cave or hovel interpreted the "fashionable home" their contract required as being a sturdy frame with plank interior walls faced by exterior weatherboards. The more fortunate added small wood or iron casements of imported glass panes set in lead; others used oiled paper, thinly shaved sheets of horn, or scraped and stretched deerskin, as windows. Some still made do only with wooden shutters. For many, their wilderness home now for the first time had the luxury of a wooden floor. The next chore would be to clapboard the outside and to replace the thatch or cover the board roof with shingles. Since both oak clapboards and shingles were finished by laborious hand-shaving, this facet of a good second home usually was delayed until well after the harvest had been brought in, if not until early the following spring.

As often as not, the first one-room weather-boarded "kitchen house" was not given such exterior elegance until there was time or special reason to add a second room on the other side of the chimney. Such was the procedure at Wenham, Massachusetts, in 1672–73 when the church called Joseph Garrish to settle as its new pastor. As salary the congregation voted to pay him £50 plus twenty cords of fireplace wood, to put up an outside fence around his house lot, and to see that he received two pounds of butter for every milch cow belonging to members. For the parsonage, the town voted to make an eighteen-foot-square addition to Robert McClaflin's house, and "also the Towne do agree to *cover the old house with [clap]boards.*"[14] (McClaflin was given additional land by the town on which to build a new house for himself.)

Kitchen-room house of plain board construction was still in use when sketched by John Warner Barber for his *Connecticut Historical Collections*, 1836. Addition at left may have been used for storage or as bedroom.

Though by later standards these first permanent homes were small and crowded, they were a vast improvement over the first shelters. The colonists' grateful appreciation for their ability to take the next step forward underlies John Hammond's description of Maryland and Virginia planters' homes in 1656, many of which by then boasted plastered interiors and some the luxury of imported windowpanes: "Pleasant is their building which although for most part they are but one story beside the loft, and built of wood, yet they [are] contrived so delightful—usually the rooms are large, daubed and white-limed, glazed, and if not glazed windows, [have] shutters which are made very pretty and convenient."[15]

Even so, too many of those hopefully permanent houses could not be considered comfortable or stylish except by those who had built them. Two visitors who toured the colonies in 1679–80 paused at Trenton to etch a harsh picture of colonial carpentry and comfort along and near the seaboard:

Most of the English, and many others, have their houses made of nothing but clapboards, as they call them here, in this manner: they first make a wooden frame the same as they do in Westphalia, but not so strong, they then split the boards of clapboard, so that they are like cooper's pipestaves, except they are not bent. These are made very thin with a large knife, so that the thickest edge is about a little finger thick, and the other made sharp, like the edge of a knife. They are about five or six feet long, and are nailed on the outside of the frame, with the ends lapped over each other. They are not usually laid so close together as to prevent you from sticking a finger between them, in consequence either of their not being well joined, or the boards being crooked. When it is cold and windy, the best people plaster them with clay. Such are most all the English houses in the country.[16]

In addition to such exterior caulking, the space between the interior wall sheathing and the exterior planking often was "nogged in," that is, filled with clay usually mixed with chopped seaweed or thatch, with moss and broken shells or sometimes with badly formed and otherwise unusable crumbly brick. Many bushels of corncobs have been removed from spaces between some ancient walls.

In spite of such efforts, the colonial house in winter never was comfortably warm, however cheerful an atmosphere it might achieve. The more carefully built and richly furnished homes of well-to-do families still provided only bone-achingly chill shelter. At church, the potential of hell-fire and brimstone may have fired their imaginations but was of no actual help in warming the New England congregation. Judge Samuel Sewall commented one Sabbath evening in 1686, "This day so cold the Sacramental Bread is Frozen pretty hard and rattles sadly broken into the Plates."[17] Almost thirty years later, the January cold of 1715 had so settled into his Salem, Massachusetts, house that the judge had to cut short his diary report because "at six o'clock my ink freezes so that I can hardly write, [even sitting before] a good fire in my wive's chamber."[18]

Benjamin Franklin, discussing his new "iron fireplace," remarked in the 1740s that it greatly increased comfort; with the stove in use, the temperature in a Philadelphia room might be raised as high as 50 degrees Fahrenheit.[19] It seemed to Dr. Alexander Hamilton, used to the warmer Virginia climate, that

> they live in their houses in Albany as if it were in prisons, all their doors and windows being perpetually shut. But indeed the excessive cold winters here obliges them in that season to keep all snug and close, and they have not summer sufficient to revive heat in their veins so as to make them uneasy or put it in their heads to air themselves. In that season (winter) they are obliged to lay in as for a sea voyage, there being no stirring out of doors then for fear of never stirring again.

They generally eat to their [winter] morning's tea raw hung beef sliced down in thin chips in the manner of parmezan cheese.

Their winter here is so excessive cold so as to freeze their cattle stiff in one night in the stables.[20]

For it was not only the people that suffered. Remarking on a common colonial boarding arrangement, John Josselyn had noticed that in late seventeenth-century Boston "the poultry had their breakfast usually in cold weather in the kitchin."[21] This kind of accommodation was necessary during winter weeks of bitter winds, snow, and ice when lean-tos or single-board-sided sheds offered scant protection. Ewes, young calves, and piglets, as well as hens, could be saved from freezing if they were moved into the shelter of the kitchen hearth.

Such care enabled certain hens, wakened by light from flames reflected through uncurtained windows, to save the lives of a Massachusetts family in December 1640, when "Mr. Pelham's house in Cambridge took fire in the dead of the night by the chimney [and was] ready to lay hold upon the stairs. A neighbour's wife, *hearing some noise among her hens*, persuaded her husband to arise, which being very cold he was loth to do, yet through her great importunity he did and so espied the fire, and came running in his shirt, and had much to do to awake anybody, but he got them up at last, and so saved all."[22]

In an age when estate appraisers took into account every scrap from the soup in the kettle, as well as the kettle itself, to the number of turnips in a cellar, each domestic animal was an important item in the household inventory. Owners, themselves uncomfortably damp and cold when too far from the hearth, took extra care, often showing what today would be unnecessary, and therefore uncommon, compassion for their stock. Thus the kitchen continued as a haven for domestic animals throughout the eighteenth century. For example, May 13, 1750, was cold, misty, and "drisley wet" in New London, Connecticut, Justice Joshua Hempsted said, and he worried that evening over the "young mare yt I had of Pierpt [which had] folded below John Plumb lot." The seventy-one-year-old diarist found the foal in "the cold almost dead, could scarcely stand. I went out & Joshua with me & he brot it hom on his horse & I drove ye mare & *wee gave it warm milk & Dryed it by the fire.*"[23]

CHAPTER 3

The Kitchen Extensions

Where's the cook?
Is supper ready, the house trimmed,
Rushes strewed, cobwebs swept?
WILLIAM SHAKESPEARE,
The Taming of the Shrew

NONE OF THE SEVENTEENTH-CENTURY one-room cottages stands as it originally was built, for these basic common-room homes with a loft or chamber above were added to by their owners as soon as practicable. A new shed or lean-to served some households as a storage place, others as a bedroom, and at times enabled those living near crossroads to become innkeepers.

In 1704 the attentive journalist Mme. Knight described one such way-stop, when from the kitchen the inn's mistress "conducted me to a parlour in a little back Lento, wch was almost fill'd wth the bedsted, wch was so high that I was forced to climb on a chair to gitt up to ye wretched bed that lay on it; on wch [I] Strecht my tired Limbs, and lay'd my head on a Sad-colourd pillow."[24]

The kitchen itself was divided, with the largest portion retaining its character as the cooking and work area. The partitioned end, preferably on the north or coldest side, was fitted with wall shelves, a stand or bench, and perhaps an old table, to provide a handy closet area for food supplies and for garden and farm utensils not in daily use. When listed in inventories, such a section was given various names, the most popular obviously having been storeroom, although little kitchen, larder, buttery, pantry, and less occasionally, dairy room, milk room, or still room,[25] were applied. A partition could also be used to create the special convenience of a separate parlor or bedroom, as well as additional catchall space for extra tools or food containers.

[28]

Door from dairy room to adjacent kitchen of the Philipsburg Manor dependency in Upper Mills, North Tarrytown, New York, is closed to show Dutch strap hinges of the early eighteenth century. Simple benches and tables hold large milk jugs.

On occasion, such a partition also served to transform a cottage into an inn. Mme. Knight described such usage in 1704 when, "I then betook me to my Apartment, wch was a little Room parted from the Kitchen *by a single bord partition*; where, after I had noted the Occurrances of the past day, I went to bed, which, tho' pretty hard, Yet neat and handsome. I set my Candle on a Chest by the bedside, and setting up, fell to my old way of composing my Resentments."[26]

Without doubt this small room sometimes served as a sickroom, although diary entries seldom support the contention. It was, after all, more convenient for the housewife who acted as nurse to keep the ill or injured member of her family in the kitchen proper; certainly it was a more comfortable arrangement for the patient to be close to the warm hearth. Justice Hempsted described one such instance in October 1747, when he "went to Stonington to Pierpt's & then to ye Widow Miner's where Molly lies sick in a Truckle bed by the fire. She seems to be very moderately visited."[27]

If, on occasion, this small room was used for a confinement, it was because the room served primarily as the parents' bedroom and not because it had been planned specifically for any other purpose. When mentioned in inventories, travelers' journals, or colonists' diaries, the most felicitous description has been Mme. Knight's "apartment." The usual probate reference simply was to the "kitchen bedroom." Sometime during the nineteenth century, when the first romanticized tales of colonial life began to appear, the phrases "borning room" and "birth and death room" crept into the novelists' vocabulary, and they have been adopted with an unfortunate and unwarranted enthusiasm in the twentieth century. Many early householders never even built such a partition; they nevertheless managed to increase the number of their offspring and care for the ill and dying without a special room assigned for these occasions.

The seventeenth-century family living in one basic kitchen room plus loft counted themselves fortunate if they owned a single good bedstead and perhaps a trundle or truckle bed which could be rolled underneath during the day. Children usually slept on the kitchen floor on what inventories of the time called beds but which in modern parlance would be described as filled comforters or pallets. (Lists of family possessions often

Food-storage area off main kitchen room of the Philipsburg separate kitchen or bake house shows use of iron ring and hooks to hold meat. In smaller or less affluent homes, meat often was hung from ceiling beams in the main-house kitchen or in loft closets adjacent to chambers. Dough-box rests on X-base table frame.

mention only one or two bedsteads, but numerous beds.) More generally than is realized today, many families living in these simple one-room homes had hired help, who usually were assigned sleeping space in the loft, without regard for separation of the sexes, and here in particularly large families they sometimes were joined by the children.

The descriptive term "keeping-room" began to be heard later (more in the eighteenth than in the seventeenth century), but was not applied to the kitchen. The phrase, used more often in southern country areas, occurs rarely in New England inventories. But when and wherever used, it was applied only to what might be most clearly understood today as the family's best room—part parlor, part hall—in which the household's best furniture was kept and its plate or porcelain was displayed, and in which chests for linens sometimes were placed as also was the best bedstead and its hangings.

As seventeenth-century houses gradually were enlarged, the old fire-room more consistently was called the kitchen; in large homes where more than one room was used for cooking, preserving, and storing food, inventories designate both a "great kitchen" and a "little kitchen." It seems probable that "little kitchen," and the less generally used term "summer kitchen," applied to a small lean-to or ell annexed to the main house.

The original common kitchen or fire-room sometimes became the ell of the family's new house. Today, when houses are designed and built with all necessary rooms completed at once, there is a tendency to think of ells or wings as later additions. For practical reasons, the reverse often was true as houses evolved in the seventeenth and eighteenth centuries. The family had to continue living in its original home while the frame for the new was constructed. On its completion a new door might be cut where once a side window had been, to allow passage from the old house to the new dwelling; and the main door of the original house became a side door.

The handsome Joseph Webb house, built in 1752 on the old Main Street in Wethersfield, Connecticut—in the elegant parlor of which Washington and his staff met with Count Rochambeau to plan the battle of Yorktown—is believed to have a 1678 kitchen ell, which thus antedates the main house by three-quarters of a century.[28]

In January 1776, although war raged in many parts of the country and three of his sons had answered the Lexington alarm, Deacon Richard Hale nevertheless planned a new "manor house" to be started as soon as the winter cold broke. Supplies and labor were short; sawyers and carpenters were among the first the colonial army had set to work, to provide carts, wagons, and warehouses, as well as to strengthen and fortify strategic buildings. The deacon and his son Enoch completed much of the framing and sheathing for the new house. Though finishing touches—perhaps much

The lower "working" kitchen, where most foods were prepared, of the restored 1720 Philipsburg Manor, Upper Mills, North Tarrytown, New York. Hearth roasting utensils include a long trammel with hooks suspended from a lug-pole, and massive wrought andirons with racks and spits at four heights.

of the plastering and wainscoting, certainly the color-staining of sheathing and casements—were not yet complete, the family prepared to move into their new home early in October. They had just done so when the "sad rumour" filtered back to Coventry that Hale's twenty-one-year-old son Nathan had been captured and hanged by the British.[29]

The new Hale home of ten rooms, a "mansion house" in the language of the period, was built with no new kitchen-room.[30] Instead, the 1776 house was constructed so that part of the original 1746 home could be utilized as a kitchen ell. The fashionable new house thus gained a rare colonial country luxury, a separate room or parlor for dining, placed in the rear of the new main building and opening into the old house, now the kitchen ell in twentieth-century terminology.

New England winters necessitated such all-in-one attached building design. In the warm south, however, as a new home replaced the original, the main house preferably became a completely detached unit. Often enough, the original house then served as a separate kitchen or bakehouse, to which additional work rooms or "offices" sometimes were attached, although where fortune provided, the tendency was to erect separate buildings for each activity.

In the Charleston (South Carolina) *Gazette* of July 28, 1733, William Dry offered for sale a plantation two miles from Goose Creek Bridge, which included an

apple and peach tree orchard, a good brick Dwelling-House, 2 Brick Store-Houses, a brick Kitchen and Wash-House, a brick Necessary-House,[31] a Barn with a large Brick Chimney, with several Rice Mills, Mortars, a winnowing House, an Oven, a large Stable and Coach-House, a Cooper's Shop, a House built for a Smith's Shop, a Garden on each Side of the House, with Posts, Rails and Pales of the best Stuff, all plained & painted, & brick'd underneath, a Fishpond well stored with Perch, Roach, Pike, Eels and Catfish, a handsome cedar Horse-block or double pair of Stairs, Frames, Plants, &c. ready to be fix'd, in and about a Spring within 3 Stones throw of the House, intended for a Cold Bath, and House over it.

By 1774, the home of the wealthiest of Virginians, Robert "King" Carter's Nomini Hall in Westmoreland County, had in addition to the great manor house a small village of such outbuildings, now usually called

Well-sweep on far side of the 1776 Hale mansion house at Coventry, Connecticut, shows above the roof line of the original one-story-with-loft home. Lightning rod protects house in this 1836 drawing by John Warner Barber. Pine trees still stand near front entrance of the restored museum house. Apple orchard at left was pruned high as protection from cattle and horses.

dependencies, including separate kitchen house, wash house, bakehouse, dairy, and storehouse.

According to tradition, no log cabins were built in New England in the colonial period—or indeed anywhere along the seaboard save in Scandinavian settlements—but this conclusion obviously depends on how "log" is defined. Bay Colony garrison houses or forts (which often doubled as private houses) were constructed of logs roughly squared off when the bark was stripped from them with an adze or axe, or by saw, as soon as pits were established for this work. These logs—which were sometimes, but not necessarily, set around four equally large corner posts—were placed atop each other, and the crevices daubed with clay. Later many were covered with shingles or clapboards. They differed from the Scandinavian cabin in the treatment of the corner joints; those in New England were mortised or dovetailed into each other, while the Swedish fashion was to notch the timbers so that they met in what was called a cob or crib style.[32]

Visitors to the home of Jacob Hendricks in Burlington, New Jersey, in 1679 compared his Swedish-style log cabin with a clapboard frame house:

> Although not much larger than where we were last night, [it] was somewhat better and tighter, being made according to the Swedish mode, and as they usually build their houses here, which are block houses, being nothing less than entire trees, split through the middle or squared out of the rough, and placed in the form of a square, upon each other, as high as they wish to have the house; the ends of these timbers are let into each other, about a foot from the ends, half of one into half of the other, the whole structure is thus made without a nail or a spike.
>
> The ceiling and roof do not exhibit much finer work, except amongst the most careful people, who have the ceiling planked and a glass window. The doors are wide enough but very low, so that you have to stoop in entering. These houses are quite tight and warm, but the chimney is placed in a corner.[33]

Whether mortised as in New England or cribbed as in the middle colonies, the log house was also a familiar sight in Maryland and Virginia. In 1728 William Byrd and his surveying party found as they charted the line with North Carolina that "most of the Houses in this part of the country are Log-Houses, covered with Pine or Cypress shingles 3 feet long and one broad. They are hung on laths with Peggs and their doors too, turn upon Wooden Hinges, and have Wooden Locks to Secure them, so that the building is finished without Nails or other Iron Work."[34]

The seventeenth-century hewed log house, with its large common room and loft, was a building type that eighteenth-century settlers would continue

Kenmore, home of patriot Fielding Lewis and his wife, Betty, sister of George Washington, was built at Fredericksburg, Virginia, in 1752. Separate office and kitchen dependencies, typical of southern planters' home styles of the period, are shown at left and right of main house.

to choose whether they moved northwest from Virginia or south into the Carolinas and thence into Kentucky and Tennessee, or west from New England into upper New York, Pennsylvania, Ohio, and Illinois. The blockhouse or log cabin was, after all, one of the most plausible uses of building materials to be found on the homestead in any section of the colonies.

Sometimes the rough-hewed exterior hid interior furnishings of better than expected worth, as Dr. Hamilton noted in the diary of his tour of the northern colonies, when he recorded a visit he and a companion made to a small farm at Greenwich Village, New York, in 1744:

> We went ashore to fill water near a small log cottage on the west side of the river inhabited by one Stanespring and his family. The man was about 37 years of age, and woman 30. They had seven children, girls and boys. The children seemed quite wild and rustick. They stared like sheep upon [us] when we entered the house, being amazed att my laced hat and sword. They went out to gather blackberries for us, which was the greatest pleasure they could make us.
>
> This cottage was very clean and neat but poorly furnished. Yet [my companion] observed severall superfluous things which

showed an inclination to finery in these poor people, such as a looking glass with a painted frame, half a dozen pewter spoons and as many plates, old and wore out but bright and clean, a set of stone tea dishes, and a tea pot. These [he] said, were superfluous and too splendid for such a cottage, and therefor they ought to be sold to buy wool to make yarn; that a little water in a wooden pail might serve for a looking glass, and wooden plates and spoons would be as good for use and, when clean, would be almost as ornamental. As for the tea equipage it was quite unnecessary, but the man's musket, he observed, was as usefull a piece of furniture as any in the cottage. We had a pail of milk here which we brought on board, and the wind coming southerly att eleven a'clock, we weighed anchor and entered the Highlands which presented a wild, romantick scene of rocks and mountains covered with small scraggy wood, mostly oak.[35]

Kalm reiterated the new emigrant-settlers' appreciation of log-cabin home-styling in 1749, when he wrote of Pennsylvania and Maryland that "formerly the Swedes built houses all of wood, with clay smeared between the logs, *like those now built here by the Irish*. They have no glass in their windows—only small loopholes with sliding shutters before them, just like our Finnish cabin windows."[36]

As the colonial era closed, Nicholas Cresswell, en route to survey Illinois lands, wrote that near Harwood's Landing on the western Virginia frontier, having taken "fourteen days to come about 120 miles [from Alexandria] . . . there are about 30 houses in [Harwoodsburg] all built of logs and covered with Clapboards, but not a nail in the whole Town."[37]

> *He from the chimney took*
> *A flitch of bacon off the hook,*
> *And freely from the fattest side*
> *Cut out large slices to be fried.*
> JOHN DRYDEN

Sometimes in autumn, when the air is sharpened by early frost, and the first real hearth fire of the season is lit, today's householder of an old farm catches briefly a scent out of the past. Flames leaping up from hickory logs or maple chunks dry out the dampened flue and evoke the smoke of kitchen "cure" fires first laid more than three centuries ago. The after-tang of the smoke brings with it the still-recognizable scent of hams and venison chimney-smoked and then stored over winter to be stewed, baked, minced, grilled, or boiled into meat-and-porridge pies. The scent is a momentary reminder of the important meat-preserving method seventeenth-century colonists learned from Indians in all the seaboard settlements.

Other, more tangible evidences are still to be found, though ever

Mid-eighteenth-century kitchen of the restored Hendrickson House, Holmdel, New Jersey, has oven built into side wall at right angle to hearth. Oven thus extends beyond wall into pantry, as seen through door in center of photo. Top of oven was used for keeping foods warm. Plates were "racked forward" as shown here for easy removal from cupboard shelf.

more rarely, when a walker in old woodlands comes upon the tumbled remains of an outdoor hearth. When the brambles and moss are removed and the settled soil dug away, crumbling stones or the powdery residue of old bricks point to the forgotten hearth, with no indication, however, of a cellar hole, or of the foundation walls that would have stood there had the fireplace and flue been part of a house, barn, or mill. The overgrown ground layer of stones is all that remains of what once was an open smokehouse.

The earliest of these smokehouses were not true sheds; that is, they were not fully enclosed. Instead, they literally were fireplaces. To form one, a hearth was laid, and perhaps a short chimney added, in the center of an area defined by four posts set in the earth and atop which stripped green boughs formed a latticework.

Colonial families north and south quickly adapted the Indian use of smoke to cure or "barbecue" meat. In the more moderate climate of Virginia, they first learned from the "locals" how to set up such sapling platforms, supported on posts five to six feet high. After meat had been salted, it was spread out on the platforms to be smoked by a fire built on the earthen floor below. It did not take much experimentation to discover that certain hardwoods imparted a special piquancy of flavor. Oak, hickory, and maple were favored.

"The tongue of a grown moose, dried in the Smoak after the Indian fashion is a dish for a Sagamor," John Josselyn declared in his seventeenth-century dissertation on New England rarities.[38] Although his notes were made at a time when "barbecue" had become part of the southern settlers' new American vocabulary, the word apparently had not yet been heard often in the northern colonies. When the first settlers in Virginia anglicized the Spanish–West Indian *barbacao* to "barbecue," it connoted the high-platform smoke method. As time passed, the word was used to describe any meat cooked, especially in the open, by being suspended above a fire. (Later, its use signified the pit-roasting method understood today.)

By 1770 many southern farmers, their homes built and barns and store-houses erected, added separate walled-in sheds for more efficient "barbe-cuing" or smoking in the house yard, eventually perfecting Virginia ham. Young Nicholas Cresswell described the smoke-curing process in 1775:

> When there is a plentiful Mast (what they call Mast are acorns, Walnuts, Chestnuts, and all wild fruits) the Hogs will get fat in the woods with little, or no corn. Great quantities are killed as soon as they are taken out of the woods, salted, barrelled and sent to the West Indies [and] sell from 12 to 27 shillings Currency per hun-dred[weight].
>
> The bacon cured here is not to be equalled in any part of the world, their hams in particular. They first rub them over with brown sugar and let them lie all night. This extracts the watery particles. They let them lie in salt for 10 days or a fortnight. Some rub them with hickory ashes instead of saltpetre, it makes them red as the saltpetre and gives them a pleasant taste.
>
> Then they are hung up in the smoke-house and a slow smoky fire kept under them for three or four weeks; nothing but hickory wood is burnt in these smoke-houses. This gives them an agreeable flavour, far preferable to the Westphalia Hams; not only that,

Gravel paths separate plant sections and lead to smokehouse at one corner of the Williamsburg Palace garden, Williamsburg, Virginia.

but it prevents them going rancid and will preserve them for several years by giving them a fresh smoking now and then. Beef cured in this manner is but very indifferent eating. Indeed the Beef in this country is not equal in goodness to the English, it may be as fat, but not so juicy.[39]

In the colder north, when extra smoke buildings were added they were more likely to be annexed to the first ell room beyond the kitchen or common room, with a separate chimney added to the new exterior end wall. Much more common were the early smoke ovens formed by the simple expedient of using the main-house chimney itself. Salted and partly dried meat could be hung from high lug-poles reached up through the flue of the kitchen fireplace; smoke rising from the logs below did the curing.

In the eighteenth century when older chimneys were rebuilt or new ones planned for new houses, a special opening for an attic smoke oven was sometimes built into, or run up several feet alongside, the chimney stack; smoke rising from kitchen fires below still cured the meat hung therein. Later many such loft areas were walled in as the once-open garrets were divided into second- and third-floor rooms. Gradually these fairly small "meat closets" became known as smoke rooms, for once cured, hams and bacon were hung here from ceiling and wall hooks to keep through the winter, and pieces were sliced off "the side" and brought down each day as needed. This descriptive name still could be heard in rural New England and in farm homes throughout Kentucky, Ohio, Indiana, and Illinois until only a generation or two ago.

A third location for an interior "smoke-furnace" was the cellar base of the chimney. These oven openings, usually one to two feet above the cellar floor, seem to date mainly from the mid-eighteenth century. Where these ovens have not been walled in or filled, the energetic, preferably small-framed, investigator will find that the oven mouth is large enough for him to crawl through. Once inside he will find himself in a small stone "room" about the same dimensions in width and depth as the cooking hearth in the kitchen above. From this vantage point the small oven flue is discoverable, as are the points between the stones where the iron lug-poles were set from three to five feet above the oven floor. Often enough the crusted lugs themselves are still in place. The higher stones of the oven wall and ceiling retain a hardened, soot-blackened coating of the grease that seeped into the porous stones during the smoking process.

In spite of colorful anecdotes woven ex post facto—some twentieth-century romantics have declared them "spy holes," pirate hideouts, or sanctuaries for runaway Civil War slaves—these openings were designed by their original owners as prosaic ovens. Few colonists had any desire to harbor pirates or planned their chimneys with this exigency in mind. Perhaps the old ovens were utilized later as spur-of-the-moment, if worrisomely obvious, slave hideouts, but it is to be doubted that even the most politically conscious eighteenth-century farmer foresaw the needs of his as yet unborn abolitionist descendants.

In one-story and one-and-a-half-story homes where constricted loft space and lack of a deep cellar obviated such extra oven areas, large sides of meat continued to be hung from lug-poles set high within the main flue and were cured by smoke rising from the kitchen hearth.

Some eighteenth-century kitchen fireplaces whose interior side walls have not been repaired too often provide evidence of a fourth chimney curing-procedure. Slender sleeper lengths of 1 by 2 or 2 by 2 hardwood, called bacon strips in New England, were set between the stones or bricks of the sides, beginning just behind the lintel and running back to the rear wall of the chimney. Even where they still exist, these old charred strips often go unnoticed, for their color has been too long blended into that of the smoke-blackened stones to be seen easily. Their ancient usefulness not recognized, other sleeper strips have been removed by restorationists in the belief that these oak or chestnut lengths were a peculiar filler used by rustic housewrights, and constitute fire hazards.

Carefully examined, however, the old bacon strip often will be found to retain at least the shanks of the hand-wrought iron nails or hooks originally studded into the wood.[40] From these spikes small slabs of ham, bacon, or other "venison" were hung to be smoked by the simplest of all colonial curing methods.

PART III

The Seventeenth-Century Kitchen

CHAPTER 1

Preparing to Set Sail

If the trumpet give an uncertain sound
Who shall prepare himself to the battle?
I CORINTHIANS XIV:8

THERE WAS LITTLE REASON to wonder, John Smith wrote, that early attempts to settle Virginia had met with such discouraging results. The prime difficulty lay in the company's having first sent over a preponderance of lesser gentry, footmen, "libertines and such like"—undoubtedly the most ill-equipped group ever to essay the frontier life.[1]

Much of the fault in the choice of early settlers originated, of course, with the stubborn Captain Smith himself, as it had with others of those first travelers who wrote rhapsodically of the New World. They pictured for their readers—in an England where forests had been thinned and each tree cherished—great stretches of thick woodlands, meadows of wild flowers and "sallet herbs," and inlets crowded with schools of fish ready to leap into the angler's net. They reported tidy cornfields scattered along the coast, cultivated by a native population anxious to trade farm produce for English trinkets.

These lyrical descriptions all too often were true as far as they went, but they tended to gloss over the individual's necessary investment in time and work and the colony's drastic need for skilled labor. They presented the New World as a kind of picnic site. They wrote of "rowes of faire houses"[2] when what actually existed was a dozen huts of roughly split green wood, crouched on the edge of the Atlantic with only a dark rim of wilderness on all other sides.

When Smith set out to persuade the yeoman and artisan to emigrate, he pictured a New England with an astonishingly short wilderness work week, wherein each day allowed a free hour or so for family fishing excur-

[45]

sions. Should that pleasure fail to entice, Smith offered the bonus of pulling a cash product out of the sea:

> What pleasure can bee more, being tired with any occasion a-shore—planting vines, Fruits or Hearbs, [or] cultivating their owne grounds to the pleasure of their owne mindes, their Fields, Gardens, Orchards, Buildings, Ships, and other Workes, etc.,—than to recreate themselves before their own doores in their owne boates upon the Sea; where man, woman and childe, with a small hooke and line, by angling, may take divers sorts of excellent fishe, at their pleasure?
>
> And is it not pretty sport to pull up 2 pence, 6 pence and 12 pence as fast as you can hale and veare a line? If a man work but 3 daies a season, he may get more than hee can spend unlesse he will be excessive. Now that Carpenter, Mason, Gardiner, Taylor, Smith, Sailer, Forger or what others, may they not make this a pretty recreation though they fish but an houre in a day, to take more than they can eat in a weeke? Or . . . yet sell it . . . or change it . . . for anything they want?[3]

While the actual phrases "land of milk and honey" or "streets paved with gold" were avoided, Smith's *Description of New England* in 1616 bore little resemblance to the frontier truth his readers who had purchased one-way tickets would face. Fields of Indian corn could be ruined by spring floods, summer droughts, and hail; there were desperate seasons when there was no grain to trade.[4] As a result, there was bound to be another seventeenth-century view of the popularity of that steady New England seafood diet, and it was presented by Edward Johnson:

"The women once a day, as the tide gave way, resorted to the mussels and clambankes, which are a fish as big as horse-mussels, where they daily gathered their families' food. . . . Quoth one, 'My husband hath travelled . . . near forty miles and hath with great toil brought a little corn home with him!' . . . Quoth the other, 'Our last peck of meal is now in the oven abaking . . . many of our neighbors have quite spent all, and we owe one loaf of that little we have.' Then spake a third, 'My husband hath ventured himself among the Indians for corn and can get none.' "[5]

Johnson's book had been written of New England in 1630–31. Unfortunately, for any effect its words of caution would have, it was not published in London until 1654. Still, he had not been able, any more than had his predecessors, to resist the impulse to proselytize; indeed, that was his main purpose in writing. The dialogue quoted ended with this declaration, " 'and yet methinks our children are as cheerful, fat and lusty with feeding upon these mussels, clambanks and other fish, as they were in England with their fill of bread.' "[6]

However much the first notes might quaver, each trumpeter managed to end his contribution to the chorus with a loud, clear call.

Many emigrants were quick to send back needed advice. Young Francis Higginson, who arrived at Salem to serve as reader in that colony's first church, was explicit in his warning of 1630: "When you are once parted with England you shall meete neither markets nor fayres to buy what you want. Therefore be sure to furnish yourself with things fitting to be had before you come, as meale for bread, malt for drinke, woolen and linnen cloath, and leather for shoes."[7]

He cautioned that the only building materials at hand would be unmilled lumber, rough stone, and clay; any other house parts must be brought from England, including "all manner of carpenters tools and a great deale of iron and steele to make nails, and locks for houses, and furniture for ploughs and carts, and glasse for windows, and many other things which were better for you to think of there than to want them here. Therefore, before you come, be careful to be strongly instructed what things are fittest to bring with you for your more comfortable passage at sea, as also for your husbandry occasions when you come to the land."[8]

Higginson emphasized that a planter must bring provisions to last each member of his family for a year, the minimum time needed to clear and cultivate a cornfield and garden. To make certain his readers understood, he provided a "Catalogue of Such Needful Things" for the individual: "8 bushels of meale, 2 Bushels of pease, 2 Bushels of Otemeale, 1 Gallon of Aquavitae, 1 Gallon of Oyle, 2 Gallons of Vinegar, 1 firkin of Butter; also Cheese, Bacon, Sugar, Pepper, Cloves, Mace, Cinnamon, Nutmegs and Fruit." Food supplies would be shipped over in their own storage containers and these would serve as pantry furnishings. To prepare and serve food, Higginson thought cooking utensils for a family's hearth should include: "1 iron pot, 1 Kettel, 1 Frying Pan, 1 Gridiron, 2 Skellets, 1 spit, Wooden Platters, Dishes, Spoons and Trenchers."[9]

Basic food was included in the average £6 fare, but each family or group was expected to cook its own meals during the voyage. Fireplaces were set up on deck. Some were well built of good brick; others were little more than an open iron pan placed on a bed of sand in which charcoal was burned. Provisions aboard ship included in the fare, William Wood wrote in 1634, would be "salt Beefe, Porke, salt Fish, Butter, Cheese, Pease, Pottage, Water-grewell, and such kind of Victualls, with good Biskets, and sixeshilling Beere."[10] If the passenger could afford the extra cost, he should carry his own

> comfortable refreshing of fresh victuall. As first, for such as have ability, some Conserves, and good Clarret Wine to burne at Sea; or you may have it by some of your Vintners or Wine-Coopers burned

here & put into Vessels, which will keep much better than other burnt Wine, it is a very comfortable thing for the stomacke; or such as are Seasicke: Sallat-oyle likewise, Prunes are good to be stewed: Sugar for many things: White Biskets, and Egs, and Bacon, Rice, Poultry, and some weather-Sheepe to Kill aboard the Ship; and some fine Flowre-baked meates, will keep about a weeke or nine days at Sea. Juyce of Lemons well put up, is good either to prevent or curre the Scurvy.

Here it must not be forgotten to carry small Skillets or Pipkins, and small frying-panns, to dresse their victualls at Sea.[11]

Deck space was shared with the pens of poultry, goats, sheep, and swine the colonists took with them either to provide fresh food during the trip of six to ten or twelve weeks or to stock their new farms. There were no staterooms and there was no steward service. Some ships offered the luxury of a small private cabin to the important passenger willing to pay a higher fare; seldom, however, was there more than one such cabin available. Passengers slept belowdeck in hammocks or on pallets wherever room could be found; those who insisted on privacy could hang up canvas strips or blankets, but this was not a popular choice, for it cut off free circulation of what little air there was. In all but the worst weather, many chose to sleep on deck.

Wood's advice obviously was based on personal knowledge when he suggested "for bedding, so it be easie, and cleanly, and warme, it is no matter how old or coarse it be for the use at Sea: and so likewise for Apparrell, the oldest cloathes be the fittest, with a long coarse coat to keepe better things from the pitched ropes and plankes."[12]

Virginia settlers differed philosophically from many of their cousins who would settle the northern colonies in not desiring separation from the Anglican church, as, for example, did those in New Plymouth. Nor did they want to establish a colony based on even a "purified form" of Anglicanism, a consideration basic to the formation of the Massachusetts Bay, Hartford, and New Haven colonies. They were spurred to Virginia by the desire to own land on which to raise raw produce to be sold in England. There was less tendency for complete families to emigrate to early Virginia. This, as well as the lack of formation into tightly knit church parishes, resulted in less inclination to settle as unified communities or townships.

The instructions given those headed for the southern colonies were basically the same as for those who set sail for New England. Thus, the young men signed by the Virginia Company to settle as tenants similarly were told that an iron pot, a kettle, a large frying pan, a gridiron, two skillets, a spit, wooden platters, dishes, and spoons were the amount of cooking equipment needed for each group of six. As Company tenants they had agreed to work for seven years to pay off the cost of their passage, at which time they would have earned the right to claim fifty acres of land. Those who (after 1616) were able to pay their own passage were each entitled to a fifty-acre section. The potential planter also could claim an additional fifty acres for each member of his household whose transportation he paid.

Fearing that adventurous bachelors might tend to stray from the colony before their seven-year terms were completed, Governor George Yeardley asked London to send over "young and uncorrupt" maids.[13] In return for her willingness to hazard an ocean voyage and life on the frontier, each woman was promised free passage if on arrival she married one of the worrisomely restless tenants. Should she decide instead on a planter who already had gained title or had come with a patent to his own land, it was understood that her bridegroom would repay the Company.

The Virginia Company also granted plantation plots—in addition to those first four settlements of James City, Elizabeth City, Charles City, and Henrico—to shareholding promoters, who in a kind of subcontractual arrangement agreed to furnish colonists and supplies. In this manner, Newport News, Southampton, Berkeley Hundred, and Martin's Hundred were planted.

Under this kind of contract, the promoters of Berkeley Hundred commissioned William Tracy in 1620 to transport fifty colonists to Virginia, including twelve women. Tracy's ship, the aptly named *Supply*, was excellently provisioned for the work ahead. In the hold were the felling axes, pickaxes, squaring axes, and spades with which the new farms would be cleared to make room for the first orchards and gardens. Weeding hoes, chisels and augers, hatchets, frows, handbills, short shovels, scythes and reaping hooks, nails, grindstones, and an anvil were shipped aboard the *Supply*, as they were on each transport later dispatched to the colony.

Barrels of tar and pitch, lanterns, bellows, hogsheads of soap and bay-salt, oil, candles, and candleholders were sent, and each man was instructed to have with him the unwieldy armor of the time: a corselet, a bandolier, a musket, a sword and belt, twenty pounds of powder and sixty pounds of shot, a pistol, and goose shot. Those who could afford it were advised to bring fishing hooks, lines and nets, kine and goats. Each emigrant was supplied with canvas to use in lieu of blankets and from which to fashion work clothes. Shipped aboard the *Supply* were chests of leather breeches, falling bands, Monmouth caps, shoes, knitted socks and Irish stockings, thread, and tailors' shears. New Virginia settlers took no chances on being without familiar English garden produce and took with them cabbage, turnip, carrot, parsnip, mustard, letttuce, and onion seeds, just as did those who sailed to New England.

John Josselyn, who visited the colonies in 1638 and again in 1663–71, wrote a more detailed catalog of necessities for the emigrant family. He anticipated the settler's ability to purchase cattle, oxen, and swine by including brands, fetters, and curry combs, and also believed the emigrant would require the solace of an occasional pipe: "Bellows, Scoop, Great pail, Casting shovel, a Sack, Lanthorn, Tobacco pipes, 5 broad howes, 5 narrow howes, 5 felling axes, 2 hand saws, 1 whip saw, 1 file and wrest, 2 hammers, 2 augers, wheels for a cart, wheel barrow, canoe, short oak ladder, plough, axle tree, cart; 3 shovels, 2 spades, 2 broad axes, 6 chisels, 3 gimblets, 2 hatchets, 2 frows, 2 hand bills; nails of all sorts; 3 locks and 3 pr. fetters, 2 curry combs, brand for beasts, hand vise, 100 wt. spikes, nails and pins (120), 2 pick axes, chain and lock for a boat, coulter (10 pound) pitch fork and plough share."[14]

By 1675, when Josselyn's notes on his two voyages were published, his list of shipboard fare differed from that given by Wood forty years earlier only in its more detailed explanation of how the captain apportioned food en route. It gives this picture of the seventeenth-century daily menu: "The common proportions of Victualls for the Sea to a Mess, being four men, is as followeth; Two pieces of Beef of three pound and 1/4 per piece; four pound of Bread; one pint 1/4 of Pease; Four Gallons of Bear, with Mustard and Vinegar for three flesh dayes in the week; for four fish dayes, to each Mess per day, two pieces of Codd or Habberdine, making three pieces of fish; one quarter of a pound of Butter, Four pound of Bread; three quarters of a pound of Cheese; Bear as before; Oatmeal per day, for 50 men, one Gallon and so proportionable for more or fewer. Thus you see the ship's provision is Beefe or Porke, Fish, Butter, Cheese, Pease, Pottage, Water gruel, [brown] Bisket and six-shilling Bear."[15]

In 1625, a little less than twenty years after the first settlement, the Virginia Company ordered a census. The record thus provided showed that 1,232 men and women, their homes scattered along the banks of the James River and on the Eastern shore, were entitled to call themselves the first families of Virginia. These old lists, still in the British Public Record Office, also included the household supplies each colonist owned at the time; in addition to the cattle and goats first brought over, swine and poultry had been added to many inventories. Some of the larger farms listed their own murderers, as cannon were called, in addition to matchlocks, swords, and cutlasses. Fewer than twenty slaves were included among the colony's chattels.[16]

Josselyn's general inventory of settlers' needs had reflected his own better-than-average income; nevertheless, he added only an extra frying pan, two more kettles, and a mortar to Higginson's kitchen list. He estimated that a family of six would require "1 iron pot, 1 great copper kettle, 1 small kettle, 1 lesser kettle, 1 large frying pan, 1 small frying pan, 1 brass mortar, 1 spit, 1 grid iron, 2 skillets, and platters, dishes and spoons of wood."[17]

That these lists cover almost exactly what each householder who could afford the cost brought to both northern and southern colonies, and to which he added surprisingly little during the seventeenth century, is borne out by the detailed inventories filed with probate courts.

CHAPTER 2

Furnishing the Great and Little Kitchens

Ay, now am I in Arden. . . .
When I was at home, I was in a better
* place:*
But travellers must be content.
        WILLIAM SHAKESPEARE,
              As You Like It

Behold, the half was not told me.
              1 KINGS 10:7

WHEN WILLIAM GOOGE DIED at Lynn, Massachusetts, in 1646, his wife and three youngsters inherited his common-room house and twelve acres of land. The appraisers for probate found five bushels of wheat, ten of Indian corn, and a bundle of flax in the loft. He left also a chest, chair, "an old chair," a stool, a trunk, and some bedding but no bedstead. Other furnishings included ex-soldier Googe's musket and bandoleers, sword and belt. Two bags or sacks, three wood trays, three wood bowls, three wood dishes, "some" pails and tubs, one "runlet," an earthen pot, a skillet, a posnet, a frying pan, a grid-iron, and six spoons completed the list inside the house. In the yard were one cow and four hogs.

Even though old court records indicate that the Googe family had at one time (if not when he died) employed a servant, the list of Googe's possessions barely included the minimum accessories advised by Higginson and Josselyn. Nor did the estate inventories of many other early colonists.

Noticeably absent is mention of a spit or any kind of hook, hake, or crow that might have been used in roasting game or fowl. Nor is mention made of a trammel, chain, or andirons. The home which could not afford these depended upon improvised utensils to which no real value—even a few pence—could be assigned by the appraisers. The lack of even the

[52]

Clock jack and weights turned spit rod between andirons so that meat could be roasted evenly. Typical seventeenth-century oven is in back of chimney wall; three trammels are suspended from lug-pole inside chimney throat. Shallow round chopping bowl at right was set on tripod base for easy transfer of food to cooking pot. Buttolph-Williams House, Wethersfield, Connecticut, 1692.

simplest iron spit was the easiest to overcome; the householder need only revert to the medieval English country method of using sharply pointed sticks or lances of hard green wood—hazel, maple, hickory, or oak branches whittled to shape as needed. The lack of andirons to support a spit in front of the fire was overcome by placing stones a couple of feet apart; the new wooden spit then was stretched between these.

As an alternative roasting method, heavy cords, twisted together for ropelike strength, were suspended from the lug-pole or galley balk set between the stones of the chimney throat. With no hooks or prongs, Mrs. Googe would have had to secure the food to be roasted by forcing a thick hardwood skewer through one end of a piece of meat; to this skewer the "roasting string" could be tied, if the string itself was not threaded through the meat. In addition to the lug-pole inside the chimney, similar wood suspension rods often were fastened in front of or just under the lintel. Sometimes pegs were inserted into the face of the lintel, from which roasting strings were suspended. In better-equipped kitchens the lug-poles were made of iron, just as iron trammel chains and hooks replaced the wood and string of the simpler hearth.

Today "skillet" and "frying pan" are synonymous in most kitchens. In the seventeenth and eighteenth centuries, a skillet more closely resembled what now would be called a saucepan of about two-quart capacity. A posnet was a small saucepot usually set on its own tripod frame or attached feet. Skillets also were set on tripod legs so that they could be used over embers, and small pieces of meat were roasted in these. What is called roasting today more accurately was termed baking by the colonial cook.

The runlet listed in the Google inventory was a wooden measure of approximately eighteen gallons; it may have been used to hold cider. The tubs in which supplies had first come from England were used to store powdered (salted) meat or other preserved food, as were the pails. One pail must have been kept for milk; another for water or cider.

Mention by the probate appraisers of wood trays, bowls, and dishes indicates that these had been turned professionally, as the spoons also must have been. If the Google family had a wooden pitcher, it was home-carved so poorly as to have no value to others. Similarly no calabashes—homemade ladles or dippers or scoops of dried and hardened gourds—would have been appraised.

The wooden trays would be those most collectors call platters or trenchers. Food was served in these common dishes, into which each member of the family dipped in turn, using a sippet of bread when bread was available. Table forks were an uncommon luxury; even in the best-appointed homes it was not until the mid-eighteenth century that they began to appear regularly in estate inventories. In lieu of forks or sippets, the agile colonial diner used the first three fingers of one hand held rigidly together, the little finger and thumb joined across the palm to keep out of the way, in a kind of horizontal Boy Scout salute. The other hand held a much-needed napkin or towel; in poor homes, however, all food was presumed "finger-licking good." Porridge or stews required spoons, as the Google inventory indicates.

In well-to-do families, the use of sippets was common at the best tables, but there, diners also used spoons and knives. Table knives in the seventeenth century, and well into the eighteenth, were sharply pointed to facilitate spearing food. As forks came into more common use in the eighteenth cen-

Captain Isaac Halsey added this early-eighteenth-century kitchen to the house built in 1648 by his grandfather, Thomas, one of the founders of Southampton, Long Island. Restored by the Southampton Colonial Society, the Halsey homestead is the oldest saltbox-style house in New York State. Cooking hearth was designed with rear beehive-shaped oven and long crane to hold cooking pots.

tury, the tip of the dining knife became rounded and gradually was ballooned out, evolving into a much tidier utensil with which to carry food to the mouth.

Higher in the economic scale than Googe was blacksmith Daniel Howard, who died in June 1675 at Hingham, Massachusetts, where he had owned some fourteen acres of land in addition to his house lot. His shop and "Coale house" were separate from his dwelling. The two-room

Howard home as described by estate appraisers may have been a second one, for the inventory listed the rooms as the "lower Roome," the "Chamber above," and a "Lean-too and Celler." The furnishings were of a quality that would indicate equal care had been given to building the house itself.

The Howard family's main common room on the ground floor was furnished with a "featherbed and Boulster, two Pillows with the Blankets and Rugg and Chests and Curtains vallens Curtaine Rod Bedstead and all things belonging to it." (The rug was a coverlet for the bed.) There were in addition "2 pare of Sheetes and four pillow Beers [cases] and three towels." Furniture included "2 Joyned Chests and one Box [perhaps placed on top of one of the chests] and a deale Board Chest; a little Joyned table, a Joyned Cradle, 6 old Chayers." The pewter kitchen accessories were "3 smale dishes and potengers, 1 pint pot and 1 Bason and 1 Chamb. pot." Brass utensils were "a warmeingpan, two Scillets and five spoones." In addition to the skillets, cooking utensils included a "frieing pan and 1 gridiron, 2 smale iron pots and pot hooks." There were also "1 payer of Andirons and one Small Speete, a firepan and tongs." Two hakes, a lamp, and an iron crow were listed.

Wood trenchers and trays were stored in the lean-to and cellar, where were also "2 powderingtubs and 3 Coolers, one Mash Tubb and 2 beere Barrels; one Spinning Wheele; Sope and Oyle; 2 Sives and 2 Payles and 2 Canns; 2 baggs and Cheese and earthen pots and pans." Other food supplies, "8 bushells of Indian Corn, Malt and Salt," were stored in the second-floor bedchamber, as were a second bedstead, supplies of sheep and cotton wool, a looking glass, tobacco box and tongs, a bridle, saddle, and two "pannels."

If a generation is counted as twenty years, Howard's possessions were inventoried during the beginning of the third generation, or forty-five years after settlement of the Massachusetts Bay Colony.

His listed house furnishings were, if not actually made to his order, certainly the work of a fellow-craftsman, as indicated by the word "joyned"; they may have been brought from England. The deal board chest probably referred to the type of low storage chest collectors today call a six-board blanket chest or box. ("Deal" indicates the use of wide, fairly thick pine or oak board.) The "little joyned table" might show up in a modern collection under the more sophisticated alias of "mixing table" or "tea table," or as one of the many misnamed tavern tables. In Howard's case, it may have served the blacksmith as a convenient writing table on which to make up his account or daybook.

Shelves, nailed or mortised into posts opposite a fireplace, were not included in listings for probate. (When the chimney was set into a gabled end, cupboards or shelves often were built into the wall on each side of

America's most completely furnished seventeenth-century kitchen, that of the 1692 Buttolph-Williams House in Wethersfield, Connecticut, includes woodenware collection displayed on wall shelves built into corner post. Early board-and-form trestle-type long work table is beneath casement; opened hutch table-chair is set with wooden bowls and porringer, covered sugar box, and covered milk jug. Children's matching high chairs are in place at table.

the fireplace.) Similarly, a kitchen work table or dresser of simple design and fairly crude home workmanship would not have been itemized, although a well-made "table board and form" executed professionally would. Many such boards and stands are better known to today's collectors as sawbuck tables. By whomever made, the table board was a single plank of the widest available wood; if a suitable single width could not be found, two or three boards were combined, held together by batten strips on the underside or at each end. Today this latter style often is called a breadboard, a term better applied to its nineteenth-century counterpart, the actual breadboard.

These tables were narrow, for they were used for serving, not sitting down to. When the table was not in use, its X-crossed legs, joined at the center by a peg, a bolt and nut or a thumbscrew, could be folded and stood upright in a corner. The table board itself was set vertically against a wall and thus out of the way of kitchen traffic. As extra storerooms and work areas were added, the need for a fold-away table gradually ceased, and the joined or permanent table took its place in the average kitchen as it had always been used in the larger homes of the well-to-do.

Before going into the pot, and once out of it, food was made ready for cooking or for serving on what the English colonist called a dresser, "the bench in the kitchen on which meat is dressed or prepared for the table."[18] This bench or table top on its own permanent frame, to which by the beginning of the eighteenth century one or more drawers often had been added to hold spices, knives, and other small utensils, today usually is disguised by the romanticized term "tavern table." This is not to say, of course, that taverns and inns did not seat customers at small rectangular tables as well as at the long "common boards," but these smaller tables had no need of drawers. They were lightly made so that at closing time they might be stacked one on top of the other; such stacking out of the way allowed easier sweeping up in taverns and in inns, where space was needed for travelers' pallets.

Almost a century of progress in the use, style, and number of kitchen tables is shown in the inventory of the estate of Mrs. Mary Bull taken at Boston on August 12, 1718. It included "2 *Tables*, four joint stools, one Greatt Chair, a Cupboard, *Drawers & Table*, a flock Bed, a *Table Board and old Frame*." (A flock bed was ticking stuffed with bits of felt or wool or scraps of other fabrics in place of feather or down filling.)

In 1662, fifty-six years after the first attempt at Virginia settlement, the inventory of the estate of Christopher Calthorpe, a York County commissioner and member of the House of Burgesses (and as such entitled to be called Captain), was filed. He left to his widow, three daughters, and son supplies of tobacco, corn, beehives, and a well-stocked dairy farm including thirteen milch cows, five heifers, four yearlings, four oxen, six steers, seven calves, three sows, two barrows, and four shoats.

Captain Calthorpe's three-room house was divided, according to probate records, into an outer room, a chamber, and a shed (lean-to). Around the fireplace in the shed, listers noted andirons, a rack, a spit and bellows, an iron pot, a gridiron, a frying pan, a dripping pan, two brass kettles, a skimmer (perhaps for cream separation), a mortar and pestle, a grater, pewter plates and three dozen napkins. The chamber furnishings were given as two feather beds, bolsters, sheets, blankets, valance, and curtains. No bedstead as such was listed, although a "couch bed and a couch" were counted, apparently a reference to a kind of day bed.

From the manner in which appraisers listed rooms in the dwelling of "Jonathan Avery, Practitioner in Physick," it would seem he had owned what originally was a four-room house to which a new lean-to kitchen had been added, thus forming a style later owners would refer to as a saltbox house. Dr. Avery, whose estate was inventoried on May 13, 1691, left a collection of "Bookes [of] Devinitie and Pisicall," and also "debts due to ye estate dificult" and other accounts receivable for which collecting also was deemed "unsertaine."

The rooms within his Dedham, Massachusetts house were listed as "the Hall Chamber" and "ye Litle Chamber" (on the second floor), with "ye Hall" and "ye bed rhome" plus "ye Kitchin" on the first. No garret, which might have been expected to have been above the kitchen, is listed.

Dr. Avery's kitchen was exceptionally well furnished, as were his other rooms; obviously not all bill collections had been difficult. Besides four chairs, a table and a "grete spining whele" there were three pot hangers, a pair of andirons, a gridiron, a toaster, a trivet, a fender, three brass candlesticks, a brass mortar and pestle, one high iron candlestick, "one with a screwed top," "two others," and a brass save-all. Pewter platters apparently were stacked atop one another or under other pieces on the shelves, for the listers noted each pile as they counted its contents: "two puter platters, four, two, five more, two more." Other pewter included a flagon, a chamber vessel, a basting ladle, and a small slice; "one bason, five more"; six plates, three porringers, a small platter, and a "sasser"; one quart pot and two pint pots; a wine cup, a salt cellar, and another chamber vessel.

When extra space was needed in Nathanael Hempsted's 1728 kitchen, the stump, or low-post bed, was easily folded up against the wall and covered by its valance and curtains. The separate, small kitchen bedroom is shown in the background. The child's go-cart, or stand-still, is similar to that listed in Dr. Avery's inventory.

Ironware included a mortar and pestle, a mustard bowl, a chafing dish, two pots and pothooks, one kettle, one spit, a peel, two dripping pans, and a frying pan. "A tin lanthorn, pastipan, cullinder and small pot" were listed together; three "bras kettles, five brase skellets and frames" similarly were grouped, followed by "a Skimmer, basting ladle & flesh forke, seven spoons" and "an Iorning box and thre heaters."

Although the listers did not so specify, their manner of grouping the next items implies they may have been stored in a partitioned-off end of the kitchen: Here wooden utensils included five trays, one platter, two pails with iron bails, two bottles, and two dozen trenchers; also a copper limbeck, a pewter limbeck and the "iron pot to it," a pewter still, a go-cart, two powdering tubs, two wort keelers, and a barrel.

A keeler was a shallow tub in which liquids were cooled; wort was an infusion of malt which if allowed to ferment became beer, or which could be distilled for spirits. In the seventeenth century the word also meant a malt infusion used to cure ulcers and scurvy. Dr. Avery may have kept a supply handy to satisfy all three possibilities: The limbecks and still were on hand to manufacture spirits and a barrel was nearby to hold beer for the table; if need be, the wort could be ladled out when the kitchen served as a pharmacy.

The doctor apparently made up and dispensed medicines to patients; listed in the kitchen were seven gallipots, five gallon-size "glases," six two-quart and sixteen one-quart bottles.

The go-cart, sometimes called a stand-stool, was a child's walker or a kind of four-sided small wooden pen on wheels; a child standing in the go-cart could hold onto the sides and propel himself forward.

The inventory of the estate of John Buttolph, successful farmer-merchant, is given here in its entirety to show the disposition of furnishings within the house as well as the values placed on furniture and accessories at the middle period of colonial settlement. Though it was entered at Wethersfield, Connecticut, Lieutenant Buttolph's listing easily could have been that of any colonist in fairly comfortable circumstances anywhere along the Atlantic seaboard at the beginning of the eighteenth century.[19] The errors in arithmetic are those of the listers.

An Inventory of Ye Estate of Leut. John Buttolph of Wethersfield who deceased Jan. Ey:ye 14th:1692–3

	£	s	d

In ye parlor or smal bed room

Ye high bed & furniture 14£: ye low bed & furniture 5£5s	19:05:00
6 pair of corse sheets 4£ & 4 pillow cases at 1£: a Cubbard 2£	07:00:00
4 chests & 2 boxes 30s: a warming pan & chimney furniture 15s	02:05:00
Earthen-ware 20s & Bookes 3£:18s: & 3 Looking-glasses 16s	05:14:00

In ye Great Kitchin

5 guns 5£: 2 belts 40s: 2 swords 20s & ammunition 20s	09:00:00
New pewter weighing 113 pound at 2s3d per pound 12£:14s:3d	12:14:03
Old pewter 27 pound at 18d per pound 2£: sixpenc & 20 porringers 30s	03:10:06
Old flagons & pewter candlesticks at 8s: 7 tinware 17s: a copper pot 10s	02:15:00
2 Brass candle-sticks at 8s: a pair of smal pistols 8s: a Jack & waits with a chain 30s	02:06:00
A chaffin-dish 10s: a mortar & pestle 6s: a Lanthorne 2s:6d	00:18:00
2 Tabels 25s: 10 chairs & stools 15s: a pair of cobirons & 3 tramels fire slice: tongs: & gridiron 50s	04:20:00
a sadle & bridle 30s: a portmantle & malepillion 15s a side saddle 25s	03:10:00

In ye Hall

2 tables 30s: a cubbard & cloath 3£ & 11 chairs 27s6d smal table & carpit 10s	06:07:06
2 corse carpits 10s: 6 cushions 12s: a fine basket 3s: cobirons 15s fine worsted yarn 3£	04:17:00

In ye smal kitchin

Ye great Brass Kettle 4£:18s: next biggest brass kettle 3£10s: next biggest kettle 42s	20:20:00
2 brass kettles 30s: smaller kettle 10s: 3 skillits 15s: & 2 iron pots & pot hooks 42s	04:17:00
2 iron skillits iron pots 20s: & iron pots 15s: 2 spits & dripping pan 15s	02:10:00

£ s d

frying pan gridiron & bellows 6s: tongs 7s: meshing tub 5s: pail
meal trough & wooden ware 15s   01:13:00
Chees press 3s: a pewter pottle pot 6s: & an iron kettle 10s   00:19:00

In ye Buttery

3 bushell of meal and barrel 10s: & 3 spining wheels 6s: 4 meal
sives 5s: a churn 3s   01:01:00
an old table & old cask 8s: Bees and hives 20s: 2 half Bushels 8s   01:16:00

In ye Shop

6 yards & 1/2 linnen cloath: 3s per yard: 19s6d: 1/2 fine Linnen
4s per yd 18s   01:17:06
a Tiffiny vail 5s: 6 bunches of Manchester 4s per bunch 24s   01:09:00
Silk frogs 2s: one ounce and half of fine thred 7s: Beeswax 2s:
gloves 3s   00:14:00
7 smal caps 7s 20 yards girt web 10s: a pair of bodyes 6s: a parcel
of spare belts 12s   02:15:00
hat linings 7s: alum 5s Rosin & Indigo 3s red & yellow oaker 10s:
a jar 1s: warming pan 6s   01:12:00
a box of drawers & drum 25s: remnant of saking 3s leather 14s.
3 Rubstone 18d   02:03:06
23 wait of flex 20s & 5 pound sheps-woll 10s a chest 12s gally-
pots & hoggshead 6s   02:08:00

In ye great Kitchin Chamber

Ye best bed and furniture 9£ & ye other bed and furniture 7£
a pair cobirons 15s   16:15:00
Old pillion and cloath 5s—a trunk 25s remnant of cloath 7s—
3 sealskins 3s   2:00:00

Hall Chamber

Bed & furniture 18£ 6 chairs 40s—ye biggest sealskin trunk 50s   22:10:00
15 pounds wollen yarn 45s—a sealskin trunk 10s trunk: covered
with leather 20s   3:15:00
a smal sealskin trunk & contents 11s—a table 8s: thre doz. &
1/2 trenchers 3s6d   1: 2:06
19 cotton napkins at 3s a napkin 57s 2 diaper table cloaths 25s,
6 napkins 13s   4:15:00

	£ s d
8 fine pillow cases 50s 2 towels 5s 15 cotton sheets 15£	17:15:00
5 fine sheets 7£ a small pr. corse sheets 12s a long table cloath 12s	8: 4:00
a corse sheet 15s: 3 boolster cases 16s: aparel for women 7£ 10s	9: 1:00
women's linnen 4£: a scarf 24s: 8 corse pillow cases 24s	6: 8:00
a remnant bedtick 2s: 2 pin cushions and hatband 7s: child's blankets 35s	2: 4:00
child's linnen 2£ 10s: a smal feather bed 3£ 10s	6:00:00

In the garret

Blankits and beding 25s—a panel 10s old cask & feathers 7s a sithe 3s	2: 5:00
35 yards sacking 18d a yard 52s6d: a timber-chain 20s a plough chain 10s	4: 2:06
old iron:Spade Beetle rings, wedges 3£ 8s carpinders tools 8s	3:16:00
3 pr. brass scales 16s: old cask 20s: salt 12s	02:08:00
six pair of sheets 6s4d: sithes 10s: old iron 5s: great stilyards 20s: least stilyards 10s	02:11:00

In the Warehouse

An iron malt mill 5s fullin mill 10s horseplow 10s a grind stone 4s, a stubin hoe 3s	1:12:00
an iron spike 1s: 10 bushels chess 20s 3 bu. barly 12s 6 bushels of rye 18s	2:11:00
5 bushel messlin 17s6d 25 bushels of Indian corne 3£2s6d	4:00:00
6 bushel of oates 12s & 16 sheep skins 12s: collars and traces 20s	2: 4:00
Flex in ye shef 20s, cart rope 2s 4 forks 4s hay knife 2s: a fan 3s	1:11:00
a cart & wheels & irons belonging with a yoke 46s: a sled 6s	2:12:00
7 baggs 10s, plow & harrow 20s, a negro woman servant 18£	19:10:00
a collar horse 40s: saddle horse 5£: mare & colt 15s	7:15:00
3 cows 12£: bull & heifer 6£: 3 steers 12£: 2 of 2 year old 4£ 2 yearlings 40s	36:00:00
4 young swine 40s, an axe 3s, led and leden weights 17s	3:00:00
a cow at 4£ 5s, three cows in reversion (i.e.) lett out to halfes: to return ye cows & half ye increase 10£ 10s	14:15:00
Sheep lett out as afresd about ten of them—5£	5:00:00
Hom lot & ye buildings thereon 200£: 4 acres & 1/2 medow 45£: 5 acres plain 40£	285:00
14 acres at Rocky-hill 70£ 15 acres west pastor 45£ 9 acres of fearfull-Swamp 27£	142:00

Clapboards for the 1692 Buttolph-Williams House, Wethersfield, Connecticut, were made of short lengths of hand-cut oak. Deep overhang of roof precluded need for eaves-troughs on this four-room hourse, designated a National Historic Site by Department of the Interior, National Parks Service.

The five seventeenth-century kitchen inventories cited, although taken in such diverse homes as those of an unsuccessful farmer, a skilled blacksmith, a burgess-dairyman, a physician, and a merchant-militia leader, and covering half a century, will be seen to have had more in common than they had differences. The real contrasts are those of quantity: some simply had "more of the same" than had their fellow colonists.

The difference in quantity is obvious when listed on tax appraisers' returns. It would not have been so noticeable on visits to the same kitchens under normal circumstances; those who owned a more than average number of utensils had also storage places for them. If the kitchen hearth and table had been set up in each of these seventeenth-century homes for the preparation of the same kind of food on the same day, little if any difference would have been found among them.

There is too often an embarrassing contrast between what inventories show would have been in such kitchens and the manner in which many equivalent "restored" rooms are furnished today.

The major purpose of historic homes should be to show how colonial families planned their rooms, decorated and furnished them—how the rooms actually looked when their original owners lived in them. This could be accomplished more easily if as much common sense, if not research, were applied by collectors to the display of utensils as they have enthusiasm for acquiring a dozen of each tool imaginable. Many restored houses suffer from such an embarrassment of culinary items. In otherwise meticulously furnished houses a veritable cartload of pots, pans, kettles, skillets, trivets, toasters, footwarmers, pothooks, trammels, flesh forks, ladles, goffering irons, griddles, bedwarmers, spits, tankards, and candlemolds often is ranged haphazardly about the chimney and hearth. The twentieth-century housewife who emptied the contents of kitchen-utensil drawers and cupboards onto the top of an electric range would be open to question, especially if the only job before her was to set a pot of soup on the back burner. Few ponder the lack of reasoning behind arrays of colonial utensils now placed obstacle-course fashion around the hearths of many refurnished seventeenth- and eighteenth-century kitchens.

For each colonial house there is somewhere a copy of the probate appraisers' inventory of the furnishings used in that house by its first owners. In many areas these records have not been retained locally but have been placed in the custody of state or county courts, libraries, or other commissions. Many householders kept daybooks; in many families it was customary to take a complete household inventory each January. These lists are the proper guides to authentic refurnishing of old houses. When such work is so guided, seventeenth- and eighteenth-century kitchens no longer will be "restored" with Oriental carpets, or even hooked or braided carpets, placed carefully before the cooking hearth—or indeed, anywhere in the "working" kitchen. Subjected to almost daily scrubbing and scouring, kitchen floors were not painted until well into the nineteenth century; nor were kitchen walls papered.

Few, except those restoring the wealthiest type of late eighteenth-century homes, will indulge in curtains at the kitchen windows. Chandeliers, however simple their wood, tin, iron, or pewter construction may seem to twentieth-century eyes, will be hung back in the churches and meeting halls from which they were taken; a few of the late eighteenth-century type may be returned to city taverns; even fewer will go back to the parlors, the ballrooms, and the rare dining rooms of those handsome larger homes whose owners could afford to squander candles by the dozen. None will be hung in the properly restored colonial "working" kitchen.

The four walls of the average early kitchen were constructed of plain sheathing; in housewrights' terms these were "weather-boarded" or "ship-lapped." In better-built kitchens, so-called feather-edged or beaded sheathing often has been found still in place, usually on the interior wall surrounding the chimney. Those who could afford the cost had the "outside" walls plastered, not only because this helped retain heat but because the white-washed plaster reflected light. However, in those kitchens for which partitions to form larders or bedrooms were planned at the time of building, such inside hidden-from-sight walls usually were of plain shiplapped boards, laid either horizontally or vertically, and sometimes in both directions within the same small room. In many cases, planks used for these walls may have represented an economical use of short timbers left after main walls and floors had been laid.

Ceiling beams in the kitchen of the average early house were at first left uncovered, serving as an unadorned base for a simple loft floor. When the original house was improved, this first plain, often irregular loft floor became subflooring. Subsequent generations usually did not further enhance the kitchen ceiling with plaster until the nineteenth century. The plaster itself was not a great extravagance but the hundreds of nails needed to secure laths to hold it were.

Doors leading to the outside from the kitchen were, almost without exception, of plain batten construction. This design called for one or two wide vertical boards exposed to the weather, faced on the room side by a series of wide boards nailed horizontally. The door opened into the kitchen as a safety measure. It was easier to bar it against intruders; it was even more important, however, for those in northern or middle colonies, to be able to open the door easily during extreme winter weather when blizzards swept high drifts of snow·and ice against it. Without ease of exit, wood for fire could not be brought in or stock tended. It could be "locked" by removing the thumb latch (in poorer homes a string or thong) or secured by an oak, chestnut, or other hardwood bar which slipped into hangers set into either side of the door frame. Except in the homes of skilled blacksmiths or locksmiths, or those of especial wealth, it is doubtful if any form of box lock and key would have been used on colonial kitchen doors.

Stairs to the loft, often of steep, narrow ladderlike construction, were set against the chimney wall. In some kitchens these were closed in as if the stairway itself were a tall narrow closet. In others, the stairs were enclosed by being built inside the small area partitioned off for a bedroom. In houses where stairway and partitions were removed long ago, evidence of their original placement nevertheless often can be determined by examining the loft or chamber floor above the kitchen. If the original floor or subfloor still is in place, the rectangular space for the stairway opening can be found. This will show up as a large patch of short-length boards. In some houses, this opening actually was a kind of trap door; when the stairs

Separate kitchen or bake house, Philipsburg Manor, New York, shows building method of the late seventeenth and early eighteenth centuries often used in middle and southern colonies for such dependencies. Here actual oven area is outside the main chimney wall; compare with New Jersey kitchen oven, which extrudes into pantry in main house.

or ladder were removed, often the door itself was nailed down and, again, appears as a rectangular floor patch today.

Interior entrances to the cellars of early houses usually were through trap doors, cut into larder floors or simply at one end of the open kitchen. Evidence of these trap doors is lacking in those houses which were better maintained through the years. Because of the constant activity in the kitchen, the amount of work that had to be accomplished there, the need for scrubbing and the consequent moisture which seeped into and rotted the boards, kitchen floors were the first to be replaced. By 1800 many homes, now rebuilt and added to, did away with the cellar-trap when the original kitchen floor was replaced. New stairs to the cellar then often were set below what once had been a closet opening off the parlor or downstairs front bedroom. When this improvement was made, the early closet shelves were removed. Where original walls remain, faint horizontal lines usually can be found indicating the old shelf arrangement.

PART IV

The Eighteenth-Century Kitchen

CHAPTER 1

"By Industry We Gained"

All greate and honourable actions are accompanied with great difficulties, and muste be overcome with answerable courages.   WILLIAM BRADFORD

ODAY MANY FIND IT DIFFICULT to understand why the colonist should have required four to six years in which to build a passable house—especially one so small—and wonder even more why so often he left improvements to later generations. Time in which to do so, however, would have been the emigrant's greatest luxury. And no matter with how bright a sheen of elegance his descendants might overlay those early efforts, they could never achieve quite the sense of accomplishment he knew. It had been, after all, the settler's indignation, despair, hope, courage, and historically unequaled determination of purpose that provided his homestead and his children's right to hold it freely.

With the exception of the pastor, for whom land and shelter usually were provided, and of the occasional other specialist whose skill also was direly needed by a new community (the blacksmith, the miller, and the tanner especially were favored), each freeman had to pay for his new home in both cash and labor. The specialists usually received theirs in return for contracting with a community to provide skilled work over a period of years. Each, whatever his particular work, almost always was the owner of farmland.

In 1620, as Plymouth was being founded and the colony in Virginia began to see hope of permanent establishment, Gervase Markham's new book,[1] designed as a helpful guide for farmers, was published. The author outlined the best use of the husbandman's sixteen- to eighteen-hour day. Subsequent editions were brought to this country; it only can be hoped that the settler had time to read the advice offered to him and his servants[2]

[71]

(a term applied interchangeably in the seventeenth century to hired help and children):

> Rising before foure of the clocke in the morning, and after thankes given to God for his reste he shall . . . first fodder his cattell[3] and make the booths cleane, rub downe the cattell . . . then he shall curry the horses . . . then he shall water and house them againe, give them more fodder . . . and whilst they are eating their meat, he shall make ready his collars, hames, treats, halters, mullens and plough-geares, seeing everything fit . . . and to these labours I will allow full two houres, that is, from foure of the clocke till sixe, then he shall come in to breakfast, and to that, I allow him halfe an houre; and then another halfe houre to the gearing and yoaking of his cattle, so that at seven of the clocke hee may set forward to his labour. . . .
>
> And then he shall plow from seven of the clock in the morning, till betwixt two and three in the afternoone, then he shall unyoke, and bring home his cattell, and having rubb'd them, drest them, and cleansed away all durt and filth, he shall fodder them, and give them meate, then shall the servants goe in to their dinner, which allowe halfe an houre; it will then be towards foure of the clocke, at which time hee shall goe to his cattell againe, and rubbing them downe, and cleansing their stalls, give them more fodder, which done, he shall go into the barnes, and provide and make ready fodder of all kinds for the next day, whether it be hay, straw, or blend fodder, according to the ability of the husbandman; this being done, and carried into the stable, oxe-house, or other convenient place, he shall then goe water his cattell, and give them more meate, and to his horse provender, as before shewed . . . and by this time it will draw past sixe of the clocke, at which time he shall come in to supper, and after supper, he shall either by the fire side, mend shooes both for himself and their family, or beat and knock hemp, or flaxe, or picke and stampe apples, or crabs for cider of verdjuce, or else grind malt on the quernes, pick candle rushes, or do some husbandly office within dores, till it be full eight a clocke: then shall he take his lanthorne and candle, and goe to his cattell, and having cleansed the stalls and plankes, litter them downe, looke that they be safely tied, and then fodder and give them meate for all night, then giving God thankes for benefits received that day, let him and the whole household go to their rest till the next morning.

Now it may be intended, that there may be in the houshold more servants than one; and so you will demand of mee, what the rest of the servants shall be imployed in before and after the time of plowing: to this I answer, that they may either goe into the barne and thrash, fill or empty the maltfat, load and unload the kilne, or any other good and necessary work that is about the yard, and after they come from plowing, some may goe into the barne and thrash, some hedge, ditch, stop gaps in broken fences, dig in the orchard or garden, or any other out-worke which is need-full to be done, and which about the husband-man is never want-ing, especially one must have a care every night to looke to the mending or sharpening of the plough-irons, and the repairing of the plough and plough-geares, if any be out of order, for to deferre them till the morrow, were the losses of a daies worke, and an ill point of husbandry.

By the end of the eighteenth century there was little if any change in the colonial farmer's daily routine from that Markham had outlined for his elder cousin in seventeenth-century England. The difference between the lives of the two was that in America the settler often had also to oversee and build at least part of his house, to forge or carve his own tools and household utensils, and if he was fortunate in being so skilled, to contrive furniture for his family's use.

Milking, gathering eggs, and responsibility for all other chores about the house were the housewife's province, and Markham had advice for her also. He demanded that she "be of chaste thoughts, stout courage, patient, untyred, watchfull, diligent, witty, pleasant, constant in friendship, full of good Neighbour-Hood, wise in discourse but not frequent therein—sharp and quick of speech but not bitter or talkative, secret in her affaires, comfortable in her counsels, and generally skillful in the worthy knowledges which all belong to her vocation."[4]

By the close of the colonial era, a cheerful disposition still was a pre-requisite for the "skilled female oeconomist," as a Pennsylvania farmer, advertising for a housekeeper, made clear. Even though the help of domestic servants was promised, he outlined a day that promised little leisure: "Wanted at a Seat about half a day's journey from Philadephia, on which are good improvements and domestics, A single Woman of unsullied Repu-tation, an affable, cheerful, active and amiable Disposition; cleanly, indus-trious, perfectly qualified to direct and manage the female Concerns of country business, as raising small stock, dairying, marketing, combing, card-ing and spinning, knitting, sewing, pickling, preserving, etc., and occasion-ally to instruct two Young Ladies in those Branches of Oeconomy, who, with their father, compose the family. Such a person will be treated with respect and esteem, and meet with every encouragement due to such a character."[5] Indeed, she would have deserved it.

Basic to the happy ending of the romance that social historians have called the American dream was the existence of a frontier. So long as there

John Gill's THE John Gill's 1786

ANARCHY
OF THE
RANTERS,

And other LIBERTINES;

THE

HIERARCHY
OF THE
ROMANISTS,

AND OTHER

Pretended CHURCHES, equally refused and refuted, in a two-fold *Apology* for the Church and People of God, called in Derision, *Quakers*.

WHEREIN

They are vindicated from those that accuse them of *Disorder* and *Confusion* on the one Hand, and from such as calumniate them with *Tyranny* and *Imposition* on the other; shewing, that as the true and pure *Principles* of the Gospel are restored by their Testimony; so is also the *antient Apostolick* ORDER of the Church of Christ re-established among them, and settled upon its *right Basis* and [F]*oundation*.

By ROBERT BARCLAY.

Phil. 2. 3. *Let nothing be done through Strife or vain Glory; but in Lowliness of Mind let each esteem other better than themselves.*
Heb. 13. 7. *Remember them that have the Rule over you, who have spoken unto you the Word of God, whose Faith follow.*

PHILADELPHIA:
Re-printed, and Sold by B. FRANKLIN, and D. HALL, 1757.

Reissue of popular English text printed and sold at Franklin's Philadelphia shop were outlands, there need not be discouragement or defeat. In the eighteenth century the colonist could trade or sell the property with which he was dissatisfied, literally pull up stakes[6] and search out and buy a new homestead farther west on which to begin again.

The result could only be a kind of contagious and sustaining belief that the limit of each family's achievement was no more than the extent of its effort. It was a belief that would have a counterpart in the development of those personalities who sought to surmount social and political hurdles rather than to win control of the physical frontier. By the end of the colonial era, America had created a new class of leader, that of the self-made man, a social status barely comprehensible to the European of the period. Some, such as chandler's-son-turned-printer-inventor-diplomat Benjamin Franklin, shared the credit:

> We have an English proverb that says, "He that would thrive must ask his wife." It was lucky for me that I had one as much dispos'd to industry and frugality as myself. She assisted me chearfully in my business, folding and stitching pamphlets, tending shop, purchasing old linen rags for the paper makers, etc.
>
> We kept no idle servants, our table was plain and simple, our furniture of the cheapest. One morning being call'd to breakfast, I found it in a china bowl with a spoon of silver! They had been bought for me without my knowledge by my wife. She thought her husband deserv'd a silver spoon and china bowl as well as any of his neighbours. This was the first appearance of plate and China in our house which afterwards in course of years, as our wealth increas'd, augmented gradually to several hundred pounds in value.[7]

Franklin's favorite breakfast at home in Philadelphia was a bowl of porridge, sweetened with honey and spiced with nutmeg, accompanied by bread and butter and a cup of tea, and which, he estimated, cost three and one-half pence.[8]

Some housewives were not as cautious as Deborah Franklin had been when she began her gradual exchange of old kitchen accessories for new porcelain and plate.

Early clergy had often inveighed against unnecessary elegance; the Reverend Mr. Hooker had been fond of quoting *Orani res ipsa negat*[9] (work which needs decoration argues its weakness of strength) whenever opportunity provided a pulpit.

Not all colonists eschewed decoration for the same reason. Their sense of fitness argued against installing in New England the kind of urban architectural grandeur that was expected of contemporary buildings in London. Such splendor would have been out of place amid raw stumps, along muddy roads, or set against a backdrop of Indian wigwams and wolf-tenanted woodlands. As a result, a variety of difficult and unpopular compromises had been made: some eyed even Harvard Hall uneasily, considering it, as Edward Johnson commented, "too gorgeous for a Wilderness, and yet too mean in other apprehensions for a Colledg."[10]

Once inside their own houses, seventeenth-century colonists could ignore the awkward prospect of the raw landscape; many families of means did. Indeed, John Josselyn declared, following his second visit to America in the 1660s, that some Bostonians were "damnable rich";[11] his astonishment presaged eighteenth-century London's who-do-they-think-they-are? attitude when the colonists finally rebelled against taxes on imported luxuries.

As the first colonial century neared its close, other visitors wondered if the Puritan image had not been exaggerated. As early as June 1680, the visiting monk Jasper Danckaerts observed with some asperity that while there were laws against profanity and neither work nor tavern-tippling was allowed on the Sabbath, "nevertheless you discover little difference between [Boston] and other places. Drinking and fighting occur not less than elsewhere; and as to truth and true godliness, you must not expect more of them than of others. When we were there, four ministers' sons were learning the silversmith's trade!"[12]

There were radical, if not ostentatiously decorative, changes in the exterior appearances as well as in the interior furnishing of the new and larger eighteenth-century houses; much of the almost medieval character of the Pilgrim era disappeared. Only an occasional second-floor overhang remained. Small-paned, leaded casements were exchanged for the larger two-sash style with eight to twelve panes in the top sash, placed over a bottom sash usually, but not invariably, of the same number of panes. In the newly built eighteenth-century houses, the kitchen, which earlier may have had only one window, often was planned with four.

A generally lighter appearance was given to old fire-rooms, even to those in older houses now being remodeled, by the use of whitewash on darkened beams and plank ceilings. Some older kitchens were modernized even more extravagantly by having the original window openings recut to take the new eight-over-twelve- to twelve-over-twelve-pane sashes. More attention was given to preservation: "*Tuesd Aug 18* [*1730*]: I tarred the clapboards on the backside of the Leantoo & mended it. *Thursd. 20.* Tard ye East End of house as high as ye Windows: [used] I gall. tar."[13]

Parlors and chambers of many later eighteenth-century homes often were described as having been "marbled" or "rubbed" or "laid in oil."

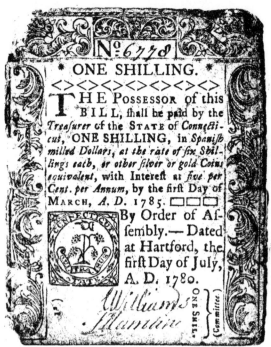

Obverse and reverse of shilling note, typical of those issued during war period, added phrase "not worth a continental" to idiomatic English. Connecticut promised 5 percent interest on shilling if held until 1785. The first signature is that of William Williams, who also signed the Declaration of Independence.

The "bed furniture"—that is, the valance, curtains, and coverlets—were made from rust and yellow-green linen woven for the Hempsted family early in the eighteenth century. The "under," or trundle, bed has a paneled headboard. Ceiling and walls were whitewashed regularly not only to preserve wood but also to reflect light. Sliding casement window at right is unique. Handy with tools, diarist Joshua Hempsted transformed a seventeenth-century window into the then-new double-sash style with no expense for new glass. Hempsted House, New London, Connecticut.

Seventeenth-century iron door handle and latch used on studded batten door. Hempsted House, New London, Connecticut.

Others were designated as the blue, green, red, black or yellow room, to indicate the use of paint on wood paneling and wainscoting. Little if any of this kind of expensive surface elegance extended into the kitchen; in fact, even when the ceilings and exterior walls of the front rooms were plastered, the four walls of the kitchen usually remained wood-sheathed.

Late in the century the kitchen—where the floor was scrubbed and scoured daily with soft soap and water to which sand often was added as an abrasive—was the first room to which mop boards (now usually called baseboards) were added as a deterrent to rot caused by moisture where sheathed walls met the floorboards.

The practice today of painting iron hardware black probably is the result of early-nineteenth century marketing. When locks, latches, and hinges were first mass-produced, they usually were given a prime coat of black paint. In the colonial household, however, door and cabinet hardware was not painted if the wood to which it was nailed was not painted, as in the case of many batten doors. If the door and door frame were painted, the iron hardware was painted the same color as the wood.

When paint began to replace the thinned-down tar mixtures of the earlier part of the century, it was used on roofs and on tools, carts, and sleds kept outside. The first use of paint in the back or "working" part of the house was likely to be as a preservative for exterior window and door frames. Only later was it used for kitchen interior doors and window frames. Paint extended into the kitchen for use on furnishings probably as much as a preserving agent as for the color it lent. Work-table tops usually were painted at the same time the table bases and legs were, although scrubbing soon removed the color, leaving tops with a light, scoured surface caused by the daily use of soap and sand. Since little that could do harm touched them, the undersides of table tops and chairs and the interiors of cupboards and chests seldom were painted.

The need to preserve the wooden parts of houses in those areas where homes commonly were built mainly of brick and stone was noted by Dr. Israel Acrelius, provost of the Swedish church in America, on his return to Stockholm in 1758: "Within, the walls and ceilings are whitewashed once a year . . . the woodwork is painted or it does not last long," he said of Delaware houses, which were "built of brick after the English fashion, without coating, every other brick glazed, or of sandstone or granite as is mostly the case in the country."[14]

A popular paint recipe, often reprinted in almanacs and copied in home manuscript books until well into the nineteenth century, directed the home owner to "melt two ounces of Rosin in an iron pot or kettle, add three Gallons of Train Oil and three or four roles of Brimstone: When the Rosin and brimstone are melted and become thin, add as much Spanish Brown, or red or yellow Oker, or any other colour you want as will give the whole as deep a shade as you like, grind them fine, as usual with oil: Then lay it on with a brush as hot and as thin as you can. Some days after the first coat is dried give it 'a second: It is well attested that this will preserve planck or timber for an age. The work can be done by a common labourer." This same formula was used for preserving tools and exterior house walls as well as for furniture and interior wooden wall surfaces.

The kitchen continued to be the room where descendants of the first settlers made their family devotions. Some visitors, such as Danckaerts, who mistrusted unseemly interest in silver among members of ministerial families, never quite approved the New Englander's home prayer service: "Our captain . . . took us to his sister's where we were welcome and from there to his father's where there was a repetition of worship, which took place in the kitchen while they were turning the spit and busy preparing a good supper. . . . The prayer was said loud enough to be heard three houses off, and also long enough, if that made it good. This done . . . he wished us welcome and insisted on our supping with him which we did."[15]

After 1640, as diary notes of the more literate householders make clear, the old Geneva Bible, read by the forefathers at Plymouth and the first Puritans in Massachusetts, had been supplanted by the new King James version. On October 1, 1697, Judge Sewall wrote that "After Dinner we sung Psalm 121." Known to many as the "Traveller's Hymn of Trust in Jehovah," it begins "I will lift up mine eyes unto the hills, from whence cometh my help," and concludes "The Lord shall preserve thy going out and thy coming in from this time forth, and even for evermore."[16]

CHAPTER 2

Furnishing the Improved Kitchen

Perhaps he who has a large fortune may not be so happy as he who has a small one; but that must proceed from other causes than from his having the large fortune. SAMUEL JOHNSON[17]

INVENTORIES REVEAL A GRADUAL but steady change in the contents of households throughout the eighteenth century. Silver serving pieces were listed more commonly in the homes of well-to-do farmers as well as in those of merchant-shippers, and there was a noticeable increase in the amount of pewter on hand. Chairs and tables, as well as cupboards and chests, were mentioned in kitchens as a matter of course. Food supplies seemed more ample.

By 1750 many inventories included at least a few knives and two-tined forks for use at better tables. By this time, appraisers were likely to speak of old pewter and to value pieces more often by weight than for their specific uses. Even if there were no other evidence, this change in inventory method alone would be enough to indicate how many more families were able to purchase pewter.

This is to give notice that a Journeyman Pewterer who is a good workman in Holloware may have constant work, and good Wages, if they will go to New York and apply themselves to Mr. David Lyell or they may write to him and know further.

Significantly enough, Lyell ran his 1711 help-wanted advertisement in the Boston *News-Letter*, for more pewterers and wire-pullers were at work in the greater Boston area than in any other section of the early eighteenth-century colonies.

[81]

Now that a family's pewter supply could be melted down and the smith asked to remold old pieces into new and more fashionable shapes, weight was the important factor. As more earthenware, Delft, and "burnt china" became available for purchase, old "sad-colored" pewter plates and porringers were changed into spoons, candlesticks, coffee and chocolate pots, pepper boxes, and other more elegant accessories.

By 1750, many workaday kitchen and table utensils, which in the last century had been carved or turned from chunks of maple and wild cherry or molded from carefully shaved sheets of horn, could be purchased made of pewter in all towns of any size. Now they were priced in shillings and pence, not in pounds. Philadelphia pewterer Cornelius Bradford advertised in 1765 that at the Sign of the Dish he offered this varied and typical stock: "dishes, plates, basons, tankards, measures, tumblers, salt cellars, spoons, milk-pots, close-stool pans, block tin and pewter worms for stills, candle molds and bottle cranes." (In estimating the number of pieces of pewter a kitchen might have when only weight is given, it should be remembered that the average plate weighed approximately two pounds; large platters and basins usually were heavier.)

Slip-decorated redware plates, bowls, and small gallipots; blue, red, green, or yellow glazed earthenware; even a single piece of "Dutch" or Delft added a splash of bright colour to the shelves of otherwise plain wooden mugs, trays, and basins in the simplest homes. Such pieces were carefully chosen, well cared for to guard against breakage, and on occasion displayed with pride: "About 12 at noon we arrived, and had a dinner of Fryed Venison, very savoury. Landlady wanting some pepper in the seasoning, bid the Girl hand her the spice in the little Gay cupp on ye shelfe."[18]

Although New England inventories occasionally included an ornamental looking glass, they rarely recorded any other attempt at wall decoration. The kitchens of the descendants of Dutch immigrants in New York, however, often were given added color by decorative porcelains, as Dr. Hamilton noticed when he visited Albany in July 1744:

> The Dutch here keep their houses very neat and clean, both without and within. Their chamber floors are generally laid with rough plank which, in time, by constant rubbing and scrubbing becomes as smooth as if it had been plained. Their chambers and rooms are large and handsom. They have their beds generally in alcoves so that you may go thro all the rooms of a great house and see never a bed. They affect pictures much, particularly scripture history, with which they adorn their rooms. They set out their cabinets and bouffetts much with china.
>
> Their kitchens are likewise very clean, and there they hang earthen or delft plates and dishes all round the walls in manner of pictures, having a hole drilled thro the edge of the plate or dish and a loop of ribbon put into it to hang it by. . . . They

Portable pewter dish rack is set on top of older carved cupboard in pantry room of the Palace kitchen house at Williamsburg, Virginia. Boxes with handles and cogwheel works similar to that shown on table under window at left had interior blades or fans for various uses: sifting grains or flour, mixing batters.

live here very frugally and plain, for the chief merit among them seems to be riches, which they spare no pains or trouble to acquire, but are a civil and hospitable people in their way, but att best, rustick and unpolished. I imagined when I first came there that there were some very rich people in the place. They talked of 30, 40, 50 and 100 thousand pounds as of nothing, but I soon found that their riches consisted more in large tracts of land than in cash.[19]

Among the luxuries owned by Henry Dering, Esquire, sold at public auction after his death at Boston in 1775, were "1 Blue and White Delph Bowl & 6 Stone patty panns . . . 1 White Gallept, Caudlecup & mugg and 11 White Delph wash Basons."

Early in the century, brass and copper were much costlier than iron, so much so that the purchase of a kettle was worth special note in the diary of the Reverend Joseph Green, of Salem, who thus recorded the major events of July 6, 1710: "Bought a brass Kettle, $3\pounds/6$ shil$/6$d; and went to Cambridge and brought my mother home with me at 6 o'clock."[20] Brass and copper were worth the investment, however, for they had special advantages over less expensive ware: they could be dropped or clattered against one another and although sustaining dents they did not crack and break as quickly as iron. The substantial numbers of brass and copper pots, kettles, and other utensils listed in colonial inventories are perhaps greater in ratio to similar accessories made of iron than is shown in restored kitchens today.

Guns, powder, and shot rarely, if ever, were racked over the kitchen hearth, where a fire was maintained throughout the year, but were rested much more safely and sensibly on pegs set into a ceiling beam or above a door. Candleholders not in use were gathered on a convenient shelf or cupboard top, although a lantern usually was kept handy near the back door to be picked up and lighted just before one left the house.

Lights for special uses, needed daily in the same kitchen work area, were left hanging or standing in place; these seem to have been listed fairly regularly as iron lamps. Under this heading would have to be placed the special lights or candleholders suspended by wire hooks or slender iron hangers above looms, spinning wheels, or other work places. A holder kept near the chimney might be one of the "tall iron sticks" sometimes noted, or an iron platelike holder for a candle, usually suspended from a wire chain and sometimes having also a pointed hook-end which could be stuck into the chimney lintel or post. Although fire burned on the hearth continuously, more cooking was done over embers than over flames. Thus light was needed to check the progress of a roast, for example, to determine when it was done to the right turn of the spit.

> *For the pleasing entertainment of the Polite part of Mankind, I have printed the most Beautiful Poems of Mr. Stephen Duck, the famous Wiltshire Poet; It is a full demonstration to me that the People of New England have a fine taste for Good Sense & Polite Learning, having already sold 1200 of these Poems.*
>
> RICHARD FRY,
> Boston *Gazette*, May 1, 1732

In most houses the family's library still was kept on a kitchen shelf. In the homes of judges, ministers, and a few especially wealthy landowners who built up large collections, personal libraries were usually stored in "closets," the small office rooms partitioned off from either a first-floor parlor or the best second-floor chamber. In rare instances some new eighteenth-century houses were planned with a special room set aside as a library.

The warm and lighted kitchen, however, was the room in which the average family's reading was done, planting records kept, and receipt books carefully copied and stitched together with flax threads. During the winter months it was the room where school lessons were studied, where samplers were embroidered, and where many adults engaged in what has been described as the colonists' favorite indoor winter sport—copying surveys, and selling and reselling bits and pieces of land.

Those many old accounts and transfers of property provide a clue to one important feature of the composite colonial portrait. By comparing the number forced to sign papers with an X and those who were able to write out and sign their own deeds, wills, and mortgages, it is possible to gauge the extent of literacy of property owners throughout early America. Thus by 1660 approximately 89 percent of the men and 42 percent of the women in the Massachusetts Bay Colony were literate; by 1700 the percentage remained steady for male property owners but female literacy had risen to 62 percent.

New England had planned it that way. In 1642, Massachusetts Bay passed its first law requiring that all children receive instruction in reading, a need reiterated in 1647, when the Bay Colony General Court recognized that "one chiefe project of ye ould deluder, Satan, [is] to keepe men from the knowledge of ye Scriptures . . . [and decreed] yt every towneship in ys jurisdiction, after ye Lord hath increased ym number to 50 householders shall yn forthwith appoint one with in their towne to teach all such children as shall resort to him to write & reade . . . and it is further ordered, yt where any towne shall increase to ye number of 100 families or householders, they shall set up a grammar schoole, ye mr thereof being able to instruct youth as farr as they shall be fitted for ye university."

In the southern colonies, where leaders such as Sir William Berkeley[21] had a different vision of the future—he had declared, "I Thank God there are no free schools nor printing and I hope we shall not have them [for] 100 years"—the literacy rate reflected the lack of public education. Sixty percent of Virginia's male property owners were literate by 1700, but only 25 percent of the women were.

The four kitchen inventories listed below reflect the new affluence and "polite interests" of fairly average home owners of the first, second, and third quarters of the eighteenth century:

Originally, William Torrey's early house had included a kitchen, a chamber on the second floor, a lean-to with a small chamber or loft above,

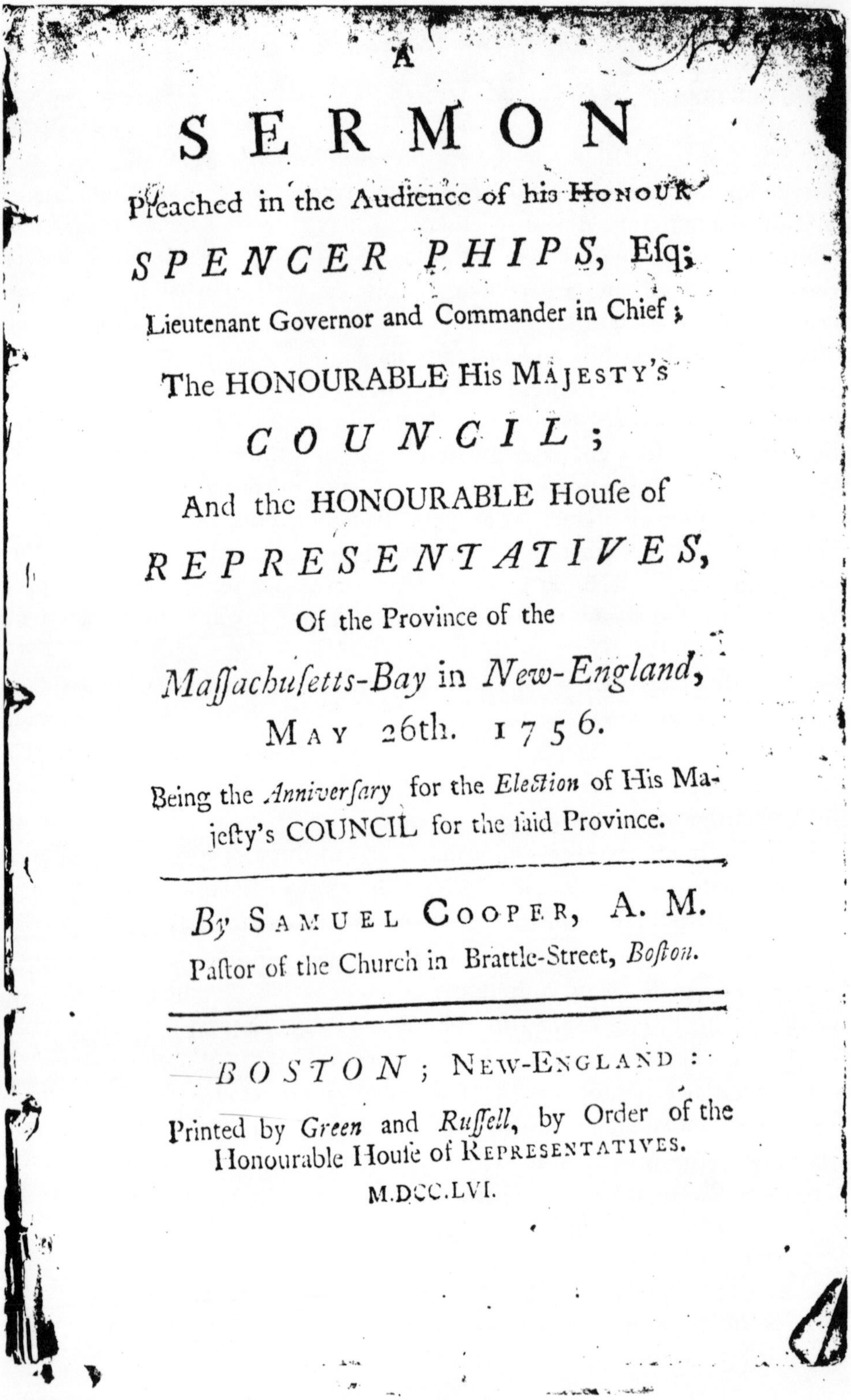

A

SERMON

Preached in the Audience of his Honour

SPENCER PHIPS, Esq;

Lieutenant Governor and Commander in Chief;

The HONOURABLE His MAJESTY'S

COUNCIL;

And the HONOURABLE House of

REPRESENTATIVES,

Of the Province of the

Massachusetts-Bay in *New-England,*
MAY 26th. 1756.

Being the *Anniversary* for the *Election* of His Majesty's COUNCIL for the said Province.

By SAMUEL COOPER, A. M.
Pastor of the Church in Brattle-Street, *Boston.*

BOSTON; NEW-ENGLAND:

Printed by *Green* and *Russell*, by Order of the
Honourable House of REPRESENTATIVES.
M.DCC.LVI.

Title page of sermon-lecture typical of those preached at various public meetings and celebrations. Colonists bought paperbound texts. Those who could afford it had books bound to order for home libraries; often several pamphlets were stitched together to form one "book."

and a cellar. Sometime shortly before February 1717 he had enlarged the old dwelling, for the inventory of the Weymouth husbandman listed at that time "the New lower room, the N. Chamber, the N. garret, and the new Cellar," in addition to the four "old" rooms and cellar.

In the kitchen were brass "kettles, pans & skillets" and some of "Bell mettle"; "pewter, earthenware, tin pans & Tunnil; 8 Candlesticks, iron ware, a Warming pan; Silver Cups & Spoons, a Cupboard with Several things in it, a Bible, Wooden Ware, Iron Tools, 3 Sives; a looking Glass, Lanthorn, & pr. bellows, a Saddle & Pillion; Bacon in the Chimney [see Part II, Chapter 3]; an old long Table; a long Gun, Tallow, Books, Chairs & Forms."

One bushel each of wheat and barley were stored in the new bed-chamber, as were three pecks of beans. Other food supplies in the new garret included twenty bushels of Indian corn, nine of malt, and eight of oats. Two more flitches of bacon hung in the old chamber; cheese was kept in the lean-to. Butter and hog's fat were preserved in the new cellar, while the old cellar held barrels of pork, beef, cider, and soap. There were an additional sixteen bushels of Indian corn in the barn.

When Lieutenant John Bridge, Gentleman, died in Roxbury in December 1748 he left his arms and cane, a little over fifty acres of farm

Roof line was changed three times to accommodate additions to 1678 Hempsted House at New London, Connecticut. Medieval English influence shows in porch, the covered front entry, of diarist Joshua Hempsted's home. Son Nathanael's 1728 addition is at right of photograph.

and meadow land, a four-room "mansion house" and barn, and a well equipped kitchen.

Appraisers counted "two brass kettles, a Brass Pan, a warming pan and 2 Skillets; six Pewter Dishes and 15 Pewter Plates; Six porrengers, 4 Basons, 1 Tankard and one Quart Pot & 1 Pint do, a Dripping Pan, Pasty Pan, Cullender & some other Tin Ware; one Iron Pott & two Iron Kittles, frying pan, Chaffindish, Gridiron and Fender; 2 tramels, Tongs, fireshovel and Andirons; a Box Iron & Heaters, Spit, Choping Knife, 2 Iron candlesticks, an Iron lamp, a Sodering Iron and Ladle; two pair of Stillyards, a Flesh Fork & Skimmer; one Table, Eight Chairs and Eleven Knives and Forks; a Bible & Sundry other Good Books & some wooden & Earthen ware."

Stored in the cellar were "30 Barrels of Cyder, some Casks of Apples, Turnips & other Sorts of Sauce, some Butter Beef & Cheese with Tubs & Earthen potts." (In the colonial vocabulary, "sauce" meant not only relishes and preserves, but any food which accompanied the main meat dish.)

Elder William Hasey of Chelsea, his social status distinguished from that of the more prominent Bridge, was listed as a yeoman when his estate was appraised in February 1754. His heirs may have been just as well satisfied; the lieutenant's estate had been valued at a total of £1497/11s/3d. Yeoman Hasey's amounted to £6165. His £8 worth of books unfortunately were not listed, but the contents of the kitchen included: "a Brass Kettle, Copper Kettle, frying pan; earthenware, 2 tramels, a Gridiron & Toaster; 1 pr cast Doggs, 2 fire Shovels & 2 pr Tongs; 2 old ironing boxes; 3 brass Skillets; Iron Kettle & Pot; meal chest & 2 pine Tables; chest & Table; 40 lb of Pewter at 4 shillings per pound." In the garret and the lean-to chamber of the four-room house were forty bushels of Indian corn and two hogsheads of cider; in the barnyard were six geese, six hogs, four cows, a heifer and two calves, two horses, and thirty-seven sheep.

Apparently grouped together for ease in listing, Elder Hasey's silver included a tankard, cann, porringer, pepper box, and three silver spoons. It is not noted whether they were kept in the kitchen or in the "best room." That parlor, however, was equally well furnished, with two bedsteads, "bedding & furniture," eighteen chairs, an oval table, chest, cupboard, ten glass bottles, a chafing dish, and "tobacco tongs."

Samuel Gardner, Gentleman, owned in December 1771 a well-stocked barn as well as a dwelling house; the furnishings included a variety of extra accessories, from a pigeon net to a damask tablecloth.

Among the "kitchen furniture," listers counted "2 brass kittles, tea kittle; brass skillet, Skimmer & peper box, 2 tramels; 12 brass Candlesticks,

2 Iron ditto, a Gridiron; 1 spit, fender & frying pann, 2 flatt irons, iron box & heaters; 2 Iron pots, 1 kittle, basting iron & skillet, tin war; 51¾ pounds of pewter, bellows & chafendish, seives; 1 Gun & bayonet & two powder horns, 1 peck, ½ peck, & morter; knives & forks, bags, meal sack & wallet; Driping pan & rolling pin, 4 trays, 3 keilers, 3 pails; kneeding trough & Churn, spinning wheels & Cards; Earthenware, Cheese press, hoops & peices of Chains, Comb; table, boxes, 2 Chests, beer Cask & Cag & wash tubs, tea pot & Cups, canister, cream pot, mustard pot, mouse trap & razor, a dozen glass bottles.''

During the years 1763 to 1765 colonial opposition to increased taxes—especially the Sugar and Stamp acts—was voiced by new leaders north and south. In Massachusetts, Samuel Adams, who ten years hence would stage-manage the Boston Tea Party, led protest groups; he was backed by John Hancock, who had just inherited a prosperous mercantile business (the profits of which he increased measurably in 1764 by smuggling). In Virginia, Patrick Henry, a farmer-turned-lawyer, proved his ability to coin quotable phrases that would become popular rallying cries. Among those who listened to him was another recent member of the House of Burgesses, George Washington, the new owner of Mount Vernon. Meanwhile, Franklin sailed again for London to plead the colonists' argument for representation in Parliament.

During this period of eighteenth-century affluence, the will of a moderately well-to-do Philadelphia merchant was submitted for probate. The inventory of his household furnishings, when compared with that of Lieutenant Buttolph at the end of the seventeenth century, points up the greater ease and comfort of life in the late colonial period. The "Inventory of the Personal Estate of Solomon Fussell late of the City of Philadelphia Rec't Deceas'd" was listed and appraised on May 5, 1762, at £3305.7.9. In addition to this sum, his £2818.0.6 worth of shop merchandise when sold brought £259.5.7½ above the appraised value. He left also £2114.19.9½ in cash, real estate which realized £1505, and £1257.2.9¼ in money owed to him "and supposed good." After his own debts were paid and probate fees deducted, and by the time accounts finally were "Examind & Pass'd" on October 25, 1765, Fussell's total estate was filed as £7907.15.11¾. His household goods, appraised at £486.7.3, included:

	£	s	d
1 Couch, 2 Arm Chairs & 7 others (all old)	1.15		
6 Maple Chairs with Leather Bottoms	4.10.0		

	£ s d
1 Diaper Table Cloth	.10.
1 Silver Spoon	.19.3
1 pr: Brass Candle Sticks	. 5.0
1 Low post sacking Bottom Bedsted & Sacking Bottom— 2 Fether Beds, 2 Bolsters 2 Pillows, 2 pr. Sheets, 1 Blankett & 1 Coverlid	8. 5.0
1 Large Bible	1. 5
6 Burnt & Enameld Plates	.10
23½ Pewter 14d.	1. 7.5
2 Brass Kettles wt. 2½ 20d.	. 4.2
4 Chkt. Curtains & a Rugg	1.15.
1 Gilt Sconce Glass with Brass Arms	3.10
Calicoe Bed Curtain, head Cloth Teaster Valiants 3 pr. window Curtains & Valients	5.10.
3 Fire Bucketts & 2 Baggs	1. 0.0
1 Silver Spoon wt. 2 oz. 1 8/6	0.17.5
6 Tea Spoons 2 8/6	0.17.
Pewter 17½ 14d	1. 0.5
1 Brass Kettle wt: 1¾ 20d	0. 2.11
A Walnut Desk	2.10.0
Feather Bed. pr: Blanketts Old	7.10.0
Bed Quilt & 2 Pillows	
Old Slate Table	0. 7.6
1 Burnt Chinia Bowl	.10.
1 Sett Green Bed Curtains & Valients	3. .
1 pr. Andirons	. 5.
2 pr: Saddle Baggs	.16.
1 Sett Pot Racks	. 5.
1 Map of Novescosia	. 2.6
1 8 Day Clock	12.10.
3 Maps	1. 0.0
2 Saddles Bridles Ec.	2. 0.0
1 Morter & Pessel & 1 Sauspan	. 5.0
1 Tea Kettle	.11.6
2 Silver Spoons wt: 2 oz. 18ds. 8/6	1.13.1
1 pr: Andirons	. 7.6
21 lb Pewter ¼d	1. 4.6
1 Sauspan	. 2.6
1 Large Brass Kettle or Pan	.10.0
1 Small Brass do. wt. 1	. 1.8
1 Chinia Plate	.10.
1 pr: old Cheretree Draws Chest and Chest	4. 0.0
A Cloth Chest & Mohogony Table	3. 0.0

	£	s	d
6 Maple Rush Bottom Chairs & a Leather Bottom Arm do.	3.	0.0	
A Sacking Bedstead, Ticking for Bed Bolsters & Pillows, 1 pr. Blanketts, 1 pr. Sheets & Quilt Cornis & Curtain Rods for Bed & Windows	8.	0.0	
3 Crack'd Chinia Bowls, 2 Small do. & 3 Plates	1.	5.	
1 pr. And Irons fire Shovel & Tongues		.15.	
A Mohogoney Dressing Box & Crack'd Looking Glass	1.	10.	
1 pr: Sheets, 1 pr: Blanketts & 1 Green Rugg (old):	2.	10.	
1 Sett of Old Blue Haretan Bed Curtains & 3 pr: Window Curtains	2.	10.	
12 Rusia & 6 Diaper Napkins		.19	
5 Table Cloths	1.		
1 Printed Cotton Counter Pin	1.	2.6	
1 Small Looking Glass		.18.	
5 Pr: sheets	2.	10.	
7 Old Chairs 21/ 6 Delph Plates & a Cloth Brush 3/6	1.	4.6	
2 pr: Old Shallow Window Curtains	.	8.	
12 Bottles & 20 Phials	.	5.	
10 Bottles Some Phials, Earthen Ware, Lamp & Tinder Box		.10.	
An Oval Table Green Cloth & Looking Glass	5.	15.	
1 Desk & Book Case	5.		
5 Leather Bottom Chairs New England fashion	2.		
Ticking of a Bed Bolster & Pillows & a pr: of Sheets & Blanketts much worn	2.	10	
A ⸺ 11 [an oval?] Table 25/ a parcel of China Glasses & stone Ware 66/3	4.	11.3	
1 pr: Endirons fire Shovel & Tongues	1.	5.	
1 Chaise whip	.	3.9	
1 Silver Tea Pott wt: 17 oz: 15 dt @ 10/ 1 Tankard 34 oz. 2 dt. 9/-	24.	4.4¾	
3 Silver Spoons 6 oz. 2. 8/6 a Cream Pott 4 oz. 10/	4.	11.10	
1 pr: Silver Tea Tongues		.12.	
6 Breakfast Basons (Pewter)	.	9.	
5 Brass Pans	1.		
A Tea Kettle 2 Coffee Potts 1 Chocolate Potts & Copper Sauspan 30/- 3 small Brass Kettles .10	2.		
4 Old Potts & Kettles & 2 pr: Hooks	.	18.	
7 Common Iron Candle Sticks 2 Pewter Muggs 1 Porenger & some Knives & forks	.	8.	
3 Salts, 3 Mustard Potts. 1 Can. 13 Pastipans 1 Cullender a Pepper Box. a Coffee Mill & Tea Kettle all Old	.	7.6	

	£	s	d
1 pr: Doggs 2 pr: Fire Shovel & Tongs	1.		
1 Joint Stool old		. 2.6	
4 Rush Bottom Chairs & 2 Small do.		.10.	
A Bread Teaster, chese Taster & pr. Bellows 4			
Sconces & 2 pr: Snuffers	5.		
1 Tea Table		.12.6	
3 And Irons Frying Pan Chaffin Dish A Stew Pan	1.15		
An Old Glass Lanthorn & Warming Pan		.12.6	
5 pr: Flatt Irons Box Iron & Choping Knife	1.		
A Parcel of Quart Bottoles Several Juggs Pails			
Bucketts 2 Iron Pans Earthen Ware Ec & Lumbering			
Articles not elce where appd.	4. 8		
A Large Ceader Tubb Iron Hoops	3.		
A Counter & Desk	2.10		
About 8 Years of a Negro Girl's time left by			
will to the Widow	30.		
Waring Apparel Including a Watch	30.		
A Large Easey Chair, Covered only with corse Linen	3.		
A Side Saddle	3.		
3 Books Sabbath of Rest 2/6		. 7.6	
1 Cambres Works		. 1.	
1 Barclays Appology		. 7.	
A Searious Call to a Devout & Holy. An Appeal.			
Christian Perfection, & a Demonsteration all by Law	1.		
Ellwood's Life		. 6.	
And Old Bible		. 7.6	
An Old Whele Barrow		· 4·	
Horse & Chair	24.		
Cash	210.		

Appraised by Us Thos: Paschall   Abel James
Philad. 5 May 1762

The "2 baggs" included on the same line with the three fire buckets refer to large carryalls, usually of canvas, kept at hand for quick removal of household goods. The "old slate table" may have been an early eighteenth-century table with a slate insert, used for mixing punch or other beverages or as a side table from which food was served. The pair of chests with cherry drawers, or chest and chest—Paschall and James seem to have had difficulty deciding on a description—often was listed as either a chest on chest or a double chest.

The cloth chest is called a blanket chest today. The "curtain rods for bed and windows" probably were custom wrought of iron, if not brass.

"Desk and bookcase" was the eighteenth-century description for that piece of furniture many now call a secretary.

The bread tester and cheese taster referred to slender plungers or metal cylinders which the cautious cook thrust into food to draw out samples. "Counter and desk" meant a small table with a portable desk-box top, a combination some today call a schoolmaster's or bookkeeper's desk.

The appraisers seem to have been surprised that Fussell, a merchant dealing in fine fabrics, owned a large easy chair "covered only with corse linen"; the chair would no doubt be considered a handsome Georgian wing chair by twentieth-century collectors. There is a temptation to speculate that the chair might have been made by Fussell himself or at least according to his knowledgeable instructions: in an earlier career the merchant had been an excellent furniture worker, at one time numbering among his apprentices William Savery.

New kitchen furnished for Nathanael Hempsted and his bride in 1728 had oven built into side wall of chimney; a crane replaced the older lug-pole and trammel chain inside the fireplace opening. Hempsted House, New London, Connecticut.

Assuredly there were those eighteenth-century builders, especially of farmhouses, who believed that Grandfather's methods were best. Throughout the century they continued to design kitchen cooking hearths and ovens much as their ancestors had. Many eighteenth-century New England houses thus retained ovens in the back of the chimney. By 1750, however, the majority of builders of new homes had begun to move the oven to one side of the main opening, with a convenient ash-storage pit set below. Both commonly still were closed by pine planks shaped to fit, although more and more owners who could afford the expense ordered iron doors, and some used heavy tin.

With the oven at one side, the size of the fireplace opening could be reduced in width and height. The sides, which in the seventeenth century had been built fairly consistently straight back at right angles to the rear wall, now with the oven gone often were raked or slanted to as much as a forty-five-degree angle. The depth of the main opening was similarly reduced; this, plus the slanted sides, helped to reflect more heat out into the room. However, as Peter Kalm noted on numerous occasions with a kind of resigned amazement, English colonists had not by 1750 installed dampers.[22] (In most homes this feature would not be added until cooking stoves were purchased in the nineteenth century.)

Notably missing from colonial kitchen inventories is the mention of cranes, although these generally were used in the kitchens of better homes in England in the sixteenth and seventeenth centuries, and would have been known as cranes to colonists. The usual early English practice had been to set the crane holders in the back wall of the chimney.

In the seventeenth century, with the oven at the rear of the fireplace, cranes set into the back or even the side wall might have interfered with easy access to the oven; a trammel chain was more easily pushed to one side and out of the way. Trammels continued to be itemized in eighteenth-century inventories. These, at times quite long, pot hangers usually were ratchets which allowed control of the distance between pot and embers and thus of the temperature at which food was cooked. The same hangers, first suspended from a hook or ring at the end of the trammel chain, later could also have been suspended from cranes.

Cranes, however, called for the installation of their own ring holders, set into the mortar between the stones or bricks of the chimney. When new houses were built around existing chimneys, it apparently was not considered feasible to remove old, settled stones in order to install new cranes. The absence of dampers also indicates the continued use of trammel chains suspended from lug-poles. It seems a safe assumption that cranes were installed more frequently in new houses for which fireplaces with side ovens had been designed than in houses which were altered by changing interior wall partitions or in those kitchens around which new additions were built.

By the mid-eighteenth century town houses in Philadelphia and other middle-colony cities were, according to Kalm, "commonly built in the English manner." In this type of better house, the lowest room was entirely underground. These walls were made of stone which was covered with mortar and then whitewashed, although the house above usually was built of brick. It was used for a cellar, pantry, woodshed, or "sometimes a kitchen."[23] The same pattern was followed in New York and in some instances also in New England, in those clapboarded houses built into the side of a hill and which thus allowed ground-floor entrances on two levels.

In all colonies where houses had finished cellars, with stone or brick floors, these areas served as workrooms for pickling and preserving as well as storage places for potted or salted foods. Justice Hempsted's diary confirms this practice and the time of year in which much preserving and salting work was done:

> Jan. 1 Wedensd (1717/18): fair & Moderate. I have been in ye Chamber garrett, Leanto & Celler pickling my Meat &c.
> Thursd. (Dec.) 26 (1747) fair. I salted up some beef in ye Garret near 2 barrills.
> Dec. 31 Rainy. Wee killed my Red Hogg. Weighed 226 lb.
> Jan. 2 (1748) fair. I helpt Salt up ye Pork & I Married James Stodder & Priscilla Mynard.
> Weds Jan 1 (1751/52): I shelled out a basket of Corn in which John's Corn was caryed up ye Garrit after husking & the Baket holds Exactly 1 bushll 2 quarts & 1 pint. I had 31 baskitts full. Natt caryed them up in ye new Garrett.[24]

As houses increased in size, additional fireplaces were built into the new second-floor chambers. The parlor in most homes continued to be the room in which the family's best bedstead was set up; the second-best bedsteads now were moved upstairs. Noticeably lacking in most inventories of these enlarged homes is the bedstead and the number of (pallet) beds, and the general sleeping accouterments which had been common in seventeenth-century kitchen inventories.

During both centuries, with rare exceptions such as that of William Googe, estate inventories of those who owned land or warehouses or who practiced skilled trades listed possession of indentured servants or slaves. No inventory examined, however, used the phrases "hired man's bed" or "under-eaves bed" to describe the type of low-post bedstead to which those names are given today. The Calthorpe "couch bed" may have referred to a narrow low-post bedstead, but the usual term for these was "truckle bed" or "trundle bed." While servants undoubtedly slept in loft or garret areas or in lean-tos behind the kitchens, no special provision for their comfort was recorded. Some, in warmer climates, may have been bedded down in barns: The Calthorpe inventory, for example, listed nine indentured servants, but even with the seventeenth-century lack of regard for privacy, these nine plus the five members of the family seem to us an overwhelming number for whom to have found sleeping space in a three-room house.

Then, as now, skilled domestic help for kitchen work was hard to find; nor was it any easier to find good plowmen for the farms or gardeners for the orchards. The preferred servant was white. Orphans were indentured to tradesmen or "farmed out" to planters in the country, as were the adult poor. This solved the potential paupers' problem of where to find food and shelter and provided needed help for those who could afford it. The largest white labor pool, however, was made up of bonded men and women who had agreed, in return for passage over, to allow themselves to be sold by shippers at public auctions, held regularly in seaports north and south. The term of such bondage averaged from five to seven years, but could depend on how high a new master had had to bid. An advertisement in January 1774 in the Pennsylvania *Messenger* was typical: "Just arrived— to be seen at the Golden Swan, kept by the widow Krieger. The lot includes (50) schoolmasters, artisans, peasants, boys and girls of various ages, all to serve for payment of passage."[25] The need for labor had been acute, of course, long before the beginning of the Revolution, so much so that in 1709 the Massachusetts General Court had decreed that the "importation of white servants [should] be encouraged."[26] These, however, were better off than Negroes similarly auctioned in the wharf markets, since there would be eventual freedom for the former to work to buy their own land but none for the latter.

Even earlier, in 1648, Massachusetts, while not actively discouraging the importation of black slaves, did provide specifically for bringing servants from Europe and for a third servant group, Indians, when it decreed: "There shall never be any bond-slavery, villenage or captivitie amongst us, unlesse it be lawful captives, taken in just warrs, and such strangers as willingly sell themselves or are solde to us."[27]

Justly captured or not, Indians were the least-sought-after servants, considered generally intractable and untrustworthy and not the best investment—they could most easily run away, for they had little fear of being identified once back with their own family or tribe. Many native servants were taken captive during the frontier wars; the Indians in turn, in collusion with the French, took captive hundreds of white English settlers who were force-marched to Canada to be sold to French colonists there.[28]

Though the entries are a dozen years apart, notes from Justice Hempsted's diary polish both sides of the old coin. On Monday, September 9,

1734, he wrote that he had gone "with Mr. Ebenezer Williams of Stonington who is Come to See a French Woman in Town that says She was the Daughter of his Brother Rev. Mr. Williams of Deerfield taken by the french & Indians from thence when that Town was Taken 30 years ago."[29] On Thursday, August 21, 1746, he noted that "old Rachel formerly a Servt to Capt John Prenttis Decd was buried in the Evening. I suppose She was near 80 years of age. She was a Captive taken in the Narhaganset war in 1675. I have known her about 60 year. . . . She always lived in the family & had many Children by her Husband (york Servt to Mr Pygan Decd). She was an Honest faithfull Creture & I hope a good Christian. She was one of our Church for many years past."[30]

> *An incredible amount of wood is squandered in this country for fuel; day and night all winter, or for nearly half the year, in all rooms, a fire is kept going.*
> PETER KALM[31]

The long skirts of the women and the petticoats worn by boys (until they were seven or eight) and the long dresses of daughters cut to the same style as that of their elders, were hazardous costumes in the seventeenth-century kitchen. They proved only slightly less so in those of the latter half of the eighteenth century when new-style ovens were set in one side of the chimney wall rather than in the back of the cavernous fireplace.

The constant maintenance of a fire, the necessary raking apart of embers and coals to provide a "slow or gentle" cooking temperature for some dishes, the need to build up brisk flames to produce "quick" heat, meant that even the most careful cook daily risked injury. Added to the danger of sparks and bits of wood which rolled out onto the hearth was the risk involved in laying the small fires with which the oven was heated. At the least this meant lifting coals from the main hearth into the oven; more difficult was starting a new oven fire with twigs and embers: "My mother's test for the degrees of heat necessary for baking was her hand and arm thrust into the oven. If she could hold it there until she could count thirty *and no longer*, it was all right," wrote Lora Case.[32]

Once the fire burned down and the oven was reckoned hot enough, the ashes had to be removed quickly with a long-handled iron shovel, the pans of food placed inside, and the oven closed by pushing its plank or sheet-iron cover or "door" into place.

Spit-roasting carried with it the chance of burns from sputtering fat. The kettles and pots, bubbling and boiling with stews, porridges, and puddings, were heavy and easily tipped when removed from their lug-pole hangers. The eighteenth-century crane, which could be swung out and away from the bed of embers, did little to reduce the tipping over of kettles. Joshua Hempsted described the danger: "April 1 sund fair (1722): Molly is scalded in ye back & neck. a dis of hot milk Spilt on her by Nathanll. *wednes 4 cloudy.* I was at home all day making a plow & looking after Molly who is bad with her Scald. Ye ague hath been in itt & she hath ye fever."[33]

The much larger caldrons used for the manufacture of dyes and the rendering of tallow for soap or candles left scars on floors and stones and on their owners as well. Unhappily the danger from burns and scaldings was not confined to daylight hours spent over the cooking pots. Fires in the dark "night season" destroyed numerous houses. Too-porous, flaky stone, or dusty brick hearth floors eroded under the ever-kindled kitchen fires, a danger sometimes unnoticed until their retained heat charred and eventually inflamed tied-in cellar beams. "The chimneys of the English . . . have no dampers for closing them up," Peter Kalm noted.[34] In the eighteenth century chimneys were generally still pointed with clay, which could disintegrate into powdery, inflammable dust. When encrustations of grease were added, and oily particles daily wafted skyward in the sooty smoke, these built-in hazards were multiplied. Chimneys were cleaned at least semiannually: first "burnt out" by deliberately lit boughs, then swept by green cedar branches thrust down them to the hearths below. The careful householder followed such burning and sweeping with a third precaution: A stone or a piece of iron was swung from the end of a chain down and against the sides of each flue to loosen lingering coom or soot. Spring and fall housecleanings were arduous.

Though many homes were more sparsely furnished than sometimes is assumed today, they often served as shops and warehouses and were cluttered with tools, utensils, and pieces of work in process. Not all a family's clothing was kept in cupboards and chests; that in daily use was hung from hooks and pegs studded in the wooden walls. The "bed furniture"—the draperies and side hangings which kept out drafts on cold nights, the netting that thwarted mosquitoes in summer—were fearful fire hazards. Flames, which woolen blankets might have hindered, were assisted by the under bedding, which was filled with down and feathers in the chambers of wealthy merchants and stuffed with dried cornhusks, straw, seaweed, or pine needles in those of "lesser worth."

Barrels of flour, splint baskets of flax, strings of dried fruits, trays of vegetables, boxed and paper-cone-covered herbs, all quickened flames toward the thatched or wood-shingled roof. The one- to three-inch layers of lard or butter which had been ladled over meat as a preservative, then covered and tied with heavy greased paper or brandy-soaked paper, caught sparks easily; crocks and pots of still-stewing foods often were retrieved from what had been the butteries and larders of burned houses. The kegs of sweet oils and the casks of home-distilled brandy were hazards below stairs.

The tired-to-the-bone weariness of servants and slaves, and of the home owners themselves, contributed to the toll. No amount of legislation against smoking along leaf-covered roadways, no amount of chimney inspectors and warnings of the need for constant vigilance could control the peril created by exhaustion. Clergymen, justices, and schoolmasters dozed over paper-strewn writing tables and neglected to snuff out sputtering candles just as often as did members of their congregations, courts, and classrooms.[35]

The master's nightly ritual of inspecting each floor before closing up the house not only was to secure his family and goods from intruders, but to make certain fires were properly banked, lamps and tallow tapers extinguished. Between the lines of Joshua Hempsted's note on the leveling of his daughter Abigail's home can be sensed sad criticism of his son-in-law, Clement Minor. Minor obviously had had to be called home when flames burst through the roof of his house. Absent when the rest of the family retired, he had not made his all-too-necessary nightly tour.

Thus in New London on Friday, April 17, 1747, Hempsted wrote, "wee had the Sad Tydings that Son Miners' Dwelling house was burn to ye ground last night by accident," and on the next day "in the aftern I went to Stonington to See my Distressed Children. . . . I found my Dejected son miner much wounded (vizt) bruised by his falling from a Chamber window in Endeavouring to Quench the fire which first began in the Lean too Chamber at the NE corner by an Indian woman Sticking a Short piece of Candle to a Cheast & falling a Sleep until it burnt through the Roof and *no man at home to prevent it Spreading.* My Daughter was the first that Discovered it about Midnight & was the Instrument to Save . . . most of the household Stuff & Shop Goods & c."

The family of another community leader, a friend of Hempsted's, suffered a similar calamity the following year. Hempsted wrote that Saturday, October 17, 1748, was "a fair and Moderate day [and so] I rid out and over Jno Comstocks ferry to Colln [Colonel] Chris averys to Carry his Deed for Record. but the Colln was gone to Preston to see his Brother Humphrey who is in a very Distressing Condition. his House burnt down to ye Ground last Tuesday night & Everything Consumed. they Saved nothing *not So much as their cloaths to their back & Some of ye Children much Scorched.*"[36]

The process of recovery was lengthy: all-consuming house fires left many facing bankruptcy; fire meant the loss of home furnishings accumulated over a lifetime and sometimes a year's supply of food, and often as well the staggering loss of shop goods and manufacturing supplies.[37] Justice

Hempsted, a skilled joiner, consequently would write of Monday, December 19, 1748, twenty months after Abigail and Clement lost their home, that on that "misty" day, "in the foren I was att home helping Danll Truman about a bedstid for Daughter Miner." On Friday he "bot ¾ yds of Duck of Capt Frost for a Bed bottom 14s p yd . . . I pd it," and on Wednesday, December 28, "in the aftern I & adam [a hired man] went to Stonington. he Carryed a New bedstid for my Daughter Miner. . . . Adm went home & I to work about the bedstid."[38]

PART V

The Wild Plenty

Many herbes in the Spring time are com-
monly dispersed throughout the woods—
good for broths and sallets, as Violets,
purslins, sorrel &c.   JOHN SMITH

JUST AS HELPFUL IN LATER YEARS when crops did poorly as they had
been in those first early starving times, the Indians taught the frontier family how to boil and eat the large acorns of the white oak, to
skim its oil for a linament to soothe rheumatic aches, and to boil its
bark for what Kalm described as the "best remedy yet found against
the dystentery."[1] In like fashion, the Indians taught settlers in Virginia a
new woodsman's dish: the acorns of the live oak when ground could be used
to thicken venison soup or could be combined with corn hominy and wild
rice, stewed with seasoning herbs over a wood-chip fire.

"The herbs and fruits are of many sorts and kinds," Smith reported,
"as alkermes, currans, mulberries, vines, respises, gooseberries . . . plums,
walnuts, chestnuts, small-nuts, pumpkins, gourds, strawberries, beans, peas
and maize; a kind or two of flax, wherewith [the Indians] make nets, lines
and ropes, both small and great, very strong for their quantities."[2]

Smith warned colonists that while "Virginia doth afford many excellent
vegetables "for the table, English cattle and sheep would not thrive the
first few years because of grass for pasturage "there is little or none, but
what groweth in low marshes: for all the country is overgrown with trees

[103]

whose droppings continually turneth their grass to weeds, by reason of the rankness of the ground, [which would have to be] amended by good husbandry." Of good trees, however, which would provide timber for building and fruit for food, there were many: "Most common [are] oak and walnut; many oaks are so tall and straight they will bear two feet and a half square of good timber for 20 yards long; of this wood there are two or three several kinds. There are also some elm, some black walnut tree and some ash—of ash and elm they make soap ashes."

Smith reported "two or three kinds" of walnuts, probably including hickories in this category, "and a kind of wood we called cypress because the wood, the fruit, and leaf did most resemble it; of those trees there are some near three fathoms about at the foot, very straight [growing] 50, 60, or 80 [feet tall] without a branch.

"By the dwelling of some savages are some great mulberry trees, and in some parts of the country they are found growing naturally in pretty groves."[3]

Smith's explorers discovered groves of "chestnuts whose wild fruit [equals] the best in France, Spain, Germany or Italy," and as for wild fruit,

plums there are of three sorts. The red and white are like [English] hedge plums [and there is another] called *putchamins* [persimmons] [which] grow as high as a palmetto; the fruit is like a medlar; it is first green, then yellow, then red when it is ripe; if it be not ripe it will draw a man's mouth awry with much torment, but when it is ripe it is as delicious as an apricot.

They have cherries [that] are much like a damson, but [because of] their tastes and color we called them cherries. We saw some few crabs, but very small and bitter.

Of vines [in Virginia there are] great abundance that climb [to] the tops of the highest trees in some places, but these bear but few grapes. [However] by the rivers and savage habitations, where they are not over-shadowed from the sun, they are covered with fruits, though never pruned nor manured. Of these hedge grapes we made nearly twenty gallons of wine, which was like our French British wine, but certainly they would prove good were they well manured.

There is another sort of grape near as great as a cherry, this they call *messamins*; they be fat, and the juice thick. Neither doth the taste so well please [as] when they are made in wine.

They have a small fruit growing on little trees, husked like a chestnut, but the fruit most like a very small acorn. This they call *chechinquamins*, which they esteem a great dainty. They have a berry much like our gooseberry, in greatness, color, and taste; those they call *rawcomens*, and do eat them raw or boiled.[4]

Colonists learned from the Indians to dry the fruit of the hackberry or "hedgeberry" and to use it in powdered form as a seasoning for meat. The honey locust provided fruit, and beer was brewed from its pulp. Seeds of the Kentucky coffee tree were used as a substitute for imported coffee beans by rural families from New York to Tennessee. Throughout New England, beach plums, as well as the red chokeberry and the chokecherry, were first boiled by the Indians into a sweet dark jelly. The shadbush fruit, although rather tasteless, was eaten raw by the Indians, who suggested its merits to early colonists. They in turn, calling it serviceberry, Juneberry, shadblow, or May cherry, baked it in tarts and bread.

Various watercresses, wild leeks, rice, milkweed shoots, peppergrass, dandelions, mushrooms, chestnuts, walnuts, hickories, and butternuts, all first were boiled with frontier game as well as served in ways more familiar to the twentieth century.

Among the other wild foods recognized by hungry colonists was the berberry, or barberry, which provided a sharp pickle. Jelly and wine early were made from the wild fox grape (known now, in impoved forms, as the Concord grape), which was found growing from New England to as far south as Georgia, and west from Tennessee to Indiana.

As for the abundance of strawberries to be found throughout the colonies (Strawberry Bank was the name first given to Portsmouth, New Hampshire), Roger Williams commented they were the "wonder of all fruits growing naturally in these parts. One of the chiefest doctors of England was wont to say that God could have made, but God never did make, a better berry. In some parts where the natives have planted, I have many times seen as many as would fill a good ship within a few miles compass."[5] Thomas Tusser's sixteenth-century verse could apply to seventeenth-century New England:

> Wife, into thy garden, and set me a plot,
> With strawberry roots, of the best to be got;
> Such growing abroad, among thorns in the wood,
> Well-chosen and picked, prove excellent good.[6]

Cranberries, John Josselyn reported, were used much by the English and Indians, who "boyl them with Sugar for a Sauce to eat with their meat; and it is a delicate Sauce, especially for roasted mutton. Some make tarts with them as with Goose Berries."[7] The cranberry not only quickly became a favorite with settlers, but quantities were sent over, preserved, to Europe and the West Indies.[8]

Josselyn's readers in 1672 learned that American cranberry leaves are "like Box but greener, thick and glistering; the Blossoms are very like the Flowers of our English Night Shade, after which succeed the Berries, hanging by long small foot stalks no bigger than a hair; at first they are a pale yellow Colour, afterwards Red, and as big as a Cherry; some perfectly round, others oval, all of them hollow, of a sower astringent taste; they are ripe in August and September [and] are excellent against Scurvy."[9]

"Cranberries are brought to market every Wednesday and Saturday at Philadelphia late in autumn," Kalm reported in 1748. "They are prepared in the same manner as we do our red lingon and they are used during winter and part of summer in tarts and other kinds of pastry." But, he warned his readers, "they require a great deal of sugar."[10]

"Sky-coloured billberries" (blueberries) were considered "a most excellent Summer Dish. They usually eat of them put into a Bason with Milk and sweetened a little more with Sugar and Spice, or for cold Stomachs in Sack [sherry]."[11]

An imaginative variety of plants was tried in an effort to find a palatable substitute for China tea. Among these were ribwort, strawberry, elderberry, blackberry, and currant leaves, goldenrod, dittany, sage, and thoroughwort. Perhaps the two best-known today, for they were among the most popular during the Revolutionary period, are raspberry leaves, the brew of which was called Hyperion tea, and loosestrife, or Liberty tea.

Probably every kind of nut or grain was parched and boiled in the effort to find a substitute for coffee; two of those most often used were rye grains and chestnuts. Dried pumpkin was boiled down to serve in place of molasses. Juice was squeezed from green cornstalks and used as a sweetener, while maple syrup, maple sugar, or wild bee's honey replaced imported sugar. Obviously, of all the substitutes, those which continued in greatest common use throughout both centuries of the colonial era were those which best took the place of these necessarily imported luxuries.

A pound of sugar, tea, or coffee may not seem an extravagance today; each was, however, in those years when hard money was a rarity in most colonial households. Twenty shillings equaled one pound sterling in the common English currency used. We loosely transcribe one colonial pound as the equivalent of five dollars, without realizing the buying power it controlled. (Its actual value today would be at least fifty dollars.) Thus, even in the mid-eighteenth century a keg of brown sugar could cost as much as a set of chairs. The estate of "Archibald McNeile, late of Kennett," inventoried in Pennsylvania on March 1, 1762–63, reflected the high cost of colonial sugar. A "Quantity of brown sugar" was valued at twenty-five shillings whereas six "black Chairs, one of them armed" were listed at just fifteen shillings for the set. "Four loaves of [white] sugar" were inventoried at one pound; so was a walnut chest.

In that same year Samuel Johnson gave an explanation of the cost of living which provides a clearer perspective of colonial money values:

Herbs dry on long, carved wood crane-type rack above the raised brick hearth of the kitchen at Kenmore, Fredericksburg, Virginia. Visitors to this restored 1750 house are served spiced tea and gingerbread prepared according to a Washington family recipe.

"If you wish only to support nature . . . let us call it six pounds. This sum will fill your belly, shelter you from the weather, and even get you a strong lasting coat, supposing it to be made of good bull's hide."[12]

Six pounds also had been the estimated cost of keeping oneself for one year in the seventeenth century; six pounds was the average charge for transporting one passenger from England to the colonies. Since the equivalent of a year's wages was needed just to get here, let alone the additional fourteen pounds to buy the first year's supplies and funds with which to purchase land, it is easy to understand why so many colonists came as indentured servants or company tenants, or in some other way mortgaged their first years in America.

Colonists during both centuries learned to adapt American woods for fashioning their household accessories. Among those they would use first, according to John Smith's inventory, were "oak, the chief wood of which there is great difference [depending] on the soil where it groweth; fir, pine, walnut, chestnut, birch, ash, elm, cypress, cedar, mulberry, plum tree, hazel, sassafras, and many other sorts, also,"[13] the last-named category including all those which did not resemble closely enough any English trees to which Smith could compare them.

Although sensibly the settler, hard-pressed for time, would have made tools from whatever dry wood was at hand, over the years certain woods were preferred for specific uses. Thus, maple was used for bowls—especially for large chopping bowls—and for trenchers, plates, spoons, ladles, stirring sticks and mashers, boxes, pails, mortars and pestles, and tubs.

Oak was preferred for hoops, chairs, table tops, and boxes. Pine was used for bucket and tub staves and for some cheese and butter containers. Birch often was made into clothespins, basket and box handles, small containers and bowls. Its paperlike bark sometimes was used for window coverings; birch saplings were shaved and splintered into brooms. Ash was excellent for barrel and keg hoops, as was hickory, which also was a favorite wood for pegs and for shaving into splints for chair seats.

Chestnut was used whenever a hard wood was called for, and often replaced oak. Cedar, probably because it resisted decay, was turned into firkins, keelers, and washtubs. Poplar and basswood, or linden, were both known as whitewood or spoonwood and were used for table utensils, undoubtedly because they had little discernible taste or odor. The sour gum, or pepperidge, tree, because of its hollowness, was easily made into mortars.

PART VI

The Standing Dishes

CHAPTER 1

The Ancient Dish

Wedensd 20th (Sept. 1721): fair til near night. I came home [from Saybrook] as far as Thos Lees & lodgd ther. I was att Black-Hall & saw a pumpkin 5 foot 11 inches Round. the Seed came out of the Streights. It was at John Griswolds.

JOSHUA HEMPSTED[1]

OF ALL THE PUDDINGS the colonial housewife was to boil or bake, the first was a kind of pumpkin stew or sauce, for the pumpkin, wrote Edward Johnson, was the "fruit which the Lord fed his people with till corn and cattle increased."[2] Pumpkin was the wilderness staple which sustained the first settlers of Virginia; it truly was deserving of the title "the Ancient New England Standing Dish," declared John Josselyn.[3]

Just as in the late nineteenth century many would speak of meat and potatoes as natural culinary companions, so throughout the seventeenth and eighteenth centuries did colonists combine "pompion sauce" with fish or flesh. Pumpkins were native to America, Josselyn reported. He found them to be "dryer than our English pompions" but thought they were "better-tasted"; so good, in fact, that he recommended eating them "green" (uncooked).[4] That the English fruit did differ in consistency had been corroborated earlier when Shakespeare in another context described it as "watry pompion."[5]

Early travelers did not always differentiate between pumpkins and squash. Robert Boyle said that "squash is an Indian kind of pompion that grows apace,"[6] and Peter Kalm spoke of "crookneck" pumpkins that kept "almost all winter" without having to be dried.[7]

Some have thought the first colonists learned from the Indians to dry pumpkins for use over winter, but this kind of tutoring would have been unnecessary; English and Continental custom had been to dry pumpkins in the same manner as apples. At home, the fruit had been sliced and placed on racks to dry in the sun, or hung to dry from kitchen beams or attic rafters, and so it was here. One hundred and twenty-five years after settlement Kalm noted no change in this old method of preservation, reporting that pumpkins were "cut in slices, drawn up on a thread and dried [to] keep all year long, and are boiled or stewed."

Others "as soon as cold weather commences, remove all the pumpkins that remain on the stalk whether they are ripe or not, and spread them on the floor where the unripe ones grow ripe, if they are not laid one upon the other. They keep fresh for several months and even through the winter, if they be well secured in dry cellars, where the cold cannot enter, or which is still better, in dry rooms which are heated now and then to prevent the cold from damaging the fruit."[8]

When Josselyn reported on the ancient standing dish of the 1660s, he provided his readers with the popular seventeenth-century recipe. The colonial housewife's manner of dealing with pumpkins, he wrote, was "to slice them when ripe, and cut them into dice, and so fill a pot with them of two or three gallons, and stew them upon a gentle fire a whole day, and as they sink, they will fill again with fresh Pompions, not putting any liquor to them. When it is stew'd enough, it will look like bak'd Apples.

"This they Dish, putting Butter to it, and a little Vinegar with some Spice as Ginger, et c., which makes it tart like an Apple, and so serve it to be eaten with Fish or Flesh."[9]

The first Dutch settlers also thought of pumpkins as substitutes for apple puddings; their method of preparation differed only slightly from that of their New England neighbors. In his description of the seventeenth-century colony along the Hudson and Mohawk rivers the Dutch official Adrien Van der Donck wrote that the "pumpkin grows with little or no cultivation and is so sweet and dry that it is used, with the addition of vinegar and water, for stewing in the same manner as apples. . . . I have heard it said, too, that when properly prepared as apples are with us, it is not inferior to them, or there is but little difference, and when the pumpkin is baked in ovens it is considered better than apples."[10]

That pumpkin pudding would remain an indispensable staple for the majority of farm and village families was reiterated in 1705 by Mrs. Sarah Kemble Knight. The travel journal she kept provides fascinating glimpses into colonial fare and kitchens, including a note that one evening she "lodg'd at Stonington [Connecticut] and had Rost Beef and pumpkin sause for supper . . . the next night at Haven's and had Rost fowle."[11]

Kalm, forty years later, also wrote of pumpkins and/or squash "eaten boiled, either with meat or by themselves," adding "in the first case, they are put on the edge of the dish round the meat."[12]

Mme. Knight remarked on the popularity of pumpkins throughout Connecticut—a colony she found a "plentifull Country for provisions of all sorts and . . . Generally Healthy [where] no one that can and will be dilligent need fear poverty nor want of food and Rayment." During her stay in New Haven, she was told a local justice "had gone into the feild with a Brother in office to gather his Pompions."[13] Kalm also remarked that "many farmers have a whole field of them."[14]

The Stonington pumpkin sauce and beef must have been prepared tastefully; had it not, Mme. Knight's criticism would have been left for our edification. That some at whose homes and inns she stopped were not good cooks was made succinctly evident. On December 6, Mme. Knight recalled, she and her guide "came to Stratford ferry, which crossing, about two miles on the other side Baited [fed] our horses and would have eat a morsell ourselves, But the Pumpkin and Indian mixt Bred had such an Aspect, and the Bare-legg'd Punch so . . . Awfull a sound, that we left both . . . and proceeded . . . to Fairfield." There, happily, the woman whom many believed to have been dame's school teacher for Benjamin Franklin finally "met with good entertainment."[15]

In his discussion of squash, Kalm said that indeed the "fruit has an agreeable taste when well prepared." He found "squashes are commonly boiled, then crushed (as we are used to do with turnips when we make porridge of them) and seasoned with some pepper or other spice, whereupon the dish is ready."[16]

Van der Donck in New York, as had Roger Williams in Rhode Island and John Smith in Virginia, did differentiate between pumpkins and other "species of this vegetable . . . called by our people quaasiens, a name derived from the aborigines, as the plant was not known to us before our intercourse with them."[17]

Quaasiens, or squash, "is a delightful fruit," according to Van der Donck, "as well to the eye on account of its fine variety of colours, as to the mouth for its agreeable taste. The ease with which it is cooked renders it a favourite with the young women. They gather the squashes and immediately place them on the fire without any farther trouble."[18]

Josselyn thought squash, whether green or yellow, long like a gourd or round like an apple, were "all pleasant food boyled and buttered and Season'd with Spice, but the yellow Squash called an Apple Squash because like an Apple and about the bigness of a Pome-water, is the best kind; they are much eaten by the Indians and the English."[19]

Pumpkin was sent to the colonial table not only as a simple boiled or baked pudding, but in other guises as well. Of these the most common must have been the heavy bread disparaged by Mme. Knight. In all colonies this seems to have been made by combining equal measures of boiled pumpkin with boiled Indian-corn meal, shaped into loaves and baked. While it may have been served as an adjunct to other food, just as often, along with a bowl of milk and perhaps some butter or molasses, it was a substitute for meal porridge at supper.

A second stew, the recipe learned from the Indians, "mingled" pumpkins, corn, peas, and beans in one porridge pot.

"The English," said Van der Donck, "who in general think much of what gratifies the palate, use it [pumpkin] also in pastry, and understand making a beverage from it."[20]

In some households, pumpkins and squash were baked whole, then brought from the oven in a large table trencher. The top was cut out, and each diner was invited to dip into the natural basin for his portion.

> The Indians boil them whole, or roast them in the ashes and eat them, or sell them thus prepared in the town; and they have indeed a fine flavor when roasted.
>
> The French and English also slice them and put the slices before the fire to roast; when they are done they generally put sugar on the pulp. Another way of roasting them is to cut them through the middle, take out all the seeds, put the halves together again and roast them in an oven. When they are quite done some butter is put in, which being imbibed into the pulp renders it very palatable. The settlers often boil pumpkins in water, and afterwards eat them alone or with meat. Some make a thin pottage of them by boiling them in water and afterwards macerating the pulp. This is again boiled with a little of the water, and a good deal of milk and stirred about while it is boiling. Sometimes the pulp is kneaded into a dough with maize and other flour; of this they make pancakes. Some make puddings and tarts of pumpkins.[21]

The English propensity for gratifying the palate not only provided a target for Van der Donck's wit, but was a source of concern for New England's own critics of its colonists. In seventeenth-century England and Europe pumpkins more often than not were considered food proper only for peasants, or, as many preferred to phrase their description, men and women of the "poorer sort." The hungry first settlers, close to starvation, had to dismiss such culinary class distinction in favor of staying alive. To some of their descendants, as time went by and fortunes grew, not having to depend on pumpkin pudding for daily fare thus became a kind of reverse status symbol.

Although Josselyn, and later Mme. Knight and others, would not refuse pumpkin sauce when it was prepared competently, for a select few second- and third-generation colonists it was difficult to imagine—as it is for us today—their ancestors' crude beginnings, those early times when neighbor shared with neighbor the same simple life.

So much changed quickly for the families of new wealth in the new cities. By the late 1630s West Indiamen and ships from Europe were sailing in and out of the increasingly crowded harbors, carrying flour, sugar, rum, molasses, and rice. The scents of these mingled along the wharves with those from kegs of pickled oysters; barrels of salt cod, pork, and beef; crates of oranges, lemons, and pineapples; bales of cinnamon sticks; bags of nutmegs; boxes of pepper and cardamom, and a hundred other delicacies for the well-stocked kitchen. It was a new world of plenty, and it tempted men and women, who could now dine on white bread and keep liveried servants to pass their gleaming pewter and silver, to forget old days and early purposes.

Such well-fed disdain for recent history prompted ministers and writers to admonish against conspicuous expenditure. Expressing true regret, Benjamin Tompson in 1676 described "New England's crisis," recalling "the times wherein old Pompion was a saint, When men fared hardly yet without complaint On vilest cates; the dainty Indian maize Was eat with clamshells out of wooden trays—these times were good, Merchants cared not a rush For other fare than Jonakin and mush."[22]

As the eighteenth century ended, Amelia Simmons wrote of preparing squash and pumpkin puddings in a manner closer to methods used today. What today's cook would style a pumpkin pie was to the "American Orphan," as Miss Simmons called herself (whether she was in fact an orphan, or whether she felt herself one because no publisher would sponsor her book, is not known), a pudding baked in a crust.

Her "pompkin" recipe specified "One quart [pumpkin] stewed and strained, 3 pints cream, 9 beaten eggs, sugar, mace, nutmeg and ginger, laid into paste, and with a dough spur, cross and chequer it, and baked in dishes three quarters of an hour." In her economical language she also suggested "one quart of milk, 1 pint pompkin, 4 eggs, molasses, allspice and ginger in a crust, bake 1 hour."[23]

The "dough spur" referred to was the same type of rotating wheel used today to cut, crimp, or decorate pastry, and which in the eighteenth century was often carved of bone, hand-forged of iron, or whittled from a hard, smooth-grained wood. The dishes in which Miss Simmons and her kitchen colleagues of the eighteenth century set their pudding pies to bake were usually red or yellow deep earthenware plates.

CHAPTER 2

The Indian Porridge

Father and I went down to camp
Along with Captain Goodwin
And there we saw the men and boys
As thick as hasty pudding.
"YANKEE'S RETURN FROM CAMP"[24]

THOMAS HARIOT, AMONG THE FIRST of Sir Walter Raleigh's company to explore Elizabeth's New Found Land in Virginia, reported that they had discovered a variety of excellent food crops on Roanoke Island.

They tasted *wickonzowr*, "called by us Pease [and] far better than our Englishe pease." They found *macocqwer*, "called by us Pompions," and picked many "mellions very good." Hariot reported a spectacular "greate herbe in the forme of a Marigolde, about six foote in height; some take it to bee Plante Solis [sunflower], of the seedes heereof they make both a kind of breade and broth."[25]

The natives offered the strangely armored and bearded English explorers of 1585 "okindigier, called by us Beanes," a plant which Hariot said grew on vines up the cornstalks. Of all the Virginia plants first reported, it was agreed that the most important by far was "Pagatowr, a kind of graine so called by the inhabitants, the same [that] is in the West Indies called Mayze. English men call it Guinney wheate or Turkie wheate." All the different kinds of corn, Hariot wrote, though they were of "divers colours—some white, some red, some yellow, some blew—yeelde a very white and sweete flowre [and] maketh a very good bread. Of these graines besides bread, the inhabitants make victuall either by parching them or seething them whole untill they be broken; or boyling the floure with water into a pappe." Hariot brought home other good news, for "We made of the same in the country some mault, whereof was brued as good ale as was to be

[116]

desired."[26] Thus, thought the exuberant adventurer, there was native cereal-grain aplenty from which English emigrants might boil their favorite pudding, and with a little time and effort, also could have good New England ale to enjoy with it.

Other early opinions differed: "The barbarous Indians who know no better are constrained to make a virtue of necessity and think it good food, whereas we judge [corn] a more convenient food for swine than for man," decided the author of the famous text *The Herball or General Historie of Plantes*, published in 1597. Turkey corn, said John Gerard, was not only hard to digest, but it was also much less nourishing than barley or oats; certainly it could not be compared favorably with the preferred English wheat or with rice.[27] A well-established London barber-surgeon, Gerard kept his own garden and maintained that of Lord Burghley. Comfortably situated, Gerard was never to have reason to emigrate to those early outposts across the Atlantic; thus he never would be forced by circumstances to dine on pudding boiled from distasteful forage.

The herbalist's disdain for corn was shared by numerous contemporaries and found reflection in the attitude of the not-so-fortunate; it was a belief that contributed in some measure to the "starving times" suffered by the first settlers along the American coast. Had not sensible leaders, notably John Smith in Virginia and Myles Standish and William Bradford at Plymouth, coerced colonists into eating stolen Indian stores and later into cultivating their own plots of corn, there might have been no precedent-setting first Thanksgiving anywhere. For as long as supplies could be stretched, English wheat and barley, though maggot-ridden and moldy—the vile cates of which Tompson wrote—were preferred.

Confronted by the "grim and grizzled face of starvation," they quickly, if grudgingly, discovered corn's virtues. Within less than two years the settlers learned to harvest maize and thus kept themselves alive.

Simultaneous revisions were made in familiar English recipes. The favorite standing dish in England had been hasty pudding, made of wheat meal boiled with milk. Here, north and south, it now was given its proper Britannia-in-Virginia name, samp, or Indian pudding. Much later, as it became ever more fashionable to disregard native influences, culinary or otherwise, the old porridge at times again went under its old title, hasty pudding. But in those early years, as Roger Williams wrote when he contradicted Gerard as to corn's suitability, "Newsamp is a kind of meal pottage unparched. From this the English call their Samp, which is Indian corn beaten and boiled and eaten hot or cold with milk and butter, and is a diet exceedingly wholesome for English bodies."[28]

Similarly, by 1668 Josselyn described it as the New England standing dish, reporting that the colonists "make a kind of loblolly to eat with Milk, which they call Sampe; they beat [corn] in a Mortar and sift the Flower out of it; the remainder they call Homminey, which they put into a Pot of two or three Gallons, with Water, and boyl it upon a gentle Fire till it be like a Hasty Pudden; they put of this into Milk and so eat it."[29]

Sometimes the "flower" itself was boiled to make an especially festive white pot, for, said Josselyn, "it makes excellent Pudden."[30] "Loblolly" was another word for thick gruel or spoonmeat; it meant food that boiled and bubbled. Similarly, the Indian name adopted by the settlers for cornmeal puddings was "suppawn" to the English; their salted version the Dutch called "sourpaan."

When that forthright Hartford, Connecticut, woman, Amelia Simmons, published (apparently at her own expense) the first cookbook specifically designed to aid her contemporaries in this country, she crammed into its meager forty-seven pages basic guides to the sensible purchase of meat and produce as well as recipes for their preparation. One of these was, naturally enough, the ancient staple of the colonies, "A Nice Indian Pudding," for which she suggested three variations. That closest to the oldest and simplest seventeenth-century form directed the cook to "Salt a pint meal, wet with one quart milk, sweeten and put into a strong cloth, brass or bell metal vessel, stone or earthern pot, secure from wet, and boil 6 hours."[31]

When Williams had spoken of unparched (that is, undried or fresh) corn being beaten, he referred to the Indian method, adopted by the colonists, of parboiling corn for half a day, then pounding the "newsamp" in a wood or stone mortar until it dried as it was beaten to a coarsely ground meal. The meal then was sifted through large shallow sieves resembling basket-woven dishes, and the larger grains pounded again and resifted.

The first colonists traded for their corn mortars or copied them from the Indians; these were simply hollowed-out sections of tree trunks from which the bark had been stripped, and usually were close to thirty-six inches high. The pestle was fashioned out of a sturdy branch slightly thicker at the working end; the thick end sometimes was whittled and rounded. Improvements on this method included the crude sweep mill, utilizing a wider mortar and a long handle or sweep which was balanced in a notch at one side of the mortar. To one end of this a horizontal block pestle or a round stone was attached, usually by thongs. The handle end was tied to a green sapling or low tree branch. When the branch was pulled down and then eased up, the process provided more pounding power more easily. Within a few years windmills took over this work.

Corn was dried after harvest in garrets and lofts and wherever else the ears could be hung from beams or spread out on floors. The dry kernels were shelled by drawing the ear over any knifelike edge: the long handle of an iron frying pan, stretched across two stools with a basket beneath to catch the grain, or the edge of a fire shovel were popular shucking tools. As time and supplies permitted, many colonists set a sharpened blade into the center of a stool-bench, cutting openings in the wood on either side of the iron. As the ear of corn was drawn over the blade, the kernels dropped into a woven basket or wooden measure below.

Shelling the corn needed for cooking on the morrow was a colonial kitchen job often done by the housewife, and sometimes by the men and children of an evening. The shelled kernels were pounded in a small table mortar and sifted for use the next morning.

Not only did the Indian maize provide colonists with their most notable standing dish; there were also other corn "dainties," to use the seventeenth-century term, to be tried. One of the first of these discoveries was corn roasted, while still in its husk, in ashes on the hearth. The settlers learned also to enjoy corn steamed over hot stones in outdoor pits, a clambake method still favored by twentieth-century New Englanders. William Strachey in Virginia described how Indians and colonists "lap their corn in rowles within the leaves of the corne and so boyle it for a Dayntie."[32] Roger Williams wrote one of the first descriptions of a fresh whole-kernel Indian-corn porridge, a curious kind of stew which, he said, the Indians made by "seething" (boiling) corn in a small amount of water, and which they called *sukquttahhash*.[33]

Second only to its adaptability as a pudding meal was corn's usefulness as a breadstuff. Josselyn provided simple mid-seventeenth-century directions for baking cornbread when he wrote that "Bread also they make of Homminey boiled, and mix their Flower with it, cast it into a deep Bason in which they form the loaf, and then turn it out upon the Peel, and presently put it into the Oven before it spreads abroad."[34]

From the Indians the first settlers learned to bake an even simpler kind of bread, antedating Josselyn's recipe. Under various names, the same cornbread has come down to us with only slight changes from colonial methods of preparation and choice of ingredients. The first name, still heard, was "oppone"—shortened by the newcomers to "pone"—which in the Algonquian language meant baked. The colonists gave pone two English names, ash cake and spoon bread.

The earliest version of colonial corn pone or ash cake called for mixing meal with water, or with bear grease—the native favorite—or with the drippings caught in pans placed beneath a bird or other flesh as it roasted on a spit. Later, bacon grease or lard was substituted. The cakes of bread, each about the size of the hand that molded them, were baked on the hearth. Later, where there was a real hearthstone, rather than a simple hard-packed earth base, the stone was brushed clean and the batter placed directly thereon, then nudged forward and covered with hot hard wood ashes. Other cooks adopted the Indian practice of laying the batter on a large "vine," or grape leaf, covering the cake with a second leaf, and then heaping ashes over the whole. Cabbage leaves, when available, were common substitutes for grape leaves. After the steaming or sputtering abated and the bread was judged done, it was pulled from the fire, brushed, and sometimes literally washed clean before being eaten.

When the colonists placed cornmeal batter on a shingle-sized piece of smooth hardwood before putting it into the ashes to bake, they reached back to the ancient English lexicon for a descriptive name and called the result "spoon-bread." The word "spoon" was used here in its original meaning, chip, large splinter or shiver, a fragment of wood. The name continued in use, although the recipe itself changed drastically. (By the nineteenth century "spoon bread" referred to batter beaten with eggs and milk and baked in tin or earthenware pans in the oven; its only resemblance to the original spoon bread was the continued use of cornmeal.)

The twentieth century also has romanticized two late-eighteenth-century names for the basic ash cake, probably because their sound to modern ears seems to hold echoes of a frontier life. "Hoecake" and "johnnycake" were not the most common early colonial descriptions. According to legend, "hoecake" is a later name that evolved when settlers in early and/or extremely crude circumstances were wont to bake cornmeal batter on iron hoe-heads. Why they should have done so when, even if tin or earthen pans were lacking, leaves and wood chips were plentiful is not explained.[35] A simpler and more likely derivation was given years ago by an amused farmer near the Indiana-Illinois line. He said the cakes were so called because they had to be "hoed out," that is, pulled or drawn from under the ashes with some kind of long iron prong if the cook's fingers were not to be burned.[36]

Close to the end of the eighteenth century, when the average kitchen was better equipped, Indian meal scalded in boiling water, with salt added, was worked into a stiff batter and baked on tins in ovens or dropped into the dripping pan at the embers' edge.

Johnnycake is today's most popular name for what once was the simple ash cake. As arguments in the library may wax over who was Shakespeare, in the kitchen the debate is whether "johnnycake" first was "journeycake" or "Shawnee cake." Adherents of the first claim that the change was the result of careless frontier pronunciation, while those of the second persuasion point to the phonetic similarity of "Shawnee" and "johnny." (The Shawnee belonged to a wide-ranging tribe known from the Carolinas to New York who eventually moved westward as the frontier expanded.)

The arguments have a common basis: most early travelers remarked on the Indians' extraordinary ability to subsist on long journeys on a few spoonsful daily of parched and ground cornmeal. William Wood wrote that the Indians parched corn in hot ashes, sifted the ashes out, beat the meal to a powder, "and put it into a long leatherne bag trussed at [their] backe like a knapsacke, out of which [they take] three sponsful a day."[37] Similarly, Van der Donck wrote a few years later that in New York, "When they intend to go a great distance on a hunting excursion, or to war, where they expect to find no food . . . they provide themselves . . . with a small bag of parched corn meal, which is so nutritious that they can subsist on the same many days. A quarter of a pound of the meal is sufficient for a day's subsistence; for as it shrinks much in the drying, it also swells out again with moisture. When they are hungry they eat a small handful of the meal, after which they take a drink of water."[38]

Needless to say, the native instant-supper was adopted by journeying settlers in each colony. By 1729, when he wrote his *History of the Dividing Line*, William Byrd recommended combining the native meal with his own portable soup (a congealed veal broth) instead of plain water: "It was more heartening if you thicken every Mess with half a Spoonful of Rockahominy which is nothing but Indian Corn parched without burning and reduced to powder."[39] Just as Byrd liked the Indian meal better when reboiled with broth, other travelers eventually preferred to mix the meal with water and bake it briefly in the ashes of the campfire.[40]

When prepared in the Indian manner, the name of the dish was translated from the native tongue variously as *nukic, nookick, nokick,* and *no-cake.* All referred to the Indian, or Shawnee, journey-cake which eventually became the Englishman's "jonny-cake." It may have been so called because almost every traveling colonist, every John in the slang of the day, carried it while journeying. (John was the popular nickname for the common man, as many cab drivers are Mac today.)

Similarly, *-kin* was the common diminutive (as in lambkin and rumkin). Remembering Tompson's lament for the days when men dined on Jonakin and mush, it seems reasonable that Jonakin referred to the small handfuls of parched meal on which the first settlers had lived through the "starving times", and that Jonakin was poetic license for Johnny. From every John's no-cake to Johnny no-cake to johnnycake was an easy transition.

The first actual cookbook reference to johnnycake was Miss Simmons' in 1796. She gave three variations of the old johnnycake recipe: "Scald 1 pint of milk and put to 3 pints of indian meal, and half pint of flower—bake before the fire. Or scald with milk two thirds of the indian meal, or wet two thirds with boiling water, add salt, molasses and shortening, work up with cold water pretty stiff and bake as above."[41]

CHAPTER 3

The First Fruit

He advised me, if possible, to have a good orchard. He knew, he said, a clergyman of small income, who brought up a family very reputably, which he chiefly fed with apple dumplings.

SAMUEL JOHNSON[42]

THE APPLE, THAT OLD ENGLAND STAPLE of rural and village families, was the first fruit tree to be cultivated diligently in the new-England colonies. Diary-keeping travelers noted the profligacy with which the trees were grown and the grafting experiments attempted, and wrote, sometimes ruefully, of the manner in which the fruit was cooked.

Though travelers' accounts were often effusive, there was solid sense behind the repeated adjuration to grow as many apple trees as possible. The fruit could be stewed, boiled, baked, or fried, used in puddings and tarts, and sliced fresh into salads. Apples were dried in the sun, and strung for use over winter, or were preserved in crocks, as apple butters and sauces. Pressed and tunned as cider, apples gave the colonial family its dawn-to-supper beverage the year around, and provided the sparkling base for wines and brandies.

"The Country is replenished with fair and large orchards," the ebullient Josselyn told his readers in 1675. "It was affirmed by one Mr. Woolcut [a magistrate in Connecticut colony] that he made Five Hundred Hogsheads of Cyder out of his own Orchard in one year."[43] Earlier, in 1633, David Pietersze de Vries had described a southern New York "garden of [two acres] full of Provence roses, apple, pear and cherry trees,"[44] and in 1686 William Fitzhugh, writing to a friend to tell of his farm in Virginia, included proud mention of a "large orchard of apple trees, well-fenced with a locust fence."[45]

Each new generation of settlers followed the apple-planting tradition.

[122]

Sixty-two years later the Swedish traveler Peter Kalm reported that he "was frequently surprised by the prudence of the inhabitants of this country. . . . As soon as one has bought a piece of ground which is neither built upon or sown, his first care is to get young apple trees and make a garden. He next proceeds to build his house and lastly prepares the land for grain." The sensible settler, Kalm discovered, divided his orchard into three kinds of apples, one "of which he sells, from another makes cider," and uses the third for "pies, tarts and the like." If one takes Kalm's sometimes sweeping statements literally, this easily was possible, for "every countryman has apple trees planted round his farmhouse."[46]

That the English farmer-colonist historically had been accustomed to planting different types of apples for varying diet needs was made evident by Philip Miller in his *Gardener's Dictionary*, one of the texts often brought here by settlers. He listed sixteen types for "kitchen use"; codling, summer marigold, summer red pearmain, Holland pippin, Kentish pippin, hanging body, Loan's pearmain, pomme violette, Spencer's pippin, Ston's pippin, oakenpin, monstrous reinette, French reinette, French pippin, royal russet, and winter pearmain; and suggested nineteen suitable for dessert: white juniting, Margaret, summer pearmain, summer greening, embroidered apple, golden reinette, summer white Colville, summer red Colville, silver pippin, aromatick pippin, grey reinette, la haute-boute, royal russeting, Wheeler's russet, Sharp's russet, spice apple, golden pippin, nonpareil, and l'api. Miller thought these six types especially good for cider: Devonshire, royal Welch, redstreaked, whitsour, Herefordshire underleaf, and John apple.

Good juicy apples in any dessert form were a treat to the American colonist in each generation. The effervescent Judge Samuel Sewall, for example, recording a "very comfortable passage thither and home again" on October 1, 1697, said he had enjoyed a breakfast of "Butter, Honey, Curds and Cream," then for dinner was served "very good Rost Lamb, Turkey, Fowls, Applepy." Fine fruit again was remarked on by the judge when on April 3, 1711, "Mr. Attorney treats us at his house with excellent Pippins." And even during the exigencies of his courtship of the hesitant Mrs. Denison, apple-supplied delights prompted Sewall to add this detail, on November 28, 1718: "She asked me if I would drink, I told her Yes. She gave me Cider, Apples, and a Glass of Wine."[47]

Apple moise, or mousse, was a long-standing English custardlike dessert, made by forcing the pulp of boiled apples through a fine sieve, adding almond milk if it could be afforded, or thick cream if it could not, and beaten egg whites, then reboiling or baking the mixture. Apple flam pie was a thick tart of spiced and sweetened apples, served with a dash of rum or sherry splashed over it.

Englishmen had for generations been true sons of Adam in their unflagging admiration of the apple; today's phrase "as American as apple pie" might more accurately have been rendered three hundred years ago "as English as an apple tart." The English colonists' continuing dedication to the traditional apple dumpling stirred Kalm to send the recipe back to Sweden, saying, "One apple dish which the English prepare is to take an apple and pare it, make a dough of water, flour and butter. Roll it thin and enclose an apple in it. This is then bound in a clean linen cloth, put in a pot and boiled. When done, it is taken out, placed on the table and served. While it is warm the crust is cut on one side. Thereupon they mix butter and sugar, which is added to the apples; then the dish is ready. They call this apple dumpling, some times apple pudding. It tastes quite good; you get as many dumplings as you have apples."[48]

Obviously, Kalm was more fortunate in his choice of a kitchen in which to be introduced to colonial apple dumplings than were some other non-English samplers of the New World menu. "Apple pie," said Dr. Acrelius, "is used through the whole year and when fresh apples are no longer to be had, dried ones are used. It is the evening meal of children. House-pie, in country places, is made of apples neither peeled nor freed from their cores, and its crust is not broken if a wagon-wheel goes over it."[49]

Every generation or so the colonists were reminded of the economic wisdom of planting apple trees, a statement reiterated at the close of the eighteenth century by that no-nonsense cook, Amelia Simmons. Not only did she address a firm lecture to the housewife concerning the great good to come of even one tree, but saw in its planting the solution to public financing and early American juvenile delinquency. "Apples," she declared, "are highly useful in families. . . . There is not a single family but might set a tree in some otherwise useless spot, which might serve the two fold use of shade and fruit; on which 12 or 14 kinds of fruit trees might easily be engrafted, and essentially preserve the orchard from the intrusions of boys, &c, which is too common in America."

One suspects the militant Miss Simmons' own engrafted garden must have been plundered regularly by neighborhood youngsters, for she continues, "If the boy who thus planted a tree, and guarded and protected it in a useless corner, and carefully engrafted different fruits, was to be indulged free access into orchards, whilst the neglectful boy was prohibited— how many millions of fruit trees would spring into growth. . . . The net saving would in time extinguish the public debt, and enrich our cookery."

Ingredients and seasoning methods for what she named "Buttered Apple Pie" differed little (except by being baked) from the dumpling recorded a half-century earlier by Kalm: "Pare, quarter and core tart apples, lay in Paste, cover with the same; bake half an hour, when drawn, gently raise the top crust, add sugar, butter, cinnamon, mace, wine or rose water q:f:." Her "Apple Pudding Dumplin" was even simpler than its forerunner: "Put into paste, quartered apples, lye in a cloth and boil two hours, serve with sweet sauce."[50] She was the cookbook author, but one cannot escape the belief that Kalm's readers followed his recipe more easily.

CHAPTER 4

The Virginia Potato

The Potatoes of Canada are by reason of their great increasing growne to be so common here with us at London that even the most vulgar begin to despise them, whereas when they were first received among us they were dainties for a Queene. Being put into water they are soon boiled tender, after which they be peeled, sliced, and stewed with butter and a little wine, being as pleasant as the bottome of an artichoke, but the too frequent use, especially being so plentiful and cheap, hath rather bred a loathing than a liking for them.

JOHN PARKINSON[51]

Now so common a staple in the American diet, the potato first was reported in the sixteenth century as a curiosity and was approached with some caution. Generally it was not until the eighteenth century that the potato was found on the tables of those who could afford anything else; or at least, before that time they seldom wrote about it. That qualification is necessary, for the first colonists soon learned of various potato dishes prepared by the Indians and easily could have observed that the natives were not poisoned by consuming the strange root.

In spite of some early and fearsome legends (for example, potatoes caused leprosy and, if not, acted as a slow poison) early plant descriptions were surprisingly factual; precise notes on how to cook the tubers were too detailed to support the belief that seventeenth-century colonists never indulged in potatoes. Closer to truth must be the assumption that the first settlers simply did not like potatoes; the European palate preferred the

[126]

heartier taste of turnips, parsnips, and cabbages to which it was accustomed.

When necessity dictated, however, the average colonial family learned to roast potatoes at the hearth, to boil them with milk or water for a pudding (a sort of mashed potato), to fry them as a kind of pancake, and to use boiled potatoes with which to bake bread.

Solanum tuberosum, Papus americanum, or the Virginia potato, was first accurately described by Gerard. Potatoes, he said, were not only "a food, but a meat for pleasure . . . being either roasted in the embers, or boiled and eaten with oile, vinegar and pepper, or dressed in some other way by the hande of a skillful Cooke."[52] He was a more adventurous diner than many of his less literate contemporaries.

Joseph Pitton de Tournefort agreed with Gerard, recording that the potato "was first brought from Virginia into England, and from thence carried to France, and other countreys. In Virginia the roots are called Openneck. The Indians use the roots for bread, which they call Chunno. There is another sort of Meat prepared from the same roots dried by the Sun's Heat and cut into small Pieces, which is called by the same Name and kept for a long time. Besides they eate the Root both green [raw] boiled and roasted. Our Countrymen, says Casper Bauhin, roast it under the ashes, and having peeled off the Skin, eat it with pepper."[53]

The average colonist's preference for greater flavor than the white potato afforded is evident in the numerous diary notes concerning the tastiness of sweet potatoes. Near Albany, Kalm found "potatoes are planted by almost everyone. The Bermuda [sweet] potatoes have likewise been planted here and succeed pretty well. Common people and gentry without distinction planted them in their gardens. They are prepared in the same manner as common potatoes and are either mixed and served with them or separately. They are bigger than the common sort and have a sweet and agreeable taste which I cannot find in the other potatoes, in artichokes, or in any other root and they almost melt in the mouth. It is not long since they were first planted here."[54]

The yam was considered a treat, for it did not grow easily save in the most southern colonies. According to Kalm, "Yams are cultivated in the hottest parts of America for eating as we do potatoes. It has not yet been attempted to plant them here [Pennsylvania] and they are brought from the West Indies on ships . . . therefore they are reckoned a rarity and as such I ate them at Dr. Franklin's today." He found yams "white and tast[ing] like common potatoes" but thought them not quite so palatable.[55]

By the middle of the eighteenth century the New London, Connecticut, justice Joshua Hempsted also noted regular harvestings of large fields of "common" potatoes. His diary entry for November 30, 1752, clearly shows that youngsters by then had none of their early seventeenth-century ancestors' reputed fear of eating potatoes. Nor did the Hempsted heirs consider their grandfather with quite the same awe the justice inspired in others: "Last night In ye Eve I went to Capt. Coits to visit his mother old Ms. Coit and I lost my old Silver Spoon markt I.A.H. it Lay with one more not markt on the Cupboard. while I was absent Natts boys Grover & Will & Josh Starr kindled a fire up & Roasted Potatoes & played a while in my Room. I suppose they all combined to hide the Spoon or Else worse."[56]

Thus, whatever might have been the fashionable disdain for potatoes in the early colonial years, by the last half of the eighteenth century potatoes obviously were a staple for the average family. This again is made amply clear for us by the forthright assertion of Miss Simmons: "Potatoes take rank for universal use, profit and easy acquirement." Further, she recommended "the smooth skin [type] known by the name of How's Potatoe" as the "most mealy and richest flavor'd," while the "yellow rusticoat [was] next best; the red, and red rusticoat . . . tolerable; and the yellow Spanish [had] their value."

As to how they added to the colonial menu, Miss Simmons declared, "A roast Potatoe is brought on with Roast Beef, a Steake, a Chop, or Fricasee; [they are] good boiled with a boiled dish; make excellent stuffing for a turkey, water or wild fowl; make a good pie and a good starch for many uses." Potatoes were to be kept from frost and dampness during the winter, she warned, and in the spring removed from "the cellar to a dry loft," where the roots should be "spread thin and frequently stirred and dryed."[57]

Early colonial families had learned from the Indians to identify and to cook other wild vegetables, each of which has been described as tasting like the white potato. One of these, hopniss, usually was boiled and was eaten instead of bread by the Indians; it was similarly enjoyed by the settlers. As a matter of fact, according to Kalm, "some English still eat them instead of the [cultivated] potatoes," preparing the peas "which lie in the pods of this plant, like common peas."[58] In much the same fashion, the root of katniss was boiled or, for variety, roasted in hot ashes, while another root, the taw-ho or taw-hum or tuckah, found in marshy areas, sometimes was roasted in pits.

PART VII

The Seventeenth–Century Garden

CHAPTER 1

Fine Flowers and Common Herbs

Now what with fine woods and green trees by land and
these yellow flowers painting the sea, all are
desirous to see our new paradise of New England.
FRANCIS HIGGINSON[1]

The Seedsman too, doth lavish out his grain,
In hope the more he casts, the more to gain;
The Gardner now superfluous branches lops,
And poles erects for his young clamb'ring hops,
Now digs them, sowes his herbs, his flowers and roots,
And carefully manures his trees of fruits.[2]

SO ANNE BRADSTREET WROTE of spring in 1650 in New England. Some would be tempted to burn her book, *The Tenth Muse*, in retribution for her "unwomanliness" in writing and unfeminine arrogance in allowing her thoughts to be published. However, all would have understood her love of natural beauty, the undercurrent of pride, the sense of special achievement that a garden represented in seventeenth-century America.

She did even more for readers today; in her exaltation of a colonial garden in springtime, Mrs. Bradstreet left us a list of its contents "as the pear, the plum, and apple tree now flourish." She counted other ancient delights, "the primrose pale, the azure violet, the double pinks, the matchless roses," and imagined for us "meads with cowslips and honeysuckles dight . . . the early cherry, the hasty peas and wholesome cool strawberry."[3]

Whatever their criticisms of her book, farmers and other gardeners in each of the colonies would have recognized the trees and plants of which she wrote, for the same kinds of seeds were sown and similar young seedlings were transplanted north and south throughout early America.

Just as the settlers' basic accents and colloquial speech patterns would

[131]

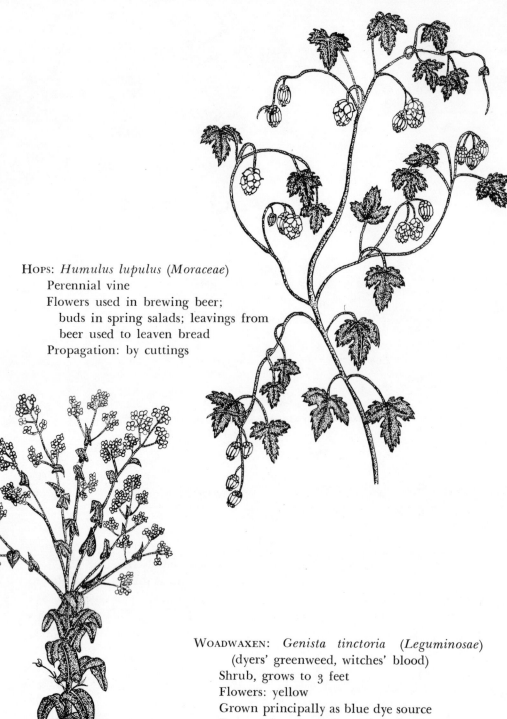

Hops: *Humulus lupulus* (*Moraceae*)
    Perennial vine
    Flowers used in brewing beer;
        buds in spring salads; leavings from
        beer used to leaven bread
    Propagation: by cuttings

Woadwaxen: *Genista tinctoria* (*Leguminosae*)
        (dyers' greenweed, witches' blood)
    Shrub, grows to 3 feet
    Flowers: yellow
    Grown principally as blue dye source
    Propagation: by seed, cuttings, layers

[132]

MADDER: *Rubia tinctorum*
　　Perennial, grows to 4 feet
　　Flowers: yellow, with berries turning
　　　from red to black
　　Roots used by dyers and
　　　calico-printers; also as a remedy
　　　for jaundice
　　Propagation: by seed or cutting

BORAGE: *Borago officinalis* (*Boriginaceae*)
　　Annual, grows to 2 feet
　　Flowers: blue, purple, or white saucers
　　Leaves used as pot herb; grown to attract bees
　　Propagation: by seed, division, cuttings

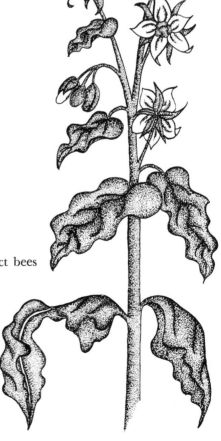

[133]

CHAMOMILE: *Anthemis nobilis*
   Perennial, grows to 12 inches
   Flowers: white rays
   Leaves used for teas, possets, syrups
   Propagation: by seed or division

MULLEIN: *Verbascum thapsus*
   Usually biennial, grows to 6 feet
   Flowers: white or yellow
   Propagation: by seed, division, cuttings

[134]

not differ too sharply until close to the Revolutionary War period, neither would their taste in food change radically from colony to colony along the Atlantic seaboard. Now-familiar regional variations in plants cultivated for food, and in cooking methods, took generations to evolve; they were achieved only after time and experience showed which of the seeds and plants imported from home would thrive best in each settlement. The first subtle differences between gardens of the north and the south would be revealed in the settlers' use of local herbs and roots discovered in nearby woodlands and marshes, and the extent to which these "spontaneous" fruits of the wilderness were recognized, accepted, and adapted.

The dishes the colonists longed to prepare were those they had known in England. The recipes and cooking methods learned at home were taught to the children born here. Without the spur of near-hunger, the wild plenty surrounding them seldom was added experimentally to the settlers' iron stew-kettles or used to season the contents of seventeenth-century brass pots. For the early colonial cook, necessity more frequently than imagination sparked menu innovation.

Even when Indian maize, or as it sometimes was called, Turkey wheat, had to be substituted for the familiar white English wheat meal, the result was still an English boiled pudding. Pumpkins and squash were stewed and baked as apples had been across the Atlantic, and to many early colonial palates the New World fruit never could compare favorably. It is not surprising, therefore, to find that by 1615 the first apple and pear trees had been planted at Jamestown, the English scions grafted to the native American "Crabbes, lesse [smaller] but not so sower as ours."[4]

A sigh of pleasurable relief no doubt accompanied the scratching of his quill pen when Edward Johnson, in 1634, set down his report that by then all in New England could enjoy apple, pear, and quince tarts instead of pumpkin pies.[5] (Not *all*, of course, or the cultivated pumpkin would not have survived. As with many such early "true relations and discourses," the facts reported and the plenty described applied to those who could afford correspondence with agents in London, who could pay the shipping charges, and who had gardening help provided by family, servants, or slaves.)

From Massachusetts Bay to the settlements that made up the colony of Virginia, a common culinary heritage produced striking similarities in the gardens and orchards planted by the English settlers. Among the "good news" sent back by Alexander Whitaker from Virginia was the report: "Our English seeds thrive very well heere, as Peas, Onions, Turnips, Cabbage, Coleflowers, Carrets, Time, Parsely, Hysop, Marjorum and many others I have tasted and eaten." He just as easily might have been describing the produce of Massachusetts, Connecticut, or any other northeastern settlement as that of Virginia.[6]

In 1628 Massachusetts colonists asked their London agents to send them fresh supplies of "wheat, rye, barley, oates, benes, pease, Peach stones, Plum stones, Filbert stones, Cherry stones, Pear Kernells, pomegranats, Woad seed, Saffron heads, liquorice seed, and roots, Madder seed and madder roots, potatoes, Hoprootes, Hempseed, Flaxse and Currant plants." Apparently they did not receive enough to satisfy their needs, or perhaps the seeds and plants sent were not able to withstand the voyage, for in 1629 the colony again wrote for "vyne plants and stones of all fruit, also wheat, rye, potatoes, barley oats, woad, saffron, lequorice seeds, hop roots and currant plants."

In 1634 William Wood described "New England's prospect" as one where "the ground affords very good kitchin Gardens, for Turneps, parsnips, Carrots, Radishes and Pumpions, Muskmillions, Isquoutersquashes, Cowcumbers, Onyons, and whatever grows well in England . . . many things being better and larger; there is likewise growing all manner of Hearbes for meate, and berries, Treackleberries, Hurtleberries, Currants . . . not only in planted Gardens but in the Woods, without either the art of help of man [such] as sweet Marjoram, Purselane, Sorrel, Peneriall [pennyroyal], Yarrow, Mirtle, Saxifarilla, Bayes, et c. There is Strawberries in abundance, very large ones, some being two inches about; you may gather half a bushell in a forenoone. In other seasons there bee Gooseberries, Bilberries, little inferiour to those that our Grocers sell in England."[7]

In that same year the new colony of Maryland was promoted as a sunlit land of plenty: "We have English peasen, and French beanes, oranges, lemons, melocotunes, Apples, Peares, Potatoes, Sugar Canes, flaxe and hempe and corne." Growing wild were "a store of large strawberries, raspices, Vines, sassafras, Wall-nuts, Acorns and the like."[8]

The following year, a pamphlet titled *A Relation of Maryland* advised emigrants bound for the middle colonies to take "seede wheate, rie, barley, oats, kernells of Peares and Apples, especially Pepins, Pearemaines, [and] Dusons for the making thereafter of Cider and Perry [as well as] the stones and seeds of whatever other fruits, roots and herbs [they] desireth to have." This promise of richly producing gardens was proffered by the pamphleteer: "English pease grow very well [in Maryland], also musk mellions, cowcumbers, with all sorts of garden roots and Herbes as carrots, parseneps, turnips, cabbages, Radish, with many more; and in Virginia they have sowed English Wheate and Barley. They have Peares, Apples and several sorts of Plummes . . . mellons and pumpions, apricockes, figges and pomegranates."

Virginia and New England planters must have shared concern over the successful cultivation of English currants. When Thomas Glover wrote in his *Account of Virginia,* "Here grow good Figges and Gooseberries, but no English currants," he echoed the Massachusetts colony's year-in and year-out plea for more currant plants.[9]

"What should I speak of cucumber, muskemelons, pompions, potatoes, parsneps, carrets, turnips which our gardens yield with little art and labour?" rather grandly inquired Captain John Smith in his *True Declaration of the Estate of the Colonie in Virginia*.[10] He had, after all, an understandably proud and possessive feeling for the colony's prospects. Today's reader only can hope the amount of hard and painful work necessary was forgiven Smith by those who joined the vaunted venture in Virginia because they had read, "The ground bringeth forth without industrie Peases, Roses, Hempe, besides other plants, fruits, herbs."

Smith assured potential colonists they would find "apples running on the ground in bigness and shape of a small lemmon, in colour and taste like to a preserved Apricock." (He may have meant a kind of squash, although he knew the Indian word. Similarly, Roger Williams had called the New England squash a vine-apple before he learned the local term.) Smith added there were "grapes and walnuts innumberable, the vines as common as [English] brambles, the walnut trees [as plentiful] as the elmes in England."[11]

Apparently describing the Carolinas, a traveler who signed himself "E. W., Gentleman" wrote of "Virginia, the south part thereof," where cultivated and wild plants included "late Cabbage, White Cole, Green Cole, Cucumber, Spinnage, Cabbage, Lettuce, Melons, Onions, Leekes, Apples of Love, Marvellous Apples, Artichokes, Radish, as well as Spike, garlike, Borage, Bugloss, Cherufe [chervil], coriander, Gourds, watercresses, Marjoram, Palme Christi [olive-oil bean], Flower gentle, White Poppy, Purslane, Rocket, Rosemary, Double Marigold, Thyme, Anise, Violets, Blittes, Skirworts, White Succory, Fennell, parsley, Holy Thistle, Hartsthorne, Sampier, Dyersgraine, Larksheele, and Burnet."[12] His list tallies interestingly with the plants and herbs Josselyn and others described as prospering in the New England colonies.

Nor was there much difference between the gardens planted by the Swedes and Hollanders in the middle colonies and those cultivated by their earlier-arriving English neighbors. Thus Dr. Israel Acrelius later said in his *History of New Sweden* that generally early Delaware colonists "cultivated beets, parsnips, onions, parsley, radish, Turkish beans, large beans, pepper grass, red pepper, lettuce, head lettuce, German lettuce and scurvy grass. Anything else is regarded a rarity."[13] His catalog of these less ambitious gardens suggests that his might have been a truly factual report. Although there is little doubt each of the leaf and root herbs mentioned in descriptions actually were grown, it is doubtful if each household each spring could have set out all of the annuals available.

"Common herbs for domestic remedies are wormwood, rue, sage, thyme, chamomile, etc.," Acrelius said. He provided a glimpse of the early homesteads and gardens along the Delaware River when he wrote that cherries, peaches, and apples were favored. "Pears are rare. Cherry trees are generally planted . . . around the houses and roads, away from the gardens. Peach trees [are grown] in an enclosure by themselves."[14]

A different landscape had been planned for early Plymouth. As a visitor from New Amsterdam noted, the first Massachusetts houses which could be called such had been "constructed of hewn planks . . . gardens [are] enclosed behind them and at the side with hewn planks, so the houses and courtyards are in very good order."[15] Stone garden walls seem more often to have been an eighteenth-century development, and one that belonged more to farm meadows in the country than as surrounds for village homes. Plank fences not only were more quickly set in place, but they could be built higher and were better able to do the job for which such fencing was intended: to keep domestic animals, small children, and garden plants a little more safe from foraging wolves, bears and foxes, raccoons and opossums.

The Plymouth houses lined First Street (later called Leyden Street), a broad roadway that was about eight hundred yards long. There was a crossing street at the middle, and the road ran southward to the rivulet and northward toward the uncultivated land. The size of these first house lots had been decided by Plymouth leaders on the logical basis that since "greater families needed larger plots [we allotted] to every person half a pole in breadth and three in width. We thought this proportion large enough for houses and gardens to impale them around."[16] (A pole was a square rod or perch and comprised $30\frac{1}{4}$ square yards in an area.)

One of the houses and gardens among the seven completed in 1620–21 had been that of Elder William Brewster. His house and plank-fenced lot were established across the new street from William Bradford's. Within the green paling, Brewster planted his garden and is said to have divided the plot with parsley, sweet chervil, sorrel, and other pot herbs set on one side of the path, and sage, thyme, spearmint, mullein, fennel, and bitter medicinal herbs along the other.

Bradford served thirty years, often unpaid, as governor of the Massachusetts Bay Colony, and was to be recognized eventually as its preeminent historian. He was also its most fervent publicist. With Edward Winslow he is believed to have been co-author of one of the first New England promotional tracts, "Mourt's" *Relation*, and under his own name contributed letters and accounts aimed at persuading other Englishmen to exchange the Old World poverty of worn-out soil and plague-polluted cities for the fresh green lands of America. One of these efforts catalogued the harvest of

Herbs from the kitchen garden hang from the original drying rack, suspended from old chestnut beams, above the stove hearth of the restored 1678 Joshua Hempsted homestead, New London, Connecticut. Other furnishings of the kitchen are of the same late seventeenth-century era, including the iron cooking pot of the type in which beans were baked, set in the algate hole, the colonial version of the modern "warming oven." (*Ektachrome by Louis H. Frohman*)

Early firearm is set safely away from the hearth on carved wooden hooks pegged into ceiling beam. Rachet candleholder kept light high when the gateleg table was used for dining, brought it close for reading or handwork at other times. English brass lantern clock and mid-drip candlesticks are typical of styles in use at the turn of the eighteenth century in comfortably well-off homes. Embroidered flame-stitch cushion covers rush seat of Carver-type armchair. According to family tradition, tall post bed was built for this corner almost three hundred years ago. Curtains are of early eighteenth-century homespun woolen lined with homespun linen; coverlet is quilted linsey-woolsey. Hempstead House, New London, Connecticut. (*Ektachrome by Louis H. Frohman*)

In this restoration of a mid-eighteenth century New Hampshire kitchen, the side oven is set just under the lintel, recessed enough to provide a warming shelf with heat provided both from the oven and the main hearth fire. Straight-back New England settle, designed to protect users from drafts, is placed against the feather-edged sheathing of the red-painted wall. X-base country stand beside settle was handy for candleholder, wine service, writing, or other work. Mantel shelf continued in use in kitchens in all colonies during the eighteenth century but seldom was added to chimneys in other rooms until after 1800. New Hampshire Historical Society Museum, Concord. (*Photo by Bill Finney*)

Upstairs kitchen and dining area at Philipsburg Manor, Upper Mills, North Tarrytown, New York, has been restored to its 1720 period with furniture and accessories of the turn of the century. Included is a rare chandelier or candlebranch, dated 1672. Most of the furniture used in the room was made in the Hudson River Valley. Sleepy Hollow Restoration. (*Ektachrome by Louis H. Frohman*)

Ladder-like stairs lead to loft above in the kitchen building of the Ferry House, Van Courtlandt Manor, Croton-on-Hudson, New York. Built-in high bed with storage space below was typical of Dutch homes in New York and other middle colonies, as was the half-door, which here leads to the pantry or storeroom. Van Courtlandt Manor, Sleepy Hollow Restoration. (*Ektachrome by Louis H. Frohman*)

The palace at New Bern, North Carolina, the first permanent capitol of that colony, was built by Royal Governor William Tryon between 1767 and 1770. Meticulously restored by Mrs. James Edwin Latham and the state of North Carolina in 1952–59, the Tryon Palace kitchen shows the use of old and new styles during the mid-eighteenth century. The huge fireplace has both lug-pole with trammels and a crane. The ancient algate hole is still in use in the left inside wall of the chimney, but the beehive oven is built into the exterior wall. At the left are three copper-lined deep wells for stews and soups, heated by fires kindled below. Brass jack and weights turn the spit before the main hearth fire. The standing iron crane at right of chimney here is used as a storage rack to keep small pots, gridirons, and tools out of the cook's way but at hand if needed. (*Ektachrome by Louis H. Frohman*)

In 1772, when Odessa, Delaware, was called Cantwell's Bridge, the town was a thriving grain port with commercial, social, and—through the Quakers—religious ties with Philadelphia. After serving his apprenticeship in Philadelphia, William Corbit set up his own tannery and also began to build a home at Cantwell's Bridge in 1772, completing the imposing brick residence in 1774. The house was restored by H. Rodney Sharp, who in 1958 endowed and presented it to the Henry Francis du Pont Wintherthur Museum to be maintained as an historic house museum. The kitchen, in an attached wing, is furnished with late-eighteenth-century pieces, the only reminder of furniture of an earlier period being the adjustable candlestand to the left of the chimney below the cylindrical candlebox. (*Ektachrome by Louis H. Frohman*)

At the close of the colonial period in 1784, those who planned the Salem Tavern work kitchen at Winston-Salem, North Carolina, made no basic changes in design from those which colonists had used more than a century before. The double hearth simply allowed room for more work to be accomplished. The fireplace at right is fitted with a clock jack and weights and with cranes set in both the left and right side walls. (*Ektachrome by Louis H. Frohman*)

Massachusetts planting. Written in couplets, it was entitled *A Descriptive and Historical Account of New England in Verse.*

Bradford knew how painfully the wilderness had been forced back; he understood the promise "the New Indies" held as well as the hard reality of the time. The word-picture he sent home may be considered more accurate than many others, for if Bradford rhapsodized, he kept nevertheless within the bounds of truthful reporting.

Hence the governor's list of what actually throve on the farms and in the gardens of early colonial Massachusetts families should be analyzed more seriously than the prettier vistas offered by part-time travelers, no matter how much more enchanting and palatable the latters' accounts may be to many today. Equally inescapable is the conclusion that Bradford made his appeal to the majority from whom the colonial population sprang, men and women who dreamed in common with Plymouth's "old settlers" of the simple life his poem described. That Bradford's account of the New World could represent a dream of plenty to so many sharpens our focus on the facts of colonial life.

Bradford wrote of the New England autumn when "all sorts of grain which our own land doth yield, hither brought and sown in every field," could be harvested to fill loft and kitchen meal-chests with "wheat and rye, barley, oats, beans and pease," for "here all thrive" and the people profit from them.[17]

The source of the average Englishman's accustomed daily diet was grown in the early days of the Bay Colony: "All sorts of roots and herbs in gardens grow, Parsnips, carrots, turnips, or what you'll sow: Skirets, beets, coleworts, fair cabbages, onions, melons, cucumbers, radishes," Bradford wrote. "Many fine flowers" blossomed, waiting to be transplanted to settlers' gardens "and 'mongst those [are] the fair white lily and sweet fragrant rose." Most colonists still were content to pick berries from bushes growing in the woods or along the cartways, for the governor speaks of finding "many good wholesome berries here, fit for man's use, almost of every kind."

Between the lines is the message that cultivated orchards had cost the first settlers long hours of hard work, for "Pears, apples, cherries, plumbs, quinces, and peach, Are *now* no dainties; you may have of each." Other wild bounty besides berries still had not been brought into every paled garden, however, for "Nuts and grapes of several sorts are here, If you will take them pains to seek for."[18]

As settlements grew, the families of greater than average wealth and of more educated palates added a cornucopia of other herbs and plants for their enjoyment and delight. Berry bushes and fruit trees eventually were set out successfully; often young trees sent from England were grafted on wild American stock.

Many of the fruits and berries yearned for in the 1620s flourished in the next two generations, so that John Davenport in 1659 could write to Governor John Winthrop, "The candied comfrey roots which my wife sendeth to you are not as white as she desired. The reason she sayeth is that they were boiled with Barbadoes sugar. My wife prayeth yourself and Mrs. Winthrop to accept a small token of marmalet and quinces, which she has made as good as she could."[19]

In 1671 John Josselyn wrote happily that "Our fruit trees prosper abundantly: apple trees, pear trees, quince trees, plum, and barberry trees. The country is replenished with large and fair orchards." As in Mrs. Davenport's, in other kitchens too, "the Quinces, cherries, Damsons set the dames a-work, marmalade and preserved damson is to be met with in every house."[20]

There seems to have remained, however, the old challenge of persuading English currants to grow in the average colonial garden, for that same year Josselyn reported: "Billberries are a most excellent Summer Dish. . . . The Indians dry them in the Sun and sell them to the English by the Bushell. [The colonists] make use of them instead of Currence, putting of them into Puddings both boyled and baked, and into water gruel."[21]

A common problem in an age when a fast Atlantic crossing still took seven weeks was to ensure proper shipboard nursery care for young plants. It was one thing to be able to order and pay for expensive seedlings; it was quite another to hope they would live to be planted and to thrive. So it was that in 1633 John Winthrop heard from a London friend to whom his order for apple trees had been entrusted. His quodling plants, Joseph Downing wrote, had been put up in an oyster firkin and it was to be hoped the ship's master would care for them en route; they needed to be set out on deck two or three days each week where they might "take fresh air."

A century later the problem persisted. When Governor Jonathan Belcher asked a Boston shipper to "bring me eight or 10 young almond trees and as many Pisa nectrins," or "anything else curious for a garden," he added explicit directions to ensure safe arrival. "The trees," he instructed, "must be grafts, not natural stocks, and very young, not thicker than your thumb. They must be carefully taken up, roots and all, and as carefully transplanted into a good box of their natural earth, and not suffered to be sprinkled with salt water, but duly served with fresh water and I do say the younger they are the more likely to live."[22]

CHAPTER 2

New England's Rarities

The country naturally affordeth very good pot herbs and sallet herbes and those of a more masculine vertue than any of the same species in England, as pot marjoram, time, alexander, angellica, purslane, violets and anniseeds in very great abundance . . . [which] I gathered in summer, dried and crumbled in to a bagg to preserve for winter store. The air is perfumed with divers other good herbes that grow without the industry of man . . . as sassafras, damaske roses, violets, balme, laurell, hunnisuckles and the like.
THOMAS MORTON[23]

THE AVID CURIOSITY with which scientists now examine moonrock bounty from outer space had its parallel in the seventeenth and eighteenth centuries. Colonial leaders regularly sent back word of America's natural phenomena, and Englishmen and other Europeans came here for the express purpose of searching out, examining, and describing America's plants and herbs. Both colonists and visitors shipped back samples of New World rarities, to be grown as novelties in the gardens of great estates, tried as new medicines against the ills and plagues of the age, or experimented with as the source of new food crops.

So it was that John Josselyn, who could sign himself Gentleman, "commenced a voyage into those remote parts of the World . . . and tendered the fruits of my Travel after this homely manner." He referred to his small book, *New England's Rarities Discovered,* in which he included also a poem "not improperly conferr'd upon" an Indian squaw "in all her

[141]

bravery" and his own chronological table of New England's history (beginning with Columbus' voyage in 1492).

His eight-year second sojourn through the woods and marshes along the northeastern sea and river banks began "in the year of our Lord 1663, May 28, [when] upon an Invitation from my only Brother I departed from London and arrived at Boston, the chief Town in the Massachusets, a Colony of Englishmen in New-England, the 28th of July following."[24]

Josselyn rested at Boston until "opportunely lighting upon a passage in a Bark bound to the Eastward, I put to Sea again, and on the Fifteenth of August I arrived at Black Point, otherwise called Scarborow, the habitation of my beloved Brother." From this headquarters he made it his "business to discover all along the Natural, Physical and Chyrurgical Rarities of this New found World."[25]

From Scarborow, Josselyn traveled through a countryside he described as rocky, mountainous, and "extremely overgrown with wood." Now and again he sighted "wide, rich valleys wherein are lakes." He went northwest as far as a ridge "known by the name of the White Mountains, upon which lieth snow all the year," but apparently did not venture northward beyond Sugarloaf, for he reported that country "is daunting terrible."

Josselyn divided his description of the plants he found, and which he compared when he could with those "known to the herbalists,"[26] into "such as are common with us; such plants as are proper [i.e., native] to the Country; such plants as are proper to the Country and have no name known to us; plants as have sprung up since the English planted and kept Cattle;[27] and of such Garden Herbs (amongst us) as do thrive there and of such as do not." All those plants—Josselyn included "herbs, flowers, trees, and bushes"—listed in the first four categories grew wild throughout New England "in great plenty," ready to be gathered or, if one wished, transferred to the home garden. The fifth grouping included "the English Herbs we have growing in our Gardens that prosper there as well as in their proper Soil."

Josselyn's first list, of ninety-one plants growing wild throughout New England, described herbs similar to those "common with us in England." As transcribed here from a copy of his book printed in London at the Sign of the Green Dragon in St. Paul's Churchyard in 1672, the order of listing, the spelling, and descriptions are Josselyn's, with the exception of the botanical names added in italics.[28]

Hedghog grass: *Carex flava*
Mattweed: *Calamagrostis areneria*
Cats-tail: *Typha latifolia*
Stitchwort: commonly taken here by ignorant people for Eyebright, it blows in June. *Stellaria graminea*

SORREL: *Rumex acetosa* (*Polygonaceae*) (dock, sour dock)
  Perennial, grows to 3 feet
  Flowers: large, deep brown
  Leaves used as pot or salad herb; in soups,
    sauces; as a cure for scurvy
  Propagation: by seed or cuttings

PENNYROYAL: *Mentha pulegium*
      (*Labiatae*) (pudding-grass, organie)
  Perennial; early descriptions
    were of upright form
  Flowers: dense blue-lilac whorls
  Used medicinally in wines or
    honey as soothing or revivifying
    drink; as ointment for aches;
    as a Liberty tea
  Propagation: by cuttings, division, runners

AGRIMONY or AGRIMONEW: *Agrimonia* (*Rosaceae*)
  Perennial, grows to 3 feet
  Flowers: yellow
  Flowers used medicinally
  Propagation: by seed or division

TORMENTIL: *Potentilla canadensis* (*Rosace*
  Prostrate, grows to 2 feet long
  Flowers: yellow
  Propagation: by seed or division

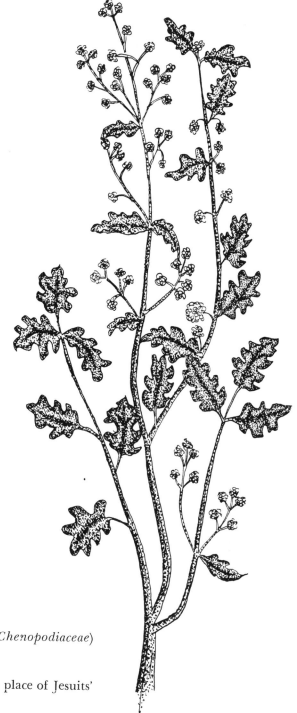

ALEXANDER: *Smyrnium olusatrum*
    (horse parsley)
    Perennial, grows to 4 feet
    Flowers: yellow clusters or umbels
    Used in salads and medicinally
        against the biting of serpents
    Propagation: by seed or cuttings

JERUSALEM OAK: *Chenopodium botrys (Chenopodiaceae)*
    (feather geranium)
    Annual, grows to 2 feet
    Used as pot herb and medicinally in place of Jesuits'
        bark
    Propagation: by seed

COMFREY: *Symphytum officinale*
(*Boraginaceae*)
Perennial, grows to 3 feet
Flowers: white, blue, pale red, or
purple
Roots used for medicinal teas and
salves, and as a source of mucilage
Propagation: by seed, division, root
cuttings

WORMWOOD: *Artemisia absinthium*
Perennial subshrub, grows to 4 f
Flowers: yellow
Used medicinally and for aroma
bitter qualities in liquors; so
times as a strewing herb
Propagation: by seed or division

FLAX: *Linum usitatissimum* (*Linaceae*)
 Annual, grows to 4 feet tall
 Flowers: small, light blue or white
 Grown for fiber and linseed oil
 Propagation: by seed

BURNET: *Poterium sanguisorba*
 Perennial, grows to 18 inches
 Flowers: greenish-white spikes
 Leaves used in wines and salads for cucumberlike
   flavor; in medicinal drinks to cure agues and
   fluxes
 Propagation: by seed or division

[147]

SAGE: *Salvia officinalis* (*Labiatae*)
    Perennial, grows from 2 to 4 feet
    Flowers: purple, violet, blue, sometimes scarlet or white
    Dried leaves used for seasonings and in medicinal teas
    Propagation: by seed or division

MUSK HERON'S BILL: *Erodium Moschatum*
    Annual or biennial, grows to 1½ feet
    Flowers: pink to purple
    Used medicinally as an astringent
    Propagation: by seed or division

[148]

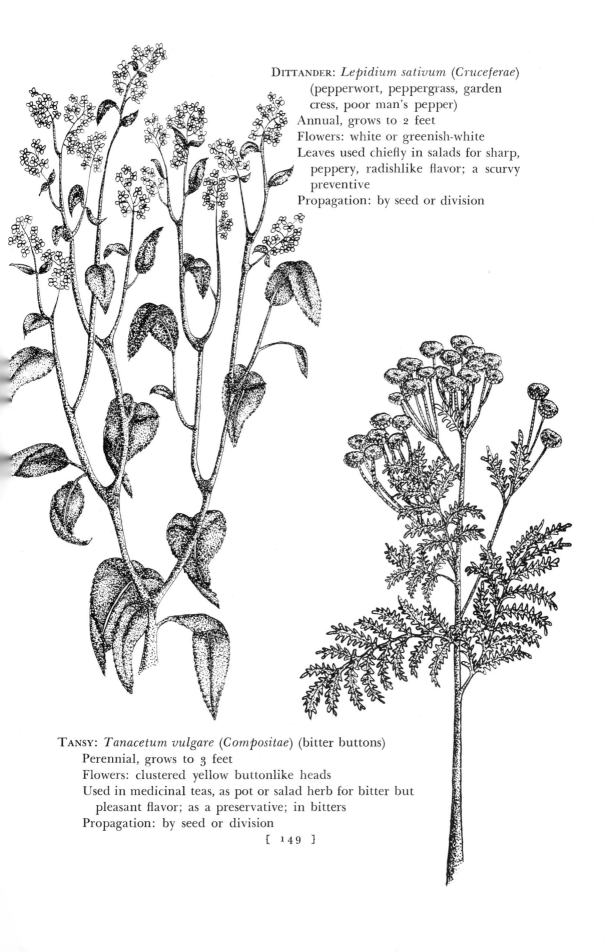

DITTANDER: *Lepidium sativum* (*Cruceferae*)
(pepperwort, peppergrass, garden
cress, poor man's pepper)
Annual, grows to 2 feet
Flowers: white or greenish-white
Leaves used chiefly in salads for sharp,
peppery, radishlike flavor; a scurvy
preventive
Propagation: by seed or division

TANSY: *Tanacetum vulgare* (*Compositae*) (bitter buttons)
Perennial, grows to 3 feet
Flowers: clustered yellow buttonlike heads
Used in medicinal teas, as pot or salad herb for bitter but
pleasant flavor; as a preservative; in bitters
Propagation: by seed or division

[149]

SUNFLOWER: *Helianthus strumosus*
Perennial, grows to 7 feet
Flowers: yellow rays
Seeds used as food and as oil source
Propagation: by seed (blooms the following year)

MARIGOLD: *Calendula officinalis* (pot marigold, calendar flower, goldes)
Annual, grows to 12 to 18 inches
Flowers: pale yellow to deep orange
Petals used to flavor stews, puddings, salads, possets, and teas; leaves used as pot herbs; fresh petals in conserves; dried petals in medicinal plasters
Propagation: from seed

ELECAMPANE: *Enula campana Helenium* (scab-wort, horse-heal, wild sunflower, elf dock)
Perennial, grows to 6 feet
Flowers: yellow daisylike heads
Juice of the root used in cough lozenges, tonics, and ointments
Propagation: by seed or division

[151]

Blew Flower-de-luce: the roots are long and streight, and very white, with a multitude of strings; they grow upon dry sandy hills as well as in low wet Grounds. *Iris*

Yellow bastard Daffodill: flowereth in May; the green leaves are spotted with black. *Erythronium americanum*, trout-lily

Dogstones: a kind of Satyrion, whereof there are several kinds in Salt Marshes. *Orchis*

Watercresses: *Nasturtium officinale*

Red Lillies: grow all over the Country innumerably amonst the small bushes and flower in June. *Lilium philadelphicum*

Wild Sorrel: *Rumex acetosa*

Adder's Tongue: comes up not till June; I have found it upon dry hilly grounds, in places where the water stood all Winter, in August and did then make Oyntment of the Herb new-gathered; the fairest leaves grow amongst short Hawthorn Bushes that are plentifully growing in such hollow places. *Ophioglossum vulgatum*

One Blade: *Maianthemum canadense*

Lily Convallie: with the yellow Flower, grows upon rocky banks by the Sea. *Convallaria majalis*

Water Plantane: here called Water-Suck leaves; It is much-used for Burns and Scalds, and to draw water out of swelled legs. Bears feed much upon this plant, so do the Moose Deer. *Alisma plantago*

Sea Plantane: three kinds. *Plantago maritima*

Small-water Archer: *Sagittaria sagittifolia* or *S. latifolia*

Autumn Bell-Flower: *Gentiana saponaria*

White Hellibore: which is the first plant that springs up in this country and the first that withers. *Veratrum viride* [probably False Hellebore, Indian Poke]

Arsmart: both kinds. *Polygonum lapathifolium, P. hydropiper*

Spurge Time: grows upon dry sandy Sea Banks and is very like to Rupterwort, it is full of Milk. *Euphorbia*

Rupter-wort: with the white flower. *Herniaria glabra* or *H. vulgaris*

Jagged Rose-penny wort: *Saxifraga virginiensis*

Sodabariglia, or Massacose: the ashes of Soda, of which they make Glasses. *Salicornia herbacea*

Glass-wort: here called Berrelia, grows abundantly in Salt Marshes. *Salicornia virginica*

St. John's-Wort: *Hypericum perforatum*

St. Peter's-Wort: *Ascyrum stans*

Speed-well Chick-weed. *Veronica arvensis*

Malefluellin, or Speedwell: *Veronica officinalis*

Upright Peniroyal: *Hedeoma pulegioides* or *Mentha pulegium*

Wild-Mint: *Mentha aquatica*

Cat-Mint: *Nepeta cataria*

Egrimony: *Agrimonia eupatoria*

The lesser Clot-Bur: *Xanthium strumarium* or *Arctium minus*

Water Lilly: with yellow Flowers. The Indians Eat the Roots which are long a boiling; they tast like the Liver of a Sheep; the moose deer feed much upon them; yellow pond lily. *Nuphar advena*

Dragons: their leaves differ from all the kinds with us; they come up in June. *Arum* [possibly Indian turnip, *Arisaema triphyllum*]

Violets of three kinds: the White Violet which is sweet; but not so strong as our Blew Violets; Blew Violets without sent, and a Reddish Violet without sent; they do not blow till June. *Viola* and *V. blanda*

Wood-bine: good for hot swellings of the Legs, fomenting with the decoction, and applying the Feces in the form of a Cataplasme. *Parthenocissus quinquefolia*

Solomons-Seal: of which there is three kinds, the first common in England [*Polygonatum multiflorum*]; the second, Virginia Solomons-seal [*P. virginianum*], and the third, differing from both is called Treacle Berries [*Smilacina racemosa*] having the perfect tast of Treacle when they are ripe, and will keep good a long while; certainly a very wholsome Berry, and medicinable.

Doves-Foot: *Geranium carolinianum*

Herb-Robert: *Geranium robertianum*

Knobby Cranes Bill: *Geranium maculatum*

Ravens-Claw: which flowers in May, and is admirable for Agues. *Geranium maculatum*

Cinkfoil: *Potentilla canadensis* or *P. reptans*

Tormentile: *Potentilla canadensis* or *P. erecta*

Avens: with the leaf of Mountant-Avens, the flower and root of English Avens. *Geum strictum* [Herb Bennet]

Strawberries: *Fragaria vesca* or *F. virginiana*

Wild Angelica: majoris and minoris. *Angelica atropurpurea*

Alexanders: which grow upon Rocks by the Sea shore. *Smyrnium aureum*

Yarrow: with the white Flower. *Achillea millefolium*

Columbines: of a flesh colour, growing upon Rocks. *Aquilegia canadensis*

Oak of Hierusalems: it is an Achariston, an excellent medicine for stopping of the Lungs upon Cold, Ptisick & c. *Chenopodium botrys*

Oak of Cappadocia: both much of a nature but Oak of Hierusalem is stronger in operation, excellent for stuffing of the Lungs upon Colds, shortness of Wind and the Ptisick, maladies that the Natives are often troubled with. *Ambrosia eleator*

Goose-Grass or Clivers: *Galium aparine*

Fearn: *Aspidium*

Brakes: *Pteris aquilina* or *Pteridium aquilinum*

Wood Sorrel: with the yellow flower. *Oxalis corniculata* or *Acetosella oxalis*

Elm: *Ulmus*

Lime Tree: both kinds. *Citrus aurantifolia, C. limetta*

Maple: *Acer*

Dew Grass: *Drosera*

Earth Nuts: of divers kinds, one bearing very beautiful Flowers. *Apiosa tuberosa*

Fuss-Balls: very large. *Fungi*

Mushrooms: some longe and no bigger than ones finger, others jagged flat, round; none like our great Mushrooms in England; of these some are of a Scarlet colour, others a deep Yellow, &c. *Fungi*

Blew flowered Pimpernel: *Anagallis caerulea* or *A. arvensis caerulea*

Noble Liver-wort: one sort with white flowers, the other with blew. *Hepatica triloba*

Black-berry: *Rubus*

Dew-berry: *Rubus*

Rasp-berry: here called Mulberry. *Rubus*

Goose-berries: of a deep red Colour. *Ribes hirtellum*

Haw-thorn: the Haws being as big as Services, and very good to eat and not so astringent as the Haws in England. *Crataegus*

Toad-flax: *Linaria vulgaris*

Pellamount or Mountain Time: *Teucrium vulgaris*

Mouse-ear Minor: *Antennaria plantaginifolia*

Oak of three kinds: white, red, and black. *Quercus*

Juniper: which Cardanus saith is Cedar in hot countries, and Juniper in cold Countries; it is hear very dwarfish and shrubby, growing for the most part by the Seaside. *Juniperus*

Willow: *Salix*

Spurge Lawrel: called here Poysonberry; it kills the English Cattle if they chance to feed upon it, especially Calves. [perhaps *Daphne laureola* or the poison sumac, *Rhus vernix*]

Gaul or noble Mirtle: *Myrica gale*

Elder: *Sambucus*

Dwarf Elder: the decoction is excellent to take the Fire out of a Burn or Scalld. *Sambucus canadensis*

Hasel: *Corylus americana*

Filberd: both with hairy husks upon the Nuts, and one setting hollow from the Nut, and filld with a kind of water of an astringent taste. *Corylus maxima*

Walnut: the nuts differ much from ours in Europe, they being smooth, much like a nutmeg in shape and not much bigger; some three-cornered, all of them but thinly replenished with kernels. [probably not a walnut, *Juglans*, but a hickory, *Carya*]

Chestnuts: very sweete in taste, and may be (as they usually are) eaten raw; the Indians sell them to the English for twelve pence the bushel. *Castanea*

Beech: *Fagus*

Ash: Quick-beam or wild ash. *Fraxinus*

Birch: white and black. *Betula*

Poplar: but differing in leaf. *Populus*

Plumb tree: several kinds, bearing long, round, white, yellow, red and black plums; all differing in their fruit from those in England. *Prunus maritima, P. americana*

Wild Purcelans: *Portulaca oleracea*

Woad-wax: wherewith they dye many pretty Colours. *Genista tinctoria*

Red and black Currans: *Ribes*

Josselyn titled his second list "such plants as are proper to the Country" and included thirty-eight.

Indian wheat: three sorts, yellow, red and blue. *Zea Mays*

Bastard Calamus Aromaticus: agrees with the description but is not barren; they flower in July, and grow in wet places, as about the brinks of Ponds. *Acorus calamus* [Sweetflag]

Wild Leekes: which the Indians use much to eat with their fish. *Allium canadense*

A plant like the Knavers Mustard, called New England Mustard. *Lepidium virginicum*

Mountain-Lillies: bearing many yellow Flowers turning up their leaves like the Martigon or Turks Cap, spotted with small spots as deep as saffron; they flower in July. *Lilium canadense*

One-Berry or Herb True Love: *Cornus canadensis*

Tobacco: there is not much planted in New England. The Indians make use of a small kind with short round leaves called Pooke. *Nicotiana tabacum*

Hollow leaved Lavender: a plant that grows in salt Marshes overgrown with Moss, with one straight stalk about the bigness of an Oat straw, better than a cubit high; upon the top standeth one fantastical flower, the leaves grow close from the root in shape like a Tankard, hollow, tough and always full of Water; the root is made up of many small strings, growing only in the moss and not in the Earth, the whole plant comes to perfection in August and then it has Leaves, Stalks and Flowers as red as blood, excepting the flower which hath some yellow admixt. I wonder where the knowledge of this plant hath slept all this while, i.e., above Forty years. *Sarracenea purpurea*

Live for ever: a kind of Cud-weed. *Antennaria margaritacea* or *Gnaphalium americanum*

Tree Primrose: taken by the ignorant for Scabious. *Oenothera biennis*

Maiden Hair or Cappellus veneru veriu: ordinarily is half a Yard in height. The Apothecaries for shame now will substitute Wall-Rue no more for Maiden-Hair since it grows in abundance in New England, from which they may have good store. *Adiantum pedatum*

Pirola: two kinds, both of them excellent Wound Herbs. *Pyrola*

Homer's Molley: *Allium tricoccum*

Loose Strife: it grows in dry grounds in open Sun four foot high, flowers from the middle of the Plant to the top, the Flowers purple, standing upon a small sheath or cod, which when it is ripe breaks and puts forth a white silken doun; the stalk is red and as big as ones Finger. *Epilobium angustifolium*

Marygolds of Peru: of which there are two Kinds, one bearing black seeds, the other black and white streak'd this bearing the fairest flowers on the very top of the stalk. *Helianthus strumosus*

Treacle berries: see before solomons seal. *Smilacina racemosa*

Earth Nuts: differing much from those in England; one sort of them bears a most beautiful flower. *Apiosa tuberosa*

Sea-Tears: they grow upon the Sea Banks in abundance; they are good for Scurvy and Dropsie, boiled and eaten as a Sallad, and the broth drunk with it. *Cakile americana*

Indian Beans: falsely called French beans are better for Physick and Chirurgy than our Garden Beans. *Phaseolus vulgaris*

Squashes: a kind of Melon or rather Gourd for they oftentimes degenerate into Gourds; some of these are green, some yellow, some longish like a Gourd, others round like an apple. *Cucurbita*

Water-Melon: is a large fruit but nothing near as big as a Pompion, colour smoother and of a sad Grass green; rounder or more rightly sap green; with some yellowness admixt when ripe; the seeds are black, the flesh or pulpe exceeding juicy; it is often given to those sick of Feavers and other hot diseases with good success. *Citrullus*

New England Daysie or Primrose: flowers in May and grows amongst moss upon hilly grounds and Rocks that are shady; It is very good for burns and scalds. *Saxifraga virginiensis*

Briony of Peru: we call it though it grow hear or rather Scamnony; some take it for Mechoacan. The green Juice is absolutely Poyson; yet the root when dry may safely be given to strong bodies. *Convolvulus sepium*

Wild Damask Roses: single, very large and sweet, but stiptick. *Rosa carolina*

Sweet Fern: the roots run one within another like a Net . . . sweet in taste, but withal astringent; much hunted after by our swine. *Comptonia asplenifolia*

Sarsaparilia: a plant not yet sufficiently known by the English: some say it is a kind of bindweed. We have in New England two plants that go under the name of Sarsaparilia; the one not above a foot in height without thorns, the other having the same leaf but is a shrub as high as a gooseberry bush and full of sharp thorns . . . it groweth upon dry Sandy banks by the sea side and upon the banks of Rivers, so far as the salt water flowes; and within land up in the country, as some have reported. *Aralia hispida* or *A. nudicalis*

Bill Berries: two kinds, Black and Sky-coloured, which is more frequent. *Vaccinium pensylvanicum* and *V. corymbosum*

Knot-Berry or Clewde Berry: Seldom ripe. *Rubus chamaemorus*

Sumach: differing from all that I did ever see in the Herbalists; our English cattle devour it most abominably, leaving neither leaf nor branch, yet it sprouts again next spring; the English use to boyl it in Beer and drink it for colds; and so do the Indians from whom the English had the medicine. *Rhus*

Wild Cherry: grow in clusters like grapes of the same bigness, blackish, red when ripe and of a harsh taste; they are also good for Fluxes; transplanted and manured, they grow exceeding fair. *Cerasus serolina*

Board Pine: a very large tree, it yields a very sovereign turpentine for the curing of desperate wounds. *Pinus palustris*

The Firr tree or pitch tree: the tar is an excellent thing to take away those desperate stitches in the sides which perpetually afflict those poor people who are stricken with the plaque of the back. *Pinus rigida*

The larch tree: *Larix*

Spruce: a goodly tree of which they make Masts for Ships; it is generally considered by those that have skill in building ships that here is absolutely the best Trees in the World. *Abies*

Hemlock Tree: a kind of Spruce; fishers tan their sails and nets with it. *Tsuga canadensis*

One Berry, Herba Paris, or True-Love: *Cornus canadensis*

Sassafras or Ague-Tree: *Sassafras officinale*

Cran-Berry or Bear-Berry: because bears use much to feed upon them. *Vaccinium macrocarpon* or *V. oxycoceus*

Vine: much differing on Fruit, all of them very fleshy, some reasonably pleasant, others have a taste of Gunpowder and these grow in swamps and low wet grounds. *Vitis labrusca* and *V. aestivalis*

Josselyn's third list, and one in which he took pride in being able to report, was titled "Of Such Plants as are proper [native] to the Country and have no Name." Some botanists still are unable to give names to all of Josselyn's third category of rarities mainly because the sketches accompanying his descriptions are so poor. Included was a plant Josselyn said was a "kind of Pirola," possibly *Goodyera pubescens*; another appears to be a type of fern; and a third was one the gentleman-explorer thought a "Wound herb not Inferiour to ours, but rather beyond it," and so he called what may have been *Verbena hastata* Clownes-all-heal of New England. One more easily recognized was the native skunk cabbage, while the fifth was called Humming Bird Tree and turned out to be *Impatiens fulva*. The sixth discovery was snake-weed, *Nabalus alba*; the seventh *Chelone glabra*; and the eighth was one Josselyn called variegated Herb Paris, but more probably it was *Cornus canadensis*. His ninth discovery, accurately named a small sunflower, was indeed *Helianthus strumosus*.

Josselyn's fourth list included "such plants as have sprung up since the English planted and kept Cattle" in New England, although, he declared, "I have not done with such Plants as grow wild in the Country in great Plenty":

Couch grass: shepherd's purse; Dandelion; groundsel; sow thistle. *Holcus mollis*; *Capsella bursa pastoris*; *Taraxacum Dens-leonis*; *Senecio vulgaris*

Wild Arrack: Night shade with the white flower. *Sonchus oleraceus*

Nettlestinging: which was the first plant taken notice of. *Urtica dioica*

Mallowes: *Malva sylvestris*

Plantain: which the Indians call Englishman's Foot as though produced by their treading. *Plantago major*

Black Henbane; Wormwood; Sharp-pointed Dock; Patience; Bloodwort; and I suspect Adders tongue: *Hyoscyamus niger*; *Artemisia Absinthium*; *Rumex crispus, R. patientia, R. sanguineus*; *Ophioglossum*

Cheek Weed: *Stellaria media*

May Weed: Excellent for the mother; some of our English house-
wives call it Iron wort and make a good unguent for old sores.
Anthemis cotula
Mullin with the white flowers: *Verbascum lychnitis*
Knot grass: *Polygonum aviculare*
Compherie: with the white flower. *Symphytum officinale*

Josselyn's fifth list was of "such Garden Herbs (amongst us) as do thrive
there, and such as do not." This catalog is of special interest; it tells what
one better-than-average observer found could be and was grown easily in
colonial gardens along the New England coast within a few years after
settlement. Each household may not have been able to grow all the plants
Josselyn included; nevertheless, these were available and could be bartered
for at markets and public fairs.

Josselyn's list of cultivated plants not only provides a picture of the
possible early garden plot, but it reveals the favorite diet staples of the
time and tells us what popular herbs were planted especially for their
seasoning or for their medicinal value. Here again, the list is in the order
used by Josselyn and retains his spelling and comments:

> Cabbidge growes there exceeding well; lettice; sorrel; parsley;
> marygold; French mallowes; chervel; burnet; winter savory; sum-
> mer savory; time; sage; carrats; parsneps of a prodigious size; red
> beetes; radishes; turnips; purslain; wheat; rye; oats; pease of all sorts
> and the best in the World; garden beans, naked oats; spear mint;
> fetherfew prospereth exceedingly; white sattin groweth pretty well;
> lavender cotton; pennyroyal; smalledge [parsley]; ground ivy or
> ale-hoof; houseleek prospereth notably; holly hocks; enula cam-
> pane; comferie with white flowers; coriander and dill and annis
> thrive exceedingly; sparagus thrives exceedingly, so does garden
> sorrel and sweet bryer; pateince and English roses very pleasantly;
> celandine; muschata as well as in England; dittender or pepper
> wort flourisheth notably and so doth tansie; musk mellons are
> better than our English; cucumbers; pompions of several kinds
> are dryer than our English pompions.
>
> Gillyflowers will continue two years; barley commonly de-
> generates into oats; rew will hardly grow [and] fennel must be
> taken up and kept in a Cellar all Winter. Clary never lasts but
> one Summer [for] the Roots rot with the frost; Bloodwort [does]
> but sorrily.

Other plants had been tried and found wanting, for Josselyn records
their failure: these include Southern wood, which he said was "no Plant
for this Country, nor Rosemary nor Bayes."

CHAPTER 3

Herbs for Witch and Wizard

Thou shalt not suffer a witch to live.
EXODUS 22:18

"AT THIS COURT one Margaret Jones of Charlestown was indicted and found guilty of witchcraft and hanged for it." So wrote John Winthrop in June 1648 of the first trial and execution in Massachusetts for the ancient crime.[29] Biblical injunction against witchcraft was the authority which would be used throughout New England to bring to trial two generations of suspects. There would be men who doubted that some of these accused actually were guilty of familiarity with Satan, but none who would doubt with any certainty that witches did exist.

Mrs. Jones was a semiliterate country-woman who grew herbs and dispensed them as medicines to her neighbors. She had an unfortunate propensity not only to diagnose and dose, but along with each dosage to provide a prognosis. She had other failings: to say the least, she lacked a healing touch. As Winthrop reported in his journal, "She was found to have such a malignant touch, many persons whom she touched . . . were taken with deafness, vomiting or other violent pains or sickness."[30]

Mrs. Jones also may have been careless in prescribing exact amounts; "she practising physic and her medicine being such things as (by her own confession) were harmless, as anniseed, liquors, etc., [nevertheless they] had extraordinary violent effects."[31] Those who tried her case thus concluded Mrs. Jones's simples must have been brewed with the help of the devil; how else could harmless herbs cause such reaction? For the Bible that held witches in abhorrence advised also that "the Lord hath created medicines out of the earth, and he that is wise will not abhor them."

Mrs. Jones appears to have had little faith in the medicines prescribed by her more learned colleagues and even less tolerance for patients who

[160]

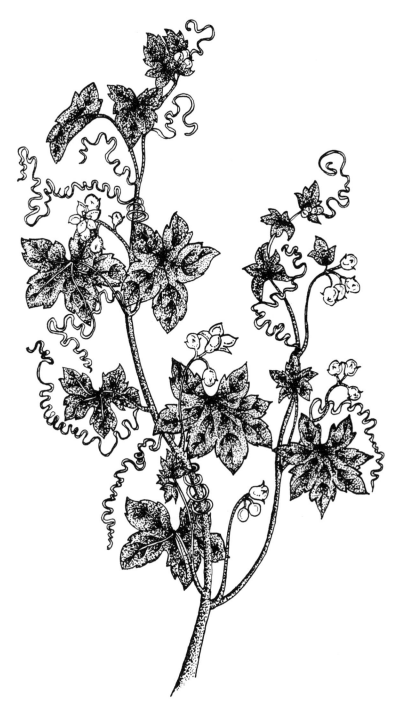

WHITE BRIONY: *Brionia alba*
  Perennial, a climbing plant often several yards in length
  Flowers: yellowish-green with smooth, red berries
  Used medicinally as a purgative and as a counterirritant
  Propagation: by seed or division

[161]

ANGELICA: *Angelica sativa* (*Umbelliferae*)
Perennial, grows to 2 feet
Stems and leaves candied, used in jellies for juniperlike flavor; in
soothing medicinal drinks
Propagation: by seed or division

ELDER: *Sambucus canadensis* (*Caprifoliaceae*) (American or sweet elder)
   Perennial shrub or tree, grows to 12 feet
   Flowers: white; edible purple-black berries
   Shoots, stalks, leaves, and bark brewed as purges; sap used for dye;
      berries in jellies, wines
   Propagation: by seed, cuttings, suckers

consulted her competitors. "She would use to tell such as would not make use of her physic that they would never be healed, and accordingly their diseases and hurts continued . . . beyond the apprehension of all physicians and surgions." Most suspect of all was Mrs. Jones's ability to diagnose fatal illness, especially since "things she foretold came to pass accordingly."[32] If more proof of guilt were needed, it was provided "the same day and hour she was executed [when] there was a very great tempest . . . which blew down many trees."[33]

George Herbert's book, *Country Parson*, advised the novice clergyman on the practicality of acting as attorney and physician (as well as pastor) to his congregation. His readers should "make the garden [the dispensery] so where the apothecary useth either for loosing, rhubarb, or for bending, bolearmena, the Parson useth damask or white roses for the one, and plantain, shepherd's purse, knot grass for the other, and that with better success."[34] The advice Herbert gave his parsons was the same Mrs. Jones had given to her neighbors. Presumably, however, those who read Herbert were able to develop a more comforting bedside manner than the witch of Charlestown had mustered, and never frightened patients out of their wits.

Among the various helpful texts brought to the colonies during those long years of witchcraft hysteria and terror was William Coles's delightful book, *The Art of Simpling*, which he described as an "Introduction to the Knowledge and Gathering of Plants." Printed in London in 1657, Coles's book divided herbs according to their uses; one chapter listed "Plants used in aid against Witchraft."[35]

Coles wrote with such restraint it is difficult to believe he put much if any credence in the efficacy of the "witchcraft" plants he catalogued. He seems to have decided to play safe by telling his readers what they wanted to hear. His statement in an earlier chapter, "Herein you may perceive that I endeavour (as much as I can) to condescend to capacities of the vulgar, whose good I heartily wish," applied equally well to his paragraphs on witchcraft. Each of the plants Coles listed in this chapter was grown in colonial gardens—if not in one's own, then in a neighbor's—or a suitable substitute was available, such as briony for the magical mandrake.

For those who wondered what the well-supplied kitchen pharmacy of a practicing witch must include, Coles explained, "The Oyntment that Witches use is reported to be made of the fat of Children digged out of their graves; of the Juices of Smallage, Woolfsbaine and Cinquefoyle mingled with the meale of fine Wheat. But some suppose that the soporiferous Medicines are likeliest to doe it, which are Henbane, Hemlock, Mandrake, Nightshade, Tobacco, Opium, Saffron, Poplar Leaves, &c. They take likewise the roots of Mandrake, according to some, or as I rather suppose the roots of Briony, which simple folke take for the true Mandrake, and make thereof an ugly Image, by which they intend to exercise their Witchcraft. Many olde wives fables are written of Vervaine, which you may read elsewhere, as Master Gerrard saith."[36]

For the benefit of those who needed help to dispel evil forces loosed against them, Coles listed "those [herbs] that are used against Witchcraft":

Mistletoe which if one hang about their neck, the Witches can have no power of him. The roots of Angelica doe likewise availe much in the same case, if a man carry them about him, as Fuchsius saith. The common people formerly gathered the Leaves of Elder upon the last day of Aprill, which to disappoint the Charmes of Witches, they had affixed to their Doores and Windowes. Matthiolus saith, that Herbe Paris takes away evill done by Witchcraft, and affirms that he knew it to be true by experience.

I doe not desire any to pin their Faiths upon these reports, but onely let them know that there are such which they may believe as they please. However there is no question but very wonderfull Effects may be wrought by the Vertues which are enveloped within the compasse of the green Mantles, wherewith many Plants are adorned.[37]

CHAPTER 4

New Amsterdam's Abundance

But may not some say, why tell
you us of these herbs? we know
not where they grow . . . I shall
therefore lead you. . . .
Come into the fields,
Then come along the streets,
by the walls and under the hedge sides;
Come into the closes, and amongst the corn;
Thence march to the woods, and
from thence into the Meadowes;
Thence to the boggs and so to the riverside;
Cast your eyes upon the banks;
And coming home into the towne againe,
Lift up your eyes, and look a little higher.

WILLIAM COLES,
The Art of Simpling

THE ONLY ATTORNEY, indeed the only graduate of a university, that Holland would send to its early seventeenth-century holdings in America was young Adrien Van der Donck, who wrote *A Description of the New Netherlands*. Published in 1653, the book provided a detailed picture of that colony's early plants.[38]

His bark arrived in the New World in 1642, and in that year Van der Donck began his work as an administrator for Dutch interests. The young Hollander lived first at Fort Orange (now Albany). Eventually he was given permission to buy his own plantation on upper Manhattan Island. A gentleman, Van der Donck was entitled to use the designation "Jonker," and as it was spelled phonetically then, and Anglicized today, his holdings were called The Yonker's Land. His estate was bounded on one side by land owned by the Bronck family, whose name, as Bronx, also continues

[166]

today. Bowerie would be the name given to other lovely park and garden areas.

Van der Donck's affection for the mountains he explored and the rivers along which he traveled, his marveling at the rich black soil and his sureness of the great promise it held, illumines each paragraph of his description of the lands that would in 1665 become the English colony of New York.[39] There, wrote Van der Donck, "when the summer progresses finely, the land rewards the labor of the husbandman; the flowers smile on his countenance; the fishes sport in their element, and the herds play in the fields, as if no reverses were to return. . . . There is plenty here for man and the animal creation."[40]

Native plants included

> mulberries better and sweeter than ours [in Holland]; several kinds of plums, wild or small cherries, juniper, small kinds of apples, many hazelnuts, black currants, gooseberries, blue India figs, and strawberries in abundance all over the country, blue-berries, raspberries, black-caps, etc., with artichokes, ground-acorns, ground beans, wild onions, and leeks like ours, with several other kinds of root and fruits, known to the Indians. . . . The Nether-landers have introduced every kind of garden vegetables, which thrive and yield well. The country produces an abundance of fruits like the Spanish capers which could be preserved in like manner.
>
> The English have brought over the first quinces, and we have brought over . . . orchard cherries, forerunners, morellaes, of every kind we have. . . . The peaches grow wonderfully well here.
>
> We have also introduced morecotoons (a peach), apricots, several kinds of the best plums, almonds, persimmons, cornelian cherries, figs, several sorts of currants, gooseberries, calissiens, and thorn apples; and we do not doubt but that the olive would thrive. . . .
>
> Although the land is full of many kinds of grapes, we still want settings of the best kinds from Germany . . . for wine.

Unlike reports from New England and the southern colonies, "In the New Netherlands, we seldom hear of any person who is afflicted with a pining disease. Many persons from the West Indies, Virginia, and other quarters of the world who do not enjoy health in those parts, when they come into the New Netherlands, there become as active as the fishes in the water. The Galens have meager soup in that country.[41] There are no heavy damps or stinking mists . . . and if any did arise, a northerly breeze would blow them away."

Although a New York settler seldom might have had need of a

LAVENDER: *Lavendula spica*
 Perennial, subshrub to 3 feet
 Flowers: blue, violet, or lilac
 One of the sweet strewing herbs, prized
  for its scent and essential oil; used in
  toilet waters, sachets, soap
 Propagation: by seed, cutting, or
  division

LEEK: *Allium porrum* (*Liliaceae*)
 Perennial, grows to 2 feet
 Flowers: purple or pink umbrels
 Bulbs and leaves used in salads, stews
 Propagation: by seed, offsets, bulblets

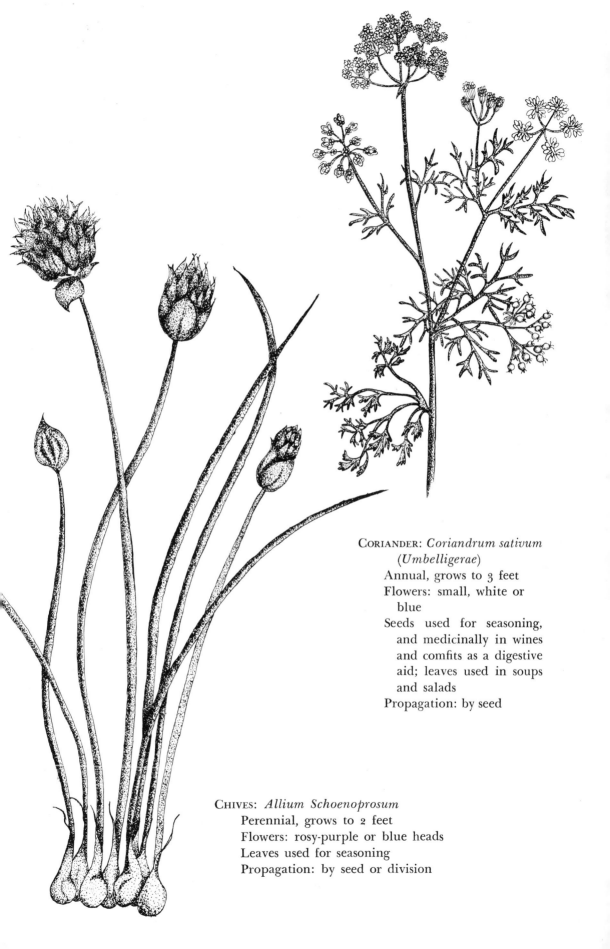

CORIANDER: *Coriandrum sativum*
    (*Umbelligerae*)
    Annual, grows to 3 feet
    Flowers: small, white or
        blue
    Seeds used for seasoning,
        and medicinally in wines
        and comfits as a digestive
        aid; leaves used in soups
        and salads
    Propagation: by seed

CHIVES: *Allium Schoenoprosum*
    Perennial, grows to 2 feet
    Flowers: rosy-purple or blue heads
    Leaves used for seasoning
    Propagation: by seed or division

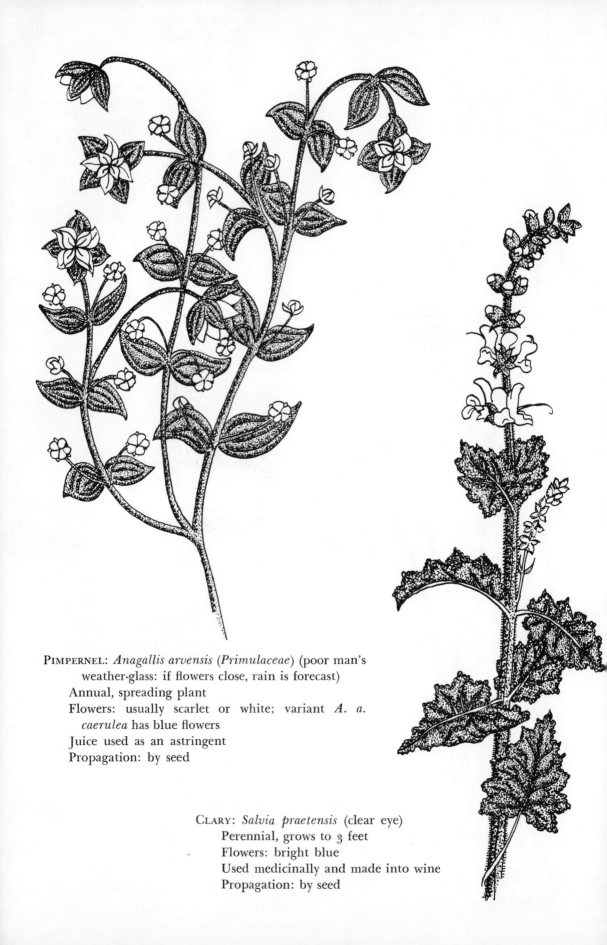

PIMPERNEL: *Anagallis arvensis* (*Primulaceae*) (poor man's
weather-glass: if flowers close, rain is forecast)
Annual, spreading plant
Flowers: usually scarlet or white; variant *A. a.
caerulea* has blue flowers
Juice used as an astringent
Propagation: by seed

CLARY: *Salvia praetensis* (clear eye)
Perennial, grows to 3 feet
Flowers: bright blue
Used medicinally and made into wine
Propagation: by seed

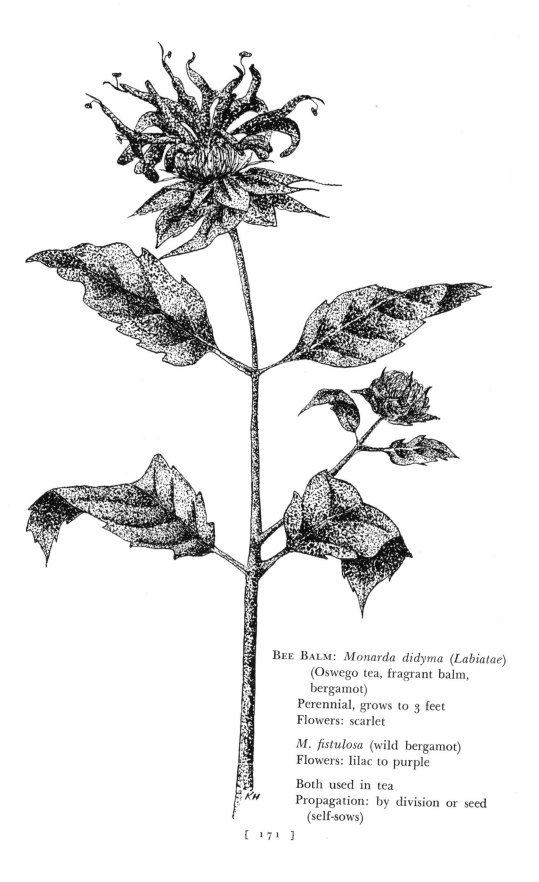

BEE BALM: *Monarda didyma (Labiatae)*
(Oswego tea, fragrant balm,
bergamot)
Perennial, grows to 3 feet
Flowers: scarlet

M. fistulosa (wild bergamot)
Flowers: lilac to purple

Both used in tea
Propagation: by division or seed
(self-sows)

[171]

physician—whether he followed Galen's principles or others—native medicinal plants and healing herbs flourished throughout the countryside for those who wished to prescribe for themselves. Van der Donck reported the plants that "are known to us include vapilli veneris, scholopendria, angelica, polypodium, verbascum album, calteus sacerdotis, atriplex hortensis and marina, chortium, turrities, calamus aromaticus, sassafras, rois Virginium, ranunculus, plantago, bursa pastoris, malva, origaenum, geranicum, althea, cinoroton pseudo, dahine, viola, ireas, indigo silvestris, sigillum, salamonis, sanguis draconum, consolidae, millefolium, noli me tangere, cardo benedictus, agrimonium, serpentariae, coriander, leeks, wild leeks, Spanish figs, elatine, camperfolie, petum male and female. . . . The land is full of many kinds besides those."

Farming was not as "heavy and expensive" as in the homeland, Van der Donck wrote, "because the fencing and enclosing of the land does not cost much. Instead of the Netherlands dykes and ditches, they set up post and rail or palisado fences. . . . Fencing timber costs nothing but the labour which is reasonably cheap to those who have their own hands."

Peas, wheat and barley, buckwheat and rye, "are plenty," he said. "The maize or turkey wheat is a hardy grain . . . fit for the sustenance of man and animals. . . . Cummin seed, canary seed and the like succeed well but are not sought after. Flax and hemp "grow fine, but since the women do not spin much, and the Indians have hemp in abundance . . . from which they make strong rope and nets, very little flax is raised."

The lands along the seaboard were "overgrown with different kinds of trees and grapevines, having many plums, hazelnuts and strawberries, and much grass." Indeed, "The whole country is covered with wood," Van der Donck said of the natural phenomena that impressed so many citizens of the old countries from which once-great stands of trees had disappeared. As a matter of fact, "there is all to much of it and in our way."

The oak trees stood sixty to seventy feet high, he wrote, and were of several kinds: "white, smooth bark, rough bark, grey bark and black bark. . . . The nut-wood grows as tall as the oak . . . it is straight and tough and hard. We now use it for cogs and rounds in our mills and for threshing flails, swivel trees, fencing and other farm purposes. It also is excellent firewood, surpassing every other kind." Ash, yellow and white pine, chestnuts—which would have been more plentiful had not the Indians "stripped the bark for covering their houses"—beech and water beech—the bark of which "turns white and resembles handsome satin"—were "ornamental and handsome for planting near dwelling houses." There were also "two kinds of ash, linden, birch, yew, poplar, sapine, alder, willow, thorn trees, persimmon, mulberry, wild cherry, crab and others . . . unknown to us."

The New Netherland autumns "are very fine, lovely and agreeable;

more delightful cannot be found on the earth; not only because the summer productions are gathered and the earth is then yielding its surplusage, but also because the season is so well tempered with heat and cold as to appear like the month of May—except that on some mornings there will be frost."

The harvest of the New Netherlanders' kitchen gardens included numerous products, "some of them known to the natives" and some brought from other parts of the world. "They consist of various kinds of salads, cabbages, parsnips, carrots, beets, endive, succory, finckel, sorrel, dill, spinage, radishes, Spanish radishes, parsley, chervil [or sweet Cicely], cresses, onions, leeks, and besides whatever else is commonly found in a kitchen garden.

"The herb garden is also tolerably well supplied with rosemary, lavender, hyssop, thyme, sage, marjoram, balm, holy onions, wormwood, belury, chives and clary; also pimpernel, dragon's blood, five-finger, tarragon or dragon's wort, etc., together with laurel, artichokes and asparagus, and various other things on which I have bestowed no attention."

However, muskmelons he did notice; they grew, he said, "in the New Netherlands luxuriantly." Some, which were called Spanish pork, "grow large and very abundant." The watermelon, which Van der Donck, as did others throughout the age, called citrull or water-citron, was "a fruit only known before to us from its being brought occasionally from Portugal [and] grows rapidly . . . their juice is sweet like that of apricots . . . they grow as large as Leyden cabbages, but in general are somewhat oblong . . . it melts as soon as it enters the mouth." So refreshing was the juicy melon "that it is used as a beverage. I have heard the English say they obtain a liquor from it resembling Spanish wine, but not so strong. . . . The vinegar that is made from it will last long.

"Cucumbers are abundant. Calabashes or gourds also grow there. . . . Turnips are good and firm as any sand-rapes that are raised in the Netherlands. There are likewise peas and various sorts of beans (including the Windsor or house-bean), and the Turkish beans grow wonderfully. . . . The blue sort are abundant."

In truth, wrote Van der Donck, "the superabundance of this country is not equalled by any other in the world."

PART VIII

The Eighteenth-Century Garden

CHAPTER 1

Flowers from Garden and Field

And se the fresshe flowres how they spryngge up!
GEOFFREY CHAUCER,
Canterbury Tales

"THE ENGLISH LADIES are accustomed to gather great quantities of life everlasting (*Folia calycina*) and to pick them with the stalks. . . . They put them into pots with or without water amongst other fine flowers which they gather in the gardens and in the fields, and place them as an ornament in the rooms."[1]

There were flowers in eighteenth-century homes wherever space could be found, Peter Kalm said, for "English ladies are much inclined to keep [them] all summer long about or upon the chimneys, upon a table or before the windows, either on account of their beauty or because of their sweet scent."[2]

Even if seventeenth-century colonists had not been able earlier to bring flower seeds with them—which they did—Kalm's English ladies nevertheless would have been able to gather bouquets from the multitude of blossoming plants and trees native to the New World. Many women, yearning for color and beauty in those simply constructed early homes, hopefully found the time to transplant seedlings and bulbs from the wild abundance that was here. Most of those flowers which they found growing wild are cultivated nursery and garden plants today.

The American wisteria blossomed from Virginia south to Florida and as far west as Texas, while bee balm, or Oswego tea, grew south from New York. From June to August throughout New York and the eastern colonies the black-eyed Susan, or yellow daisy of the sunflower family, could be gathered. Blue monarda, or wild bergamot, and wild sweet william, a kind of phlox, grew in New England, while southern colonists in April and May picked Carolina jessamine and wild woodbine anywhere south of Virginia. Both New England and Virginia planters searched out cattails, or bog plant, learning from the Indians to eat the sweet tuberous roots and to weave mats of the flags, as well as to dry them for winter bouquets.

Clematis, a midsummer member of the buttercup family, grew wild in all the colonies and was one of the first American plants to be cultivated, whether it was called traveler's-joy, old-man's-beard, devil's-hair, wild hops, or virgin's-bower. The columbine blossomed from Pennsylvania north, and the first colonists learned from the natives to brew tea from columbine seeds for relief from headaches. The flame azalea flourished from Pennsylvania to Georgia and west as far as Kentucky and Ohio. What was described as the fragrant sumac (*Rhus canadensis*) was one of the first native shrubs to be transplanted for its ornamental beauty. The fringe tree, growing from Georgia to Florida, was known also as the flowering ash or the snowflower.

Hydrangea was native south of New England, as was the lily of the valley, long known also in Europe. Pink locust, or rose acacia, grew from Virginia to Alabama. Rose mallows were found in freshwater marshes from Massachusetts to Florida. Silver bell and snowdrop greeted settlers traveling from West Virginia to Florida, southwest to Texas, and west into Illinois.

Trumpet creeper grew from Pennsylvania southward and the trumpet honeysuckle from New England to Florida. Many kinds of violets grew all along the colonial coast, as did turtlehead, or balmony, a native of the snapdragon family. The Indians called *Impatiens biflora*, or jewelweed, the crowing cock flower.

Flowering plants brought here from Europe during the seventeenth century included bearded blue iris; bouncing Bet; cabbage rose; marigold, or calendula; gilliflower or carnation clove pink; daffodil; and veronica.

Here by the eighteenth century were autumn crocus, scilla, nasturtium, periwinkle, Canterbury bell, pansy, peony, China aster, poet's narcissus, Oriental poppy, lilac, day lily, chinaberry, cornflower, box, jonquil, hyacinth, moneywort, hollyhock, grape hyacinth, English daisy, primrose, larkspur, English ivy, and yew. By the middle of the century, newspaper readers from Boston to Charleston were accustomed to advertisements offering "garden seeds and flower roots, amongst which are the best orange carrots . . . Turkey renunculas roots, Dutch tulips, fine anamonies, double poppies, double larkspur, with many other articles" imported from London and the Continent.[3]

I know a bank whereon the wild thyme blows,
Where oxlips and the nodding violet grows,
Quite over-canopied with luscious woodbine,
With sweet musk-roses, and with eglantine.
WILLIAM SHAKESPEARE,
A Midsummer Night's Dream

Of all the flowers the colonists would plant for beauty, as well as for usefulness when transformed into simples and conserves, the rose seems always to have been their first choice. The Reverend Higginson wrote in 1634 of the "abundance of damaske roses" in the Bay Colony.[4] Even that disgruntled exile from Merrymount, Thomas Morton, became almost lyrical when he described the "air perfumed with divers good herbes that grow without the industry of man," listing musk roses, "violets, balme, laurell, hunnisuckle and the like."[5]

Roses were part of the English tradition; they perfumed hedgerows and formal garden walls alike, and were in Gerard's words, even the "ornament of our English sceptre."[6] Scots chose the thistle, the Welsh the magical leek, the Irish the shamrock, but the English even when divided chose either the red rose of Lancaster or the white of York, and when united, the variegated red and white of the House of Tudor. In New England as it had been across the Atlantic, the rose was a favorite design worked in crewel embroidery or carved in the wood panels of chests and the cornices of parlors and corner cupboards. As the herbalist Gerard said, being so "esteemed in his beautie, vertue and his fragrance, the rose doth deserve the chiefest and most principall place among all flowers whatsoever."[7] Settlers in the mid-seventeenth century who brought with them John Parkinson's *Theatrum Botanicum* were reminded by the author that the crimson beauty of the rose "is the light of the earth, the faire bushe of the spring, the lightning of the land."[8]

The apothecary's rose—the red rose of Lancaster, *Rosa gallica officinalis* —had been known in England since at least the time of the Roman invasion, and was developed during the Middle Ages for its medicinal qualities. It was brought early to the colonies, where it was distilled into rose water, powdered for sachets, and made into ointments, jellies, and conserves. Thus when the wife of Governor John Winthrop was stricken with a "fit of the mother"—the Saxon term for hysteria—colleague John Endecott of Salem advised soothing her with syrup of roses.[9]

The number of roses known to the colonists was small; today's familiar hybrids generally were not developed until the beginning of the nineteenth century. Those roses the settlers would have listed began with the ancestor of the *gallica*, the *officinalis*, which Parkinson described when he wrote of its large, often double, blossoms of clear, brilliant red with gold stamens.

Ancient also by our later standards is the *alba*, the white rose of England, for it was listed by Albertus Magnus in the thirteenth century; it too was prized by the colonial apothecary and planter. The summer damask, *Rosa damascena*, and the autumn damask, *R. damascena bifera*, may have been introduced into England by the Romans.

The *centifolia*, or cabbage rose, was not developed until 1700, when Dutch nurserymen crossed the *Rosa damascena* and *R. alba* to create the blossom seen in so many paintings of the early eighteenth century. What the colonists called a pink moss rose was the *centifolia muscosa*, developed also in seventeenth-century Holland. Noted by Philip Miller in 1759, the moss rose he described was, he said, a descendant of one he had received from Holland just thirty years earlier.[10] The simple rose began to disappear from American gardens after 1800, when scores of new hybrids were introduced as the tea roses of China were combined successfully with older English flowers.

To see the roses of the seventeenth and eighteenth centuries it is necessary to look for those that still grow wild and are less popular garden choices. The sweetbrier, *Rosa eglanteria*, with its small pink blossoms and scent reminiscent of a ripe apple, was the hardy shrub Judge Sewall planted —one rose to two junipers—for a hedge fence around his Salem yard. It blooms as a wild rose today from Maine to Virginia and west to Tennessee. The dog or canker rose, or wild brier, *R. canina*, has creamy pink or white blossoms similar to those of the sweetbrier and is found along roadsides from Maine to Pennsylvania. The swamp rose, *R. carolina*, is known from Maine to Florida and into Mississippi, while the smooth meadow rose, *R. blanda*, with large pink blossoms on thornless stems, is found throughout New England and New Jersey.

It was the distilled water of such roses, Gerard said, that strengthened the heart and refreshed the spirits; he recommended its use in "junkettings, cakes, sawces and many other pleasant things, for it gives a fine and delectable taste."[11] Rose petals were crushed, "ground in a mortar" and boiled with equal amounts of sugar for a conserve, or added to honey as an elegant syrup. Rose hips were used not only for jelly, but for pies and tarts. One such recipe was provided by Robert May in 1671 when he told the cook to "take hips, cut them and take out the seeds very clean, then wash them and season them with sugar, cinnamon and ginger, close the tart, bake it, scrape on sugar and serve it in."[12]

CHAPTER 2

Jefferson's Notes on Virginia

*A house though otherwise beautifull, yet
if it hath no Garden belonging to it, is
more like a Prison than a House.*
WILLIAM COLES[13]

"THE DECLARATION OF INDEPENDENCE, the Virginia Statute for Religious Freedom, the University of Virginia"—these were the lines Thomas Jefferson, Washington's Secretary of State and third President of the United States, said he preferred for his epitaph.

Although he was not so wealthy as some other Revolutionary leaders, Jefferson's holdings and manner of living, both before and during the war, were, to say the least, far removed from those of the average colonist. An intellectual equal of Franklin, Jefferson also enjoyed the ability to learn whatever could be taught by others or gleaned from books, and sometimes to invent what he found lacking. As did his Philadelphia elder, the master of Monticello appreciated epicurean delights. And, just as Franklin had been criticized by contemporaries for his enjoyment of good food generally and Paris cuisine particularly, so was Jefferson; Patrick Henry declared he "abjured his native victuals" in favor of dishes concocted by a French chef.

Long before he installed a foreign cook in the presidential kitchen, however, Jefferson had required a good table at Monticello, and he often planned the daily menus. For of all facets of his life—attorney, planter, burgess, political philosopher, statesman—he preferred, he said, that of a landowner whose farm "supplies a good table, clothes himself and his family, furnishes a surplus to buy salt, sugar, coffee, and a little finery for his wife and daughters, enables him to receive and visit his friends, and furnishes him pleasing and healthy occupations."

[181]

Jefferson's description of the bucolic life might have been written by any prosperous colonial farmer, but his interpretation of a simple formula for a happy farm existence differed hugely, just as the garden he planned for Monticello had little relation to the kitchen patch cultivated by farmers of lesser means.

In 1774, aided by an expert Italian gardener and vignerons from Tuscany, Jefferson designed a long, fairly narrow garden 686 feet long by 80 feet wide with a triangular bed at each end. Into this one and one-third acres were set, according to his garden book for that year, "Pisa carrots, Salmon radishes, Lattuga lettuce, Windsor beans, cluster peas, spinach, vetch, peas, green lentils, black-eyed peas, seven rows of Tuscany wheat, celery, radishes, cress, nasturtium"; these in addition to somewhat more prosaic turnips, cabbages, spinach, potatoes, cauliflower, onions, beets, cucumbers, brussels sprouts, succory, endive, salsify, and eggplant. The orchard included apple, cherry, almond, olive, greengage plum, plum peach and French chestnut trees and mulberries from England.

"I shall confine myself to native plants," Jefferson wrote in his *Notes on Virginia*, completed when he was governor of the colony, for "a complete catalogue of the trees, plants, fruits, &c. is probably not desired. I will sketch out those which would principally attract notice as being 1. Medicinal, 2. Esculent, 3. Ornamental, or 4. Useful for fabrication; adding the Linnaean to the popular names [in order to] convey precise information."[14]

Native plants useful in medicine, he wrote, were:

Senna, *Cassia ligustrina*; Arsmart, *Polygonum Sagittatum*; Clivers or goose-grass, *Galium Spurium*; Lobelia of several species; Palma Christi, *Ricinus*; James-town weed, *Datura Stramonium*; Mallow, *Malva rotundifolia*; Syrian mallow, *Hibiscus moschentos, H. virginicus*; Indian mallow, *Sida rhombifolia, S. abutilon*; Virginia marshmallow, *Napaea hermaphrodita, N. dioica*; Indian physic, *Spirea trifoliata*; Euphorbia Ipecacuanhae; Pleurisy root, *Asclepsias decumbens*; Virginia snake-root, *Aristolochia serpenteria*; Black snake-root, *Actaea racemosa*; Seneca rattlesnake-root, *Polygala Senega*; Valerian, *Valeriana locusta radiata*; Gentiana, Saponaria, Villosa & Centaurium; Ginseng, *Panax quinquefolium*; Angelica, *Angelica sylvestris*; Cassava, *Jatropha urens*.

Among native Virginia succulents, Jefferson included:

Tuckahoe, Lycoperdon tuber; Jerusalem artichoke, *Helianthustuberosus*; Long potatoes, *Convolvulas batatas*; Grenadadillas, Maycocks, Maracocks, *Passiflora incarnata*; Panic, *Panicum* of many species; Indian millet, *Holcus laxas, H. striosus*; Wild oat, *Zizania aquatica*; Wild pea, *Dolichos* (Clayton); Lupine, *Lupinus perennis*; Wild hop, *Humulus lupulus*; Wild cherry, *Prunus Virginiana*;

Cherokee plumb, *Prunus sylvestris fructu majori* (Clayton); Wild plumb, *Prunus sylvestris fructu minori* (Clayton); Wild crab-apple, *Pyrus coronaria*; Red mulberry, *Morus rubra*; Persimmon, *Diospyros Virginiana*; Sugar maple, *Acer saccharinum*; Scaly bark hiccory, *Juglans alba cortice squamoso* (Clayton); Common hiccory, *Juglans alba fructu minore rancido* (Clayton); Paccan, or Illinois nut, Not described by Linnaeus, Millar, or Clayton. Were I to venture to describe this . . . I should specify it as the *Juglans alba, foliolis lanceolatis, acuminatis, serratis, tomentosis, fructu minore, ovato, compresso, vix insculpto, dulci, putamine, tenerrimo*. It grows on the Illinois, Wabash, Ohio, and Missippi.

Black walnut, *Juglans nigra*; White walnut, *Juglans alba*; Chestnut, *Fagus pumila*; Hazlenut, *Corylus avellana*; Grapes, *Vitis*, Various kinds; Scarlet Strawberries, *Fragaria Virginiana* of Millar; Whortleberries, *Vaccinium uliginosum?*; Wild gooseberries, *Ribes grossularia*; Cranberries, *Vaccinium oxycoccos*; Black raspberries, *Rubus occidentalis*; Blackberries, *Rubus fruticosus*; Dewberries, *Rubus caesius*; Cloud-berries, *Rubus chamaemorus*.

In his third group, ornamental Virginia bushes and trees, Jefferson listed several that colonists a century earlier would have included as medicinal, notably the sassafras and elder:

Plane-tree, *Platanus occidentalis*; Poplar, *Liriodendron tulipfera, Populus heterophylla*; Black poplar, *Populus nigra*; Aspen, *Populus tremula*; Linden, or lime, *Tilia Americana*; Red flowering maple, *Acer rubrum*; Horse-Chestnut, or Buck's-eye, *Æsculus pavia*; Catalpa, *Bignonia catalpa*; Umbrella, *Magnolia tripetala*; Swamp laurel, *Magnolia glauca*; Cucumber-tree, *Magnolia acuminata*; Portugal bay, *Laurus indica*; Red bay, *Laurus borbonia*; Dwarf-rose bay, *Rhododendron maximum*; Laurel of the western country, Qu. species?; Wild pimento, *Laurus benzoin*; Sassafras, *Laurus sassafras*; Locust, *Robinia pseudo-acacia*; Honey-locust, *Gleditsia*; Dogwood, *Cornus florida*; Fringe, or snow-drop tree, *Chionanthus Virginica*; Barberry, *Berberis vulgaris*; Red-bud, or Judas-tree, *Cercis Canadensis*; Holly, *Ilex aquifolium*; Cockspur hawthorn, *Crataegus coccinea*; Spindle-tree, *Euonymus Europaeus*; Evergreen spindle-tree, *Euonymus Americanus*; Itea Virginica; Elder, *Sambucus nigra*; Papaw, *Annona triloba*; Candle-berry myrtle, *Myrica cerifera*; Dwarf-laurel, *Kalmia angustifolia, K. latifolia*, called ivy with us; Ivy, *Hedera quinquefolia*; Trumpet honeysuckle, *Lonicera sempervirens*; Upright honeysuckle, *Azalea nudiflora, A. viscosa*; Yellow jasmine, *Bignonia sempervirens*; Calycanthus floridus; American aloe, *Agave Virginica*; Sumach, *Rhus*, Qu. species?; Poke, *Phytolacca decandra*; Long moss, *Tillandsia Usneoides*.

Among those plants and trees he thought suitable for manufacturing purposes, Jefferson included:

Reed, *Arundo phragmitis*; Virginia hemp, *Acnida cannabina*; Flax, *Linum Virgianum*; Black, or pitch-pine, *Pinus taeda*; White pine, *Pinus stroba*; Yellow pine, *Pinus Virginica*; Spruce pine, *Pinus foliis singularbus* (Clayton); Hemlock spruce fir, *Pinus Canadensis*; Arbor vitae, *Thuya occidentalis*; Juniper, *Juniperus Virginica*, called cedar with us; Cypress, *Cupressus disticha*; White cedar, *Cupressus Thyoides*; Black oak, *Quercus nigra*; White oak, *Quercus alba*; Willow oak, *Quercus phellos*; Red oak, *Quercus rubra*; Chestnut oak, *Quercus prinus*; Black jack oak, *Quercus aquatica* Query?; Ground oak, *Quercus pumila* (Clayton); Live oak, *Quercus Virginiana* (Millar); Black birch, *Betula nigra*; White birch, *Betula alba*; Beach, *Fagus sylvatica*; Ash, *Fraxinus Americana*, *F. Novae Angliae* (Millar); Elm, *Ulmus Americana*; Willow, *Salix* Query species? Sweet Gum, *Liquidambar styraciflua*.

In addition, Jefferson wrote, six other plants were found in Virginia "when first visited by the English," but he believed they "most probably were natives of more southern climates and handed along the continent from one nation to another of the savages." These were:

Tobacco, *Nicotiana*; Maize, *Zea mays*; Round potatoes, *Solanum tuberosum*; Pumpkins, *Cucurbita pepo*; Cymlings, *Cucurbita verrucosa*; Squashes, *Cucurbita melopepo*.

Besides these plants, which are native, our Farms produce wheat, rye, barley, oats, buck wheat, broom corn . . . rice well enough . . . tobacco, hemp, flax and cotton . . . indigo. We cultivate potatoes, both the long and the round, turnips, carrots, parsneps, pumpkins, and ground nuts (*Arachis*). The Gardens yield musk melons, water melons, tomatas, okra, pomegranates, figs, and the esculent plants of Europe. The Orchards produce apples, pears, cherries, quinces, peaches, nectarines, apricots, almonds, and plumbs.

More than a hundred years after settlement, there was no discernible change in the basic vegetables and seasonings the colonial family planted and used. In April 1738, John Little advertised "new garden seeds" for sale at his shop on Milk Street, Boston. Had the shop been open for business in 1638, there could not have been any appreciable difference in its inventory. Presumably, if the shrewd retailer offers what his customers want to buy, then fifth-generation Boston colonists still preferred to plant the same foods their ancestors had brought over; compare Little's seed list with lists given in preceding chapters: "Choice good Windsor and Sandwich beans, Hot Spur and Marrow Fat Peas, Radish seed, Spinage and Orange

Local commissary agents purchased cereal grains, vegetables, and meat from farms for Revolutionary army troops and oats for horses. John Wilcox's request for the Connecticut Committee to pay him for six tuns (barrels) of flour and a load of oats sent to men camped at Roxbury in 1776 suggested payment be made through Haddam Town Clerk Hezekiah Brainerd's office.

Carrot, Sweet Marjoram and Colliflowers, hard Time Seeds, Large Summer Cabbage, Golden Purslan, Cabbage Lettuce, Parsnip and Double Marygold seed; all of the best sort and at a very reasonable rate."

With the approach of war, there was an obvious lessening of inclination to purchase luxuries; colonial advertising reflected a renewed concentration on gardening for sustenance. Thus, in February and March 1773, James and Arthur Jarvis, New York City agents for another slow-selling luxury line, Henry William Stiegel's Pennsylvania glass, divided their advertising space between the "American made glass" and a "very large and general assortment of earthen, delf, etc.," with a "variety of English garden seeds of the last year's growth, viz; Early Charlton, marrowfat, badmans dwarf and golden hotspur peas; winsor scarlet runners and large white kidney beans; lettuce and cabbage of various kinds, carrot, parsnip, radish, turnip, &c &c." With the exception of the lettuce, the seeds were all for foods that could be dried or otherwise preserved, just as they had been in the seventeenth century.

> *The world, and the fashion thereof, is so variable, that old people cannot accommodate themselves to the various changes and fashions of their day, and will not surrender their attachments to the good old way—while the young and the gay bend and conform readily to the taste of the times, and fancy of the hour. . . . The candor of the American Ladies is solicitously intreated by the Authoress, as she is circumscribed in her knowledge, this being an original work in this country.*   AMELIA SIMMONS[15]

During the seventeenth century, when Josselyn and other observant travelers reported on the herbs, vegetables, and wild fruits and nuts found growing here, as well as those which had been introduced by the first settlers, they listed as many plants as came to their attention—or at least all those they felt qualified to identify. Of these edible plants able to thrive in colonial soil, including the myriad herbs for seasoning and medicines, the actual number most commonly sent up to table comprised a comparative handful. No matter how industrious she might have been, the average colonial housewife simply did not have time to tend a garden of as many plants as were available to her. Sensibly, she planted only those which needed special care and cultivation. Those others which would grow well in their naturalized homes along hedgerows, between hills of corn, near the marshes, or deep in the woodlands were gathered when needed from the "wild" spot where they grew.

Thus even as late as the 1740s, Peter Kalm remarked while touring in New Jersey, "We frequently saw asparagus growing near the fences in a loose soil or [in] uncultivated sandy fields. It was also plentiful between the corn." Although some gardeners did tend and cultivate asparagus in their home plots, Kalm added, "I have likewise seen it growing wild in other parts of America."[16]

The grand English and French garden plans published in Europe at the time, with plantings in intricate mazes and formal separations by types of flowers and trees, had little relation to the kind of plot development possible—or even preferable—on the edge of a wilderness clearing. Only on a few estates in the more settled areas, such as those of men of superior wealth and vast holdings, as were the Faneuils, Franklands, Washingtons, Carters, and Jeffersons, could this kind of horticultural fancy be indulged. For the greater majority in New England farm and village homes and in small mid-colony and southern plantations, the housewife was fortunate who had time and help enough to keep separate her flower garden from her bed of culinary herbs, and to keep both of these apart from the necessary, and much larger, vegetable plot, mainly planted with turnips, cabbages, potatoes, and beans.

The common-sense planning of these various garden areas called for setting sweet-smelling and colorful "pleasure" plants near parlor or hall windows; the herbs were planted handily near the kitchen door or by the well; the strongly scented vegetables, which required large planting areas, were placed if at all possible where prevailing winds would blow their odors away from the house.

CHAPTER 3

The Other Necessaries

STILL SIX MILES OUT TO SEA, "more than one sense was agreeably affected," Peter Kalm wrote, "when the wind brought the scent of plants and flowers or that of fresh mown hay" to the eager passengers sailing toward the American coast in 1748.[17] The sentiment was a common note in other travelers' journals, for as the Reverend Andrew Burnaby said in 1759, sixty leagues from land "the air was richly scented with the fragrance of the pine trees."[18]

Many of the gardens which helped to supply this airborne welcome were painstakingly planned as well as tended. Whether necessary kitchen plot or formal flower garden, each almost invariably was laid out in a pattern. The simplest was made up of two narrow rows divided by a path, preferably wide enough for two people to walk down side by side, and usually bisected at intervals by narrower walkways. These facilitated the tasks of weeding and cutting as well as providing divisions of beds.

Such patterned plots were noted by Josselyn when, considering New England's "rarities,"[19] he remarked on the common use of beds. To the colonial gardener a seed, flower, or vegetable bed meant literally a square or rectangle built up from the ground surface, its sides strengthened by planks to prevent washing or falling away of soil. In the words of a popular encyclopedia of the time, a "bed is a piece of ground raised a little above the level of the adjoining ground and in which seeds are sown or plants set."[20]

Paths between beds were made of crushed shells or, in many seaboard gardens, of fine sand. The hard-packed earth, usually covered with a layer of gravel or small stones, or set with flat stepping stones, formed others. Grass paths would have been a luxury. Indeed, there seems no record they ever were planted even by the wealthiest homeowners. Those who could afford the expense of a gardener enjoyed small squares, oblongs, circles, or diamonds of grass—kept neat by tedious hand shearing—as soft decorative accents in formal flower gardens. Grass allowed to grow near the house was cropped by sheep, cows, or grazing horses; where such quadruped help was not utilized, the grass was cut less tidily by scythe or sickle.

Delight in a garden's loveliness appears in every diary of the time, the description varying with the diarist's temperament; some seemed different, if only momentarily, from their usual selves. Superior Court Judge Samuel Sewall, whose fear for his children's possible inability to find salvation often bordered on mania, wrote one April morning in 1699, "I saw and heard the Swallows proclaim the Spring." Judge Sewall makes clear, if only indirectly, that gardens were planted as close to the house as possible. On October 21, 1720, he wrote: "I heard Madam Winthrop's voice enquiring somthing. After a good while, *Clapping the Garden door* twice or thrice, she came in."[21] The proximity of animal pens to the house was pointed out years earlier by the judge when on July 18, 1687, he said, "I was startled in the morning as I was at prayer in the Kitchen, at a sudden unusual noise; which prov'd to be two Cows running in to our little Porch entry the iike to which never fell out before that I know of."[22]

The herb garden in front of the John Blair House kitchen and smoke-house gains a formal appearance from the clipped hedge and picket fence, double-diamond parterre patterns, and brick walks. Colonial Williamsburg, Virginia, restoration.

The New London justice Joshua Hempsted, who seldom mentioned flowers, was constrained to write in June 1730 that he spent the "afternoon at home picking up yellow blossoms in the lot," as pleasant a description of tending to an overabundance of dandelions as has ever been written— especially by a diarist whose garden records were usually of cabbages or turnips set near the cellar entry. His remarks, invariably preceded by the phrase "I was at home all day," recited the practical: "We sett out Cabbages"; "stackd ye cornstalks and gathered pumpkins"; "[we were] pruning Appletrees and covering the Ground over where the hogs had Rooted & [were] breaking Dung"; we plowed the turnip yard"; "I was helping Nathll about enlarging the Garden on ye back side the house by the wall and setting out Peach Trees their." Youngsters early learned to work in home gardens; those in the Hempsted family were so taught, according to the justice: "I hoed corn with Josh and Natte part of the day to Larn them to hoe."[23]

The many notes on nurturing fruit trees will make more sense to readers today if it is remembered that most trees were grown from seed in beds, then when five or six years old were set out in a permanent orchard space, often planned so that the same area could be used as grazing land. Fruit trees were pruned high to avoid damage by sheep or cattle. Judge Sewall wrote of grafting a "Stock pretty high out of the Cows reach, with cions from Mr. Moodey's Orange Pear, and grafted two Appletree Stocks with Mr. Gardener's Russetings; the Cow having eaten last year's Grafts all save one Twigg."[24]

Fencing near the houses usually was of wood palings set vertically, of triple or quadruple rows of horizontal planking, and sometimes of split rails set in what was called a snake fence, the description fitting its meandering line. Fences to keep animals within pastures often were combinations: "We made a fence of Brush, & poles & thorn trees to stop the place." Fences required mending each spring and fall to repair the ravages of weather and sometimes that of neighbors: "I top poled the fence & found several poles & Stakes wanting . . . Stole this winter in hard times."[25] Justice Hempsted surmised a fellow townsman had appropriated his fence rails to split for kindling.

Most colonists kept bees. A common practice was to plant those garden beds nearest the beehive with herbs that the busy inhabitants seemed to prefer: bee balm, lemon balm, thyme, and winter savory, thus following Thomas Tusser's sixteenth-century husbandry advice for May:

> Set hive on a plank, not too low by the ground
> Where herb with the flowers may compass it round
> And boards to defend it from north and north east,
> from showers and rubish, from vermin and beast.[26]

Bricks help to contain the gravel path and also form the floor of the hexagonal gazebo in the Benjamin Wales House garden at Williamsburg, Virginia.

Almost two centuries later expert advice was lengthier than Tusser's rhyme but had changed little: "[Beehives] made of straw are the best. The ingenious Mr. Wildman's hives are 'seven inches in height, and 10 in width. The sides are upright so that the top and bottom are of the same diameter. A hive holds nearly a peck!' Each hive should stand single on a piece of deal somewhat larger than the bottom of the hive for the bees to rest on when they return from the field . . . supported on a single post two and one half feet high. Weeds should not be permitted to rise near the hive. The stands should be four yards asunder so that the bees will find their way [to their proper hives]."[27]

Some of the orchards may not have been so tidy as their owners would have wished. Prudent husbandry, however, demanded careful control of insects. A common preventive measure required that "as soon as fruit trees are in blossom take a list of cloth or any other substance [thick vines sometimes were used, as were twists of corn husks] and dip it in tar and tie it round the body of your tree; from time to time supply the list with fresh tar until the fruit is ripe. This prevents ascent of insects up the tree."[28]

Other fruit trees must have presented a ghostly appearance on moonlit summer evenings when those who battled worms and moss followed advice to "scour and wash the trees with soap suds and whitewash the tree with lime."[29] Stone fruits, especially plums and peaches, were best protected if "two or three of the common land toads be confined in a pen of a foot diameter around the root of the tree; they will catch every insect that comes in the pen."[30]

Such remedies must have worked, for travelers in each century reported good yields. Labadist monks Danckaerts and Sluyter said in 1679 that "as we walked along Broadway we were astonished by the abundance and variety of its food supplies, its crop of wheat, apples and pears and still more wonderful peaches."[31]

Writing of Virginia in 1705, Robert Beverley noted that colonists had "for their recreation the farms, orchards and gardens [which] constantly afford them fragrant and delightful walks. In their woods and fields they have an unknown variety of [wild] vegetables to discover."[32]

As the eighteenth century progressed, many colonial gardeners built bowers with seats for leisurely enjoyment of flowers and herb beds. Some such retreats were grander, if no happier, than others, as Colonel Byrd wrote: "The afternoon was devoted to the Ladys who shew'd me one of their most delightful Walks. They conducted me thro' a Shady Lane to the Landing, and by the way made me drink some very fine Water that issued from a Marble Fountain and ran incessantly. Just behind it was a cover'd bench where Miss Theky often sat and bewail'd her fate as an unmarried woman."[33]

The garden house or gazebo—Byrd's "cover'd bench"—afforded a challenge to the colonial builder who enjoyed designing. Some gazebos were replicas of the Chinese temples that were painted on enameled chests; others were decorated with finials, copies of drops used on other furniture; and some reflected the design of the main house itself.

According to Mrs. Grant, "Every family had its garden, its well, and before every door a tree was planted" to provide a shaded summer work area "surrounded by seats."[34]

Whether or not bowers, tree seats, or gazebos could be afforded, there was one building, rarely considered today, that was always incorporated into the design of each colonial house lot. Earlier in this century, Chic Sale illuminated the craft and philosophy of "the specialist" and thus gave his name to a new American slang phrase when he publicized those small essential buildings almost unknown to today's younger generation.[35] Indeed, few meticulous restorationists of early American homesteads repair or replace the ancient privy.

The water buckets and shoulder yoke were hung at the entry nearest the well; thus, these at the 1678–1728 Hempsted House were kept in the porch, as the covered front entry room was called, handy to the typical New England plank-and-post well curb. Cedar pole sweeps, cradled in tree crotches, were used to drop and fill the bucket, then raise it. The natural branch-crotch formations and poles usually were brought to the house yard from the woodlot in winter and allowed to season for a year before use.

Two hundred and more years ago colonists gave special attention to the design and accouterments of the "necessary." It was given a well-chosen site and often concealed by flowering shrubs, these sometimes espaliered. At the least, a covering of ivy or honeysuckle was provided. Some necessaries were of simple board-and-batten construction. Others were replicas of the main house, clapboarded or laid in brick; some were given roofs of slate rather than of simple wood shingles. Many, especially in colder, more northerly climes, had interior walls as carefully plastered as the mistress's parlor.

Interior accouterments reveal a gregarious aspect of colonial life, another reminder that the seventeenth- and eighteenth-century American family accepted the Elizabethan indifference to privacy. Victorian prudery was far in the future: the average colonial necessary accommodated three visitors.

Neighbors of Colonel and Mrs. Joseph Webb called the Webb House in Wethersfield, Connecticut, Hospitality Hall, a community compliment often bestowed on a colonial town's most handsome house. The owner usually was the area's most successful merchant or its largest landowner; he was likely to be well traveled and better educated than many. It was expected that celebrities—social, military, or political leaders—would be received at the manor house, and it would have been no surprise for them to find that the necessary attached to the Hospitality Hall was of the same elegance as the manor house; in this instance it was provided with a semicircle of seats.[36]

The loss of a handsome necessary was cause for colonial outrage. Even now, after so many years, we sympathize with the advertiser in the Boston *News-Letter* of October 7, 1736, who announced, "On Tuesday Night the Fifth Instant, some evil-minded Persons stole out of the Garden of Nathanael Wardell, Chaise-maker, a Necessary-House, and carried it away. Whoever will discover the Person or Persons that did it, so as they may be brought to Justice and convicted thereof, shall have Ten Pounds Reward."

Genuine anger no doubt prompted Mr. Wardell to promise what in 1736 was a princely reward—10 pounds was more cash money than many families counted in a year. The amount also indicates the high cost of replacing a necessary suited to Wardell family standards, not to mention the high income enjoyed both by urban colonial carriage-makers and carpenters.

PART IX

The Kitchen Manufactory

CHAPTER 1

The Common Beverages

*Every family or every two families [have]
a spring of sweet waters betwixt them,
which is farre different from the waters
of England, being not so sharpe, but of a
fatter substance, and of a more jetty
colour; yet I dare not prefer it before
good Beere, as some have done, but any
man will choose it before bad Beere,
Wheay or Buttermilk.* WILLIAM WOOD[1]

MILCH COWS WERE SO SCARCE in many communities in the early days of settlement that butter and cheese were not commonly set on the table, but by the turn of the eighteenth century they were so plentiful that Massachusetts divine John Cotton observed ruefully in 1704 that the only things cheap in New England were milk and ministers.[2]

Travelers expected to be served a bowl of hot milk or pottage when they stopped at country inns, although sometimes attempts to vary the common dish proved disastrous. Mme. Knight, en route to New Haven in 1704, spoke of one unfortunate encounter with an innovative cook near "Suiting Devil else Kingsbridge," New York, where "They had nothing but milk in the house, which they Boiled, and to make it better, sweetened with molasses, which I not knowing of till it was down and coming up again . . . I believe it did me good in clearing my stomach."[3]

European travelers throughout the eighteenth century declared no colonial cheese ever met the standards of English Cheshire or Stilton; even the usually complimentary Kalm tended to dismiss the subject, saying, "there are [only] two kinds of cheese here, good and bad."[4] Whenever an inn or public house had managed to gain a reputation for dispensing good

A 1760 recipe to make currant wine at home: "Take your Currants full ripe Pick them [over]; & mash them—Then squeeze out the juice thro a Hare Bag or Sive—& to every Gallon of juice put Two Gallons of Water & to every gallon of Liquor put 3 pound & half of the best white Lisbon Sugar Lett it stand In the Tubb two days stirring it twice a day—then put it in a cask & lay a paper over the Bung. But not stop it Down close while [until] it has done Singing or working then let it stand for Nine or ten months. then rack it off thro: a fine flannell Bagg —then Rench the cask with some of the own wine and put it into the cask again & then let it stand for two or three months before you Bottle it off. When you rack it, to every 15 Gallons put in a pound of sugar and a quart of the Best Brandy & water—cold are Best."

cheese, those who could took advantage of the opportunity to enjoy the rarity; thus Judge Sewall during the summer of 1687 "carried my two sons and three daughters in the Coach to Danford; the Turks head at Dorchester, eat sage Cheese, drank Beer and Cider and came homeward."[5]

Whether it was served as a kind of curds and whey, as soft pot cheese, or with porridge, with bread and butter, or with berries or other fresh fruit, a bowl of milk was expected at the tables of the wealthy just as it was in the farm kitchen. Philip Fifthian, a tutor in the home of Robert Carter, Nomini Hall, in July 1774 said, "[we have] every Day good fruit for Dinner, caudled apples, hurtle-berries with milk." By the end of summer, of course, the diet changed with the season and the young tutor said that late in September, "Peaches & Fruit are omitted at Dinners, & Soup or Broth is brought in; milk and Hominey at Breakfast too are laid by & Coffee & Sage Tea brought in [instead]; Our Suppers are Coffee & Bred & Butter."[6]

Only slight regional menu variations were noted by Kalm in 1749 in his travels through New York:

The whole region about the Hudson River above Albany is inhabited by the Dutch: this is true of Saratoga as well as other places. During my stay with them I had an opportunity of observing their way of living, so far as food is concerned, and wherein they differ from other Europeans.

Their breakfast here in the country was as follows: *they drank tea in the customary way* by putting brown sugar into the cup of tea. With the tea they ate bread and butter and radishes; they would take a bite of the bread and butter and would cut off a piece of the radish as they ate. They spread the butter upon the bread and it was each one's duty to do this for himself. They sometimes had small round cheeses (not especially fine tasting) on the table, which they cut into thin slices and spread upon the buttered bread.

At noon they had a regular meal and I observed nothing unusual about it. (Dinner usually was meat served with turnips or cabbage.) In the evening they made a porridge of corn, poured it as customary into a dish, made a large hole in the center into which they poured fresh milk, but more often buttermilk. They ate it taking half a spoonful of porridge and half milk. As they ordinarily took more milk than porridge, the milk in the dish was soon consumed. Then more milk was poured in. This was their

Beverage accessories: glass wine bottles also used for oil or vinegar, in use from 1650 to 1740

Beverage accessories: three styles of canteens or kegs; ale shoe; brass mortar; toddy irons

supper nearly every evening. After that they would eat some meat left over from the noonday meal, or bread and butter with cheese. If any of the porridge remained from the evening, it was boiled with buttermilk in the morning so that it became almost like a gruel. In order to make the buttermilk more tasty, they added either syrup or sugar, after it had been into the dish. Then they stirred it so that all of it should be equally sweet.

Pudding or pie [which was] the Englishman's perpetual dish, one seldom saw among the Dutch, but they were indeed fond of meat.[7]

Few doubted that solid meat, cheese, and milk made up the healthiest diet. New Englanders had occasion to worry over the fate of the vegetarian, especially when they had before them the example of such as "Thos Lee Junr [who] died October the 20th 1733 in the 28th year of his age, a hopefull young man [who] never Eat any flesh or Cheese."[8]

In any colony where temperatures fell below freezing, one of the late-fall chores for the housewife was to churn butter to store for winter use. A thick layer of salt was tamped down on the bottom of a wooden firkin or stone crock, the butter then packed in as solidly as possible and another inch of salt ladled over the top before a tight lid or cover was set in place and the container stored in the cellar.

> *The ladies make wine from some of the fruits. . . . They principally take white and red currants for that purpose, since the shrubs of this kind are very plentiful in the gardens.*   PETER KALM[9]

Women were the brewers and distillers of colonial wines, brandies, and cordials, and usually also the ones who experimented with a variety of mashes to produce palatable beer and ale for the family. Sorting and washing berries and larger fruits, measuring out sugar and water, and chopping the herbs, spices, and other ingredients that went into the earthen crocks and copper pots were midsummer and autumn tasks for the kitchen, just as the pressing of cider was an undertaking for the men and boys in the backyard or orchard.

Berries and fruits, which grew in the open fields, beside the narrow unfenced roadways, and throughout the woodlands, were gathered for wine by country families; townspeople purchased their supply from farming Indians, who often peddled fruits and vegetables door-to-door, or from rural neighbors who brought produce to the weekly market fairs.

Kalm thought raspberries and cherries "which are cultivated and well taken care of" gave a finer wine than did wild varieties. However, he said

Beverage accessories: pewter tankard; leather jacks; wooden mugs and tankards

equally good wines were produced from "strawberries which grow in great plenty in the woods," from blackberries, which were "everywhere about the fields," and from the wild grapes that could be gathered from thick vines edging the woods of every colony.[10]

Other than sugar, the most expensive necessities in making home wine, cider, or beer were crocks in which the beverages were mixed and fermented, and the kegs, casks, and barrels in which to store each family's supply. Even more expensive were glass bottles and demijohns, the vast majority of which had to be imported from England and Ireland, for it was not until near the end of the colonial period that any American glassworks could be counted a stable and established manufactory.

In January and February 1773, Henry William Stiegel advertised that he, "Proprietor of the first American flint-glass manufactory in Pennsylvania, is just arrived in this city . . . and that the glass he offers to the public will be found to rival that which is imported and [will be] sold at lower prices." Stiegel offered "Quart, pint and half-pint decanters, pint crafts [carafes]; pint, half-pint and jill tumblers; syllabubs and jelly glasses; wine and water glasses, phials and other bottles for Chymists and Apothecaries, &c.". Among the "&c" had to be counted the householders who brewed their own liquors.[11]

Beverage accessories: polychrome Delft cups or mugs; pewter cup; burl cup; wood mug; blown wine tasters

[203]

CHAPTER 2

The Home Apothecary

Good housewives provide, ere sickness do come,
Of sundry good things in her house to have some.
Good aqua composita and vinegar tart,
Rosewater and treacle to comfort the heart;
Cold herbs in her garden, for agues that burn,
That ever strong heat to good temper may turn,
White endive and succory, with spinage enough,
All such with good pot herbs should follow the plough;
Get water of fumitory liver to cool,
And others the like, or else go like a fool.
Conserves of barberry, quinces and such
With sirops that easeth the sickly so much.

THOMAS TUSSER[12]

ROM THE TIME OF THE FIRST ENGLISH OUTPOST at Jamestown and the cold, huddled beginning at New Plymouth—as long, in fact, as America remained a frontier country—medicine often was of necessity a do-it-yourself project. It is no simple coincidence that the worn and yellowed journals mused over by collectors today include more recipes for soothing jellies and broths, medicinal herb teas, poultices, and general directions for care of the ailing than for preparing food. As a matter of fact, Johnson's eighteenth-century dictionary defined "recipe" as a medical formula.

The home cures and self-treatments prescribed for the ills and injuries most colonists sustained were those which had been handed down through the generations, often carefully memorized, sometimes garnered in small notebooks, now and again added onto the flyleaves of cherished copies of such popular texts as Samuel Sharpe's *Surgery*, first published in 1710.

For the vast majority of settlers, the woods and marshes, their doorstep gardens and hard-won orchards, served as their pharmaceutical supply

[204]

houses. The kitchen hearth and work table provided the laboratory in which astringents, liniments, salves and poultices, herb teas and soothing cordials, syrups, lozenges, and other comforts were brewed, distilled, and dispensed—as often by the colonial man as by his wife. The necessary utensils and equipment were at hand: mortars and pestles; bowls, crocks, bottles, and jugs; pots, saucepans, and cauldrons; sieves, ladles, spatulas, skimming spoons, knives, and hatchets;[13] homespun cloth for bandaging; needles and strong flaxen thread for sutures, borrowed if necessary from the home cobbling bench.

By way of comparison with home kitchen inventories of the time, Dr. William Salmon in his 1671 *Compendium of Physick* named the instruments and necessaries useful, besides "honesty and a good conscience," in the professional compounding of medicines. He suggested few articles that could not have been found disguised as cooking utensils in the well-furnished colonial kitchen, nor did he list needs for which other such utensils could not have been adapted if occasion demanded.

Chiefly, Dr. Salmon declared, the physician required a "brass Kettle; a Sieve, a Gord, Tongs, a Cauldron, a File; an iron Mortar; a Pestle; a glass Mortar and Pestle; a seperator; a Funnel; a Press; a Tile; a pair of Sheers; Vials; Boxes; Gally-pots; Corks, Spoons; Strainers and Spatulas." In addition, he needed

> an alembick [a gourd-shaped vessel for distilling, with a cap or alembic to convey products to a receptacle]; a seirce [or searce, which was a fine strainer]; a Press; Crucibles [any vessels, usually earthenware, which could endure great heat]; Retorts [usually glass vessels with a long downward-bent neck in which liquids being distilled were heated]; Bags, Weights and Scales, together with a pair of Goldsmith's bellows.
>
> The Chyurgical Instruments [with] which the Artist ought to be furnished are chiefly these: a Plaister Box; an Uvula Spoon; a Pair of Forceps, a spatula Lingua, an Incision knife, a Pair of Scizzors, a Small Razour, a stitching Quill and three Square Needles; with a case of good Launcets and a Salvatory; letting all be kept very sharp, clean and bright.

From their recipes, books, and diaries, the colonists' own knowledge of what probably ailed them can be deduced. A disproportionate number of cures and treatments suggested for certain categories of illness reveals the frequency with which they struck, as well as the average settler's lack of specific knowledge and his inability to diagnose except in the most general terms. By this method of deduction, of all ailments throughout colonial America ague must have headed the list as the most common (epidemical diseases such as smallpox aside), taking in southern colonies the form of

Polychrome Delft gallipot

malaria and in northern settlements that of influenza. To cure her family's frequent colds and agues, the colonial housewife picked medicines from herb garden and woods, well instructed by folklore and contemporary texts. Of all the books available, few were as popular as *English Herbals, or The English Physician Enlarged*, published by Nicholas Culpepper, apothecary-turned-physician, in London in 1653. The book, which enjoyed twenty-three editions until its last printing in this country in 1824, distilled Culpepper's knowledge of simples culled from ancient lore as much as from his own use and prescription of them.

For more than 170 years those who followed his advice believed that coltsfoot was "admirable for coughs" mixed with a "little oyle of annis seeds" and smoked in a tobacco pipe and that bryony, either white or black, would purge phlegm and "watery humours." Balm, taken inwardly, Culpepper said, proved an excellent remedy for a cold. Columbines, according to John Josselyn, would cure sore throats, for they "have a drying, binding quality." Culpepper's readers believed cottonwood "taken in a pipe" eased "coughs of the lungues" and "vehement headaches," while horehound "cleanses the breast and helps old coughs." Similarly, thyme cured coughs and shortness of breath, but persons troubled with a combination of coughs, shortness of breath, wheezing, a sore throat, and noises in the ears could best be comforted by hyssop, presumably taken as a tea. Culpepper deemed orpine inferior to no medicine in helping "quinsie of the throat." Rosemary cleared "stuffings in the head," and sweet marjoram was declared "an excellent remedy for cold diseases in the brain"; it also "easeth pains in the belly."

A decade after Culpepper's text first was published, the traveler John Josselyn had returned on his second voyage to note New England's "Rarities." Here he found "watermelon is often given to those sick of Feavers and other hot diseases with good Success," and reported that raven's-claw, "which flowers in May, is admirable for Ague." He wrote that colonists had been taught by the Indians the virtues of "sumach . . . to boyl it in

Mid-eighteenth-century home cures for asthma

Cure for the Asthma
Water Cresses, Brook Lime, Wild Sallendine,
garden Scurvy Grass — Three Spoonfulls of Each
of the Juices — Prickley Ash bark, black
Cherry bark — two Spoonfulls of Each of the
Bark to be put in to a Quart of good Rum and
to Make a bit bitter; Half a Jill at a time, to
be taken, three times a Day —

Cure for the Asthma
Turnips Slic'd up, and garlick, Lay one

Beer and drink it for Colds" and that cranberries were "good to allay the fervours of hot Diseases," indicating they may have been used thus in the form of a conserve.

Josselyn had admired the Indians he met in New England and particularly respected the hard-working webbes or wives. While he found the men "somewhat horse-faced," many of the women "have very good Features, seldom without a Come to Me or *Cos Amoris* in their countenance." All were "black Eyed, having even short Teeth, and very white; their Hair black, thick and long." The Indian women "generally [were] as plump as Partridges," and here and there he even met one "of a modest deportment." In his poem, Josselyn suggested that if others questioned "Whether White or Black be best, Call your Senses to the quest; And your touch shall quickly tell The Black in softness doth excell."

Josselyn's acceptance of native beauty, discussed at such length in a fairly small book, came as little surprise to English readers at home or in the colonies. Racial antagonism, in terms of bans against marriage between settlers and natives, was to develop later, particularly after the Revolution, and more often than not as a social byproduct of fearsome wars over land ownership.

Certainly, in his search for other natural rarities Josselyn needed the help of the Indians and their friendly acceptance of his motives in roaming the woodlands and marshes. At times they exchanged recipes for medicines. The somewhat casual manner in which Josselyn described one instance of on-the-spot medical collaboration suggests there must have been more free exchange of recipes between the original residents and the colonists than often has been believed.

The Jerusalem oak, Josselyn wrote, provided an excellent remedy for allaying the "stuffing of Lungs upon Colds, shortness of Wind and the Ptisick, maladies that the Natives are often troubled with," and he told of his experiments with additions to the local brew: "I helped several of the Indians with a Drink made of two Gallons of Molasses wort into which I put Oak of Hierusalem, Cat mint, Sowthistle, of each one handful; of Enula Campana Root one Ounce; Licuorice scrap'd, bruised and cut in peices, one Ounce; Sassafras root cut into thin chips, one Ounce; Annyseed and sweet Fennel-seed of each one Spoonful bruised."

After providing the list of ingredients as given to the Indians, Josselyn's description of the proper preparation of the tonic sounds as if he then directed his advice to the colonial housewife: "Boil these in a close Pot, upon a soft fire to the consumption of one Gallon, then take it off and strein it Gently. You may if you will boil the streined Liquor with Sugar to a Syrup, then when it is Cold, put it up into Glass Bottles, and take thereof three or four spoonfuls at a time letting it run down your throat as leisurely as possibly you can; do thus in the morning, in the Afternoon, and at Night going to bed." (A "close pot" was a kettle with a cover, and "soft fire" meant long brewing and simmering over glowing embers rather than hard-burning high flames.)

A second remedy using chips of sassafras, "the Ague tree," was given by Josselyn, perhaps for those less well equipped or able to afford the time the first necessitated: The chips of the root, he advised, should be "boyled in Beer" and were "excellent to allay the hot rage of feavers, being drunk."

Pains and aches except as to location (there are many notes on "pains in the side," which may have indicated unrecognized appendicitis): Headaches of migraine proportions, toothaches, gout and cramps, gripes and dysentery in a dread variety of degrees of seriousness, and fits—a general category which encompassed difficulties from mild epilepsy to killing strokes—were all treated with home remedies.

Josselyn noted that men and women kept their complexions but that many lost their teeth: "The women are pittifully Tooth-shaken, whether through the coldness of the climate, or by sweetmeats of which they have store, I am not able to affirm." Whatever the cause, a century later Peter Kalm recorded in his *Travels* that while the colonists used toothbrushes (made from the frayed twigs of dogwood and used with salt and water), toothache still was a common complaint. As a remedy, some colonists had learned from the Indians to boil the inner bark of the Canada elder, which they tied in a poultice, as hot as could be borne, on the cheek where the "ache was most violent."

Remedies for toothache were many; herbs believed to soothe these pains included burdock or clot-bur, which also was good, according to Culpepper, to soothe "the biting of mad dogs." Celandine, Josselyn said, the root of which "is manifestly hot and dry, if chewed helps toothache," as would the "juyce of Marigolds held in the mouth."

Kalm also noted that some colonists rubbed the bitter seed capsules of Virginia anemone into pieces, then dipped the small, rough pellets, which looked like cotton, into strong brandy and applied them to an aching tooth. When the ache was "attended by a swelling," the colonist was advised by Josselyn to boil "gruel or corn meal and milk [and] add while yet over the fire some lard or other suet and stir it well." The gruel then was placed on a piece of cloth and applied as "hot as possible" to the cheek, where it was kept "till cool again."

"White Hellibore," wrote Josselyn in *New England's Rarities Discovered*, grows in such abundance "that you may in a small compass gather whole Cart-loads of it." The Indians used it as a salve for their wounds, "annointing the wound first with Raccoons greese, or Wild-Cats greese and strewing upon it the powder of the Roots; and for Aches they scarifie the grieved part and annoint it with one of the foresaid Oyls, then strew upon it the powder. The powder of the Root put into a hollow tooth, is good for the Tooth-Ach. The Root sliced thin and boyled in Vineager, is very good against Herpes Milliares."

Where some medical recipes might include ingredients difficult to obtain in a hurry, Dr. Salmon and other writers of such compendia included alternative dosages, one of which presumably was sure to be available. For the distress of "Deafness and slow Hearing," for example, the choice of potions was between "The juyce of Radishes; fat of a mole, eele or serpent; juyce of an Onyun soaked in Sperrit of Wine and roasted; essence of a man's or bullock's gall, all very excellent. In difficulty of hearing, distilled Boyes Urine is Good; but better is the Oyl of Carawayes." What the age and gender of one's family might fail or falter in supplying, the kitchen herb garden surely could provide.

Vapors and qualms now have a connotation of emotion or weakness of will more than of physical distress. In the seventeenth and eighteenth centuries, however, they were causes of eventual if not immediate death. Then the meaning of "qualm" was closer to its Saxon source—"stroke of death"—and would have been explained by the educated colonist as "a sudden seizure of sickly languor."

No matter with what high degree of hope or with what calm of resignation they had boarded ship to partake of the promise of a better life in a new land, the stark reality they found reduced many emigrants to hysteria: "Besids, what could they see but a hidious & desolate wildernes, full of wild beasts & wild men? . . . which way soever they turned their eyes [save upward to the heavens] they could have little solace. . . . Summer being done all things stand upon them with . . . a wild & savage heiw. If they looked behind them ther was the mighty ocean which they had passed, and was now as a maine barr & goulfe to separate them from all the civill parts of the world . . . what could now sustaine them but the spirite of God & his grace?"[14]

The promise of what might someday be was little match for the tangled shadows of the all-too-real wilderness forests; truly this was the darkness that could be felt. The sudden and silent approach of unintelligible savages exceeded the accustomed fear of footpads and press gangs; the howling of wolves, the baying of loons, the myriad never-before-imagined "lizards and strange fish," the wild fowl screaming overhead—none had been envisioned on the civilized side of the Atlantic.

The terrifying horizon the colonists faced was incredibly different from the skyline at home, from which most trees long before had disappeared. The lack of even the dingiest stone-and-plaster city building, the filthiest and most crowded alley or lane, brought too forcefully, too suddenly, to many the realization of their aloneness and the unaccustomed need for true self-dependence; and too often, when they landed here, "It was winter . . . sharp & violent & subject to cruell & feirce stormes, dangerous to travill to . . . serch an unknown coast."[15]

Thus the repetition in seventeenth-century records of so many colonists suffering from hysteria and fits, of so many who "languished and died," of the stark hints of suicide.[16] Even the long delays in girding themselves to begin building adequate shelters can be explained fully only by recognizing the emigrants' overwhelming fear and despair at the seemingly impossible task they had essayed. Their fears are underlined again and again by the great number of potions and charms, the recipes and prescriptions devised to cure hysteria. Indeed, the need seems to have lessened little for many who arrived well past the beginning of the eighteenth century.

Although "all the wig-wams, huts and hovels the English dwelt in at their first coming [would be turned] into orderly, fair and well-built houses,"[17] what Bradford and other diarists had cried out against as a great howling wilderness was to remain just that for long stretches of both time and geography. Later emigrants to those first settlements would be greeted by the comforting sight of inns in palisaded forts and of common houses in which they could find temporary shelter while they searched for new hope. And eventually, there would be fair cities. A scant century after Plymouth, an English traveler would write he "could almost think himself at home in Boston,"[18] and by 1753 homes along the lovely Ashley in South Carolina —"Delightful villas—be they long renowned"—would be the subject of *London Magazine* verses.

These, however, were later havens for the sophisticated visitor. The first travelers over that "vast and furious ocean" who had little, as William Bradford said, but the "spirit of God and his grace" to sustain them were more fortunate than many of their less religious companions. For no matter how quaint the speech and spelling now seem, nor how easily three centuries have obscured the terror in colonial settlement history, the stark truth stands out.

The recipes for the old herbal potions with which the colonists sought to assuage fear and anguish had as their most effective ingredient the one never listed: the attentive kindness, patience, and love of some other person —the one who brewed the simples and spooned them up. Whether these recipes were memorized and handed down from generation to generation, or whether settlers sought advice from more learned members of the colony, the prescriptions available against sorrow and fear were much the same. Thus Dr. Bright, Culpepper reported, ordered hellebore "for such as are mad with melancholy," and his own seventeenth-century text recommended balm, "taken inwardly," or borage to cure "swooning and heart qualms." Spleenwort, he wrote, was "excellent good" for melancholy people: "Boyl it and drink the decoction but because a little boyling will carry away the strength of it in vapours, let it boyl but very little; this is the general rule for all Simples of this nature."

Among sweet marjoram's many virtues was its ability to soothe "such as are given to sighing." Thyme, too "resisted fearfulness and melancholy," and rosemary helped the memory. Rhubarb helped one to withstand melancholy when two drams of it were sliced thin, steeped overnight in white wine and then, the following morning, strained out, and the wine alone drunk.

The ancient herb of grace, rue, "strengthens the heart exceedingly," said Culpepper. "There is no better herb than this in pestilential time"— a description the young physician must have given with sadness and bitterness, for he wrote in an age that regularly knew the terror of wholesale death during epidemical plagues.

Physicians and laymen agreed that a conserve made of the "floures of the Clove Gillofloure and sugar is exceedingly cordiall and wonderfully above measure doth comfort the heart." Josselyn apparently was such a believer, for he included gillyflowers in the list of herbs and spices which he recommended to the emigrant in his book *Two Voyages*. Similarly, Culpepper suggested that the leaves and flowers of the marigold, brewed into a posset or other warm drink, were a "comforter of the heart and spirits." Tea made of southernwood was an old English palliative for hysteria.

Unless a few dried herbs, ready for use, had been tucked away among clothing or blankets, however, many such recipes could be prepared by newly arrived colonists only after the harvest of a second spring, or unless they were fortunate enough to arrive when it was possible to discover familiar leaves and roots during the growing seasons.

A small manuscript receipt book discovered amongst a trunkful of eighteenth-century papers and pamphlets near Hartford, Connecticut, recorded twenty-six medical formulas kept by one New Englander between 1721 and 1756. The receipts, in the order entered in the twenty-page homemade notebook, were titled:

> For the gravel; Mr. Hawes Green Oil how to make: To make a Stiptick Water; for a Fever; For a Rash or any Fever attended with an Eruption; A Gargle for a Sore Throat; For a Bruise or Rhumatick pains; For Cutts or wounds; A Purge Mixt in a Little Gruel; the Dose of Jallop; To Make Tincture of Hiera Piera; The Dose of Ipecacuanha; the Dose of Venice Treacle; The Dose of Rhubarb; Dose of Glauber Salt; For a Cough; for Consumption; For a Cough; Jalop for a Purge; Venice Treacle for a sweat in a

Cold; For an Ague; an other for an Ague; To make Snail Water or the Worm Cordial; A Receipt that Haels Blood; To Stop a Scouring in a Cow or Calf; To Cure an Ague.

The "green oil" formula directed the home practitioner to "Take of the tops of red sage in flower, Rosemary in flower, Baum, Green Chamemile, Wild Valerian root & Eight Ounces of the best Olive Oil; Infuse three pints for ten days or a fortnight & two or three spoonfulls of this Oil, taken inwardly is very good in any inwards Bruises or Spitting blood & Cases in the dread Palsey If attended with a Cough. 1756."

Among the other receipts were these:

For Consumption take Valerian root dried & made into tea.

For a Cough Take Three pints of Water abt half an Ounce of Liquorish one Ounce of Raisons in the Sun stoned two fige Sliced in a little Barley boiled till it comes to quart then strain it off.

The Dose of Rhubarb: 30 or 40 grains chew'd or Grated into a glass of wine & water.

an other for an Ague: Take 12: Grains of Saffron & dry it by the fire then Beat it to powder put it into a Glass of Canary take it for ye Ague about an hour before you think Ye fitt will come then warm your bed & go into coverd very close after the Hott fitt uncover the cloths gently & their lye till next morning. my Fathers receipt.

For a Fever: Take Salt of Wormwood three Drams put it into a large Bason and pour upon it six Spoonfulls of Juice of Lemons, and stir them together with a spoon till the fermentation is Over. then add to it half a Pint of white wine & water Equall parts & sweeten it with fine Sugar and take a wine glassfull every four hours, Purge & bleed.

A Gargle for a Sore throat: Take honey one Spoonfull Desolve it in half a pint of sage Tea. then add two Spoonfulls of Vinegar, Brandy or Rum: three Spoonfulls of Salvolatile, Two or three spoonfulls—Gargle your throat three or four times a day warm— But don't neglect to Purge with mana & Glauber Salt & Bleed in time if Violent.

"Mana" (or "manna") referred in the pharmacy to a gentle laxative derived from the juice or sap of the ash tree or the larch; the reference here may, however, have been to coarsely ground wheat of the consistency used in puddings. Glauber salt was named for the German chemist Johann Rudolf Glauber (1604–68), who first made sulphate of sodium artificially.

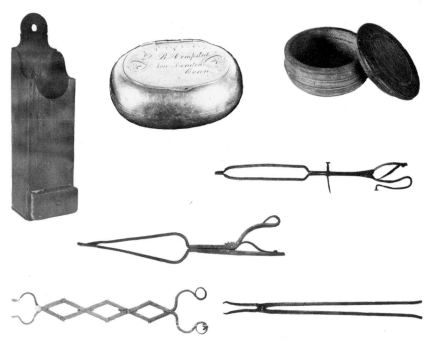

Tobacco accessories: wall box for pipes and tobacco; silver and wood snuffboxes; pipe or coal tongs

CHAPTER 3

The Dye Pot

Apparel is to distinguish and put a difference between persons according to their Places and Conditions.

URIAN OAKES[19]

ANY GREAT BRASS AND IRON KETTLES listed in old inventories survive as mute reminders of colonial love of color in household linens and wearing apparel. Huge by later standards, such vessels held five to forty gallons and had a special usefulness each spring and autumn for the long boiling and simmering needed to manufacture dyes at the hearth or in the kitchen dooryard. These same caldrons later would be hauled back close to the chimney when salvaged grease and tallows were reboiled and skimmed (or, in some areas, waxy bayberries harvested) for the seemingly endless work of providing candles.

The tedious, steamy transformation of flower petals and stems, leaves and grasses, roots and barks, nut hulls and berries into dyes could not have been a favorite chore save for the promise it held of bright colors and subtle shadings. Dyeing was work done out of necessity by those who also grew flax and who spun and wove their own linens.

Dyeing and weaving were a challenge to the ingenuity of the greater number of housewives in average circumstances early and late in colonial history: during the first generations of settlement because family fortunes and social stature were still evolving, and later because it had become unpatriotic to import fabrics. During prosperous periods, after towns and commerce had been established, the wives of merchant-shippers; of planters who grew money crops of tobacco, rice, corn, or wheat; of professional men; and of the more successful artist-craftsmen could well afford to purchase finished and dyed fabrics.

[216]

It was with pride that Benjamin Franklin wrote from Paris in 1766, "It was a Comfort to me to recollect that I had once been cloth'd from Head to Foot in Woolen and Linen of my Wife's Manufacture, that I never was prouder of any Dress in my Life, and that She and her Daughter might do it again if it was necessary." Lest Deborah fear her husband intended a return to a life of austerity, Franklin was quick to add, "Joking apart, I have sent you a fine piece of Pompadore Sattin, 14 yards, cost 11 shillings a yard; a silk Negligee and Petticoat of brocaded Lutestring for my dear Sally; with two dozen Gloves."[20]

These more fortunate women were a fairly small minority, even in the best of times. The families of the overwhelming numbers of village artisans and small farmers, from the Bay Colony to the later Carolinas and Georgia, spun, wove, dyed, and seamed, if not all, as much as possible of the clothing they needed.

This was an era (now dimmed almost out of memory by mass manufacture, minimum wages, and insured mortgages) when one's costume, like the size and furnishing of his house, provided instant identification of his place in the social and economic scheme. The old saying that "a place showeth the man, and it showeth some to the better and some to the worse" had a hard, literal meaning in early America: the color of his apron proclaimed the journeyman and his apprentice, as did homespun the farmer, and silk and fine woolen the clergy. The amount of silver and gold used in buckles and points, the extent of waistcoat satin and lace, similarly accounted the hard-money wealth of the merchant or planter. Such visual identification of rank and fortune through color, fabric, and styling was maintained consciously and at times enforced by law.[21]

North or south, the seventeenth- and eighteenth-century settler would have been amused, if not outraged, by any pretension, even in costume, to equality among individuals. All might be equal in the eyes of God, but no such leveling was allowed in man's relationship with man.

The notion that the first Plymouth settlers or the Puritan-Congregationalists at Boston and New Haven daily wore drab blacks and grays was a romantic invention imposed on popular history in the nineteenth century. Included among the silks and velvets in the wardrobe chest that William Bradford brought when he arrived to help build a new Eden were a violet-colored cloak and a crimson waistcoat. Elizabethans by heritage and inclination, the lesser members of the *Mayflower* company wore the russets, greens, yellows, reds, and blues they would have worn had they remained carpenters, tailors, coopers, yeomen, or servants in England. Though some of their religious philosophy differed radically, this fondness for colorful costume changed only as the colonists' pocketbooks and social circumstances ordained.

This intends that we keep within the line and place, *that providence has set us. We must not without God's call quit our post, thrust our selves into* anothers prov-ince, *with a conceit that* there *we may best serve, and promote the good of the world. But herein observe the will of God by keeping to the service that belongs to our station, which providence has made our peculiar business. Thus every man is to serve his generation by moving in his own orb; and discharging those offices that belong to that order that the government of heaven has assigned him to.* EBENEZER PEMBERTON[22]

The English sense of social order—which distinguished between royalty, noble aristocracy, and the "other ranks," between the worth of landowners and tradesmen, merchants and clerks, yeomen and tenant farmers—sur-vived the Atlantic crossing with fewer bruises than did its emigrant-advo-cates. Thus in New England the intellectual and educated (thereby giving the clergy a great edge), outranked the not-so-literate majority. The land-owner was superior to the shopkeeper, who often was not a property holder and hence could not vote. The physician was a notch above the dentist, sur-geon, or apothecary, and the merchant-shipper outranked most of those who supplied the goods he traded.

Children were inferior to adults, as were women to men, although most would have agreed with John Cotton that "women are creatures without which there is no comfortable living . . . it is true of them what is wont to be said of governments, that bad ones are better than none."[23] Lest even this unenviable compliment tempt her to slip out of her place in the natural order, Cotton added that a wife should stay "at home, edu-cating of her children, keeping and improving what is got by the industry of man."[24]

Better to stand at the wheel, ply the needle, weed the garden, and watch that interminable kettle than to chance the fate which dealt so terrifyingly with women who read and wrote in preference to household chores. For who had not heard the whispered details—when indeed they were not thundered from pulpits—of witchcraft accusations against Ann Hutchinson for her theological debate, or did not fear the insanity that plagued the wife of Governor Edward Hopkins? She, it was said, might have kept her wits had she not meddled "in such things as are [more] proper for men whose minds are stronger."[25]

In the nominally Anglican south, the position of the clergy was kept closer to the lower social esteem granted its members in England. Similarly, there was not the same admiration for those who had only intellectuality to market. However, as in the north, the larger a family's landholdings and the greater the number of tenants, the higher its rung on the social ladder. And their clothes were used to show it. The handful of truly large landholders (whose property encompassed the hundreds of acres necessary for a planting system that seldom replenished the soil) had an extra advantage on this social scale. The nature of the southern economy, with great distances separating the larger plantations, caused each owner often to act as his own merchant-shipper, maintaining his own warehouses and wharves. Living usually within or near the boundaries of these early semifeudal estates were the small farmer-artisans who would have been found working in villages in the north. Thus the early plantation might support its own mills, tanneries, and repair shops, each run for the owner by white tenants or contractors, who in some areas later were replaced by slaves they had trained. (Although some slaves were set to work assisting these tenant-farmer–craftsmen, the vast majority of the black thousands worked in the fields.)

Obviously, keeping the average colonial family, who had come here in hopes of a better standard of living, within these bounds of social rank was no easy task. Both the clergy-influenced leaders of New England and the governors of the more southerly provinces were in agreement that "virtue is like a rich stone, best plain set." Both passed laws—generally unsuccessful of enforcement—against sumptuous use of laces and colorful imported finery. Their reasons for doing so seem to have been influenced not so much by their right-hand positions as by common sense.

The English investors who backed plantations with ships and food and clothing staples expected the return on their investment to be achieved by regular export from the colonies of native raw produce, hence the tendency to remind the settlers that time and money spent in attempts to keep up with London fashion might better be used to pay old debts. Plain clothes were more suitable for hard frontier work and certainly effective reminders to the common man and woman of their mortgaged position.

In 1639 Massachusetts churches exhorted against those prone to follow "new fashions and to fall into excessive costliness," and in 1650–1651 the General Court expressed its "detestation that men and women of meane condition, education and calling, should take uppon them the garbe of gentlemen by wearing of gold or silver lace or buttons or poynts at their knees, or walke in great boots, or women of the same ranke wear silke or tiffany hoods or scarfs." The court in 1718 worried that "long credit" was causing "extravagance and excessive consumption," and in 1721 took action against the hospitality and gift-giving features of funerals as causing "impoverishment of many families."

To curb a tendency toward excessive finery in the wilderness, the Virginia assembly in 1619 saw to it that cash was spent on colonizing equipment rather than unseemly fashion by imposing a tax on a bachelor's apparel; a married man was taxed on his own wardrobe and that of his family. In 1650 Virginia legislated against ribbons woven with silver and gold threads, and against silks generally, to the extent that should any be imported, they were ordered confiscated.

Costly attire in itself might not have been a sin, but bankruptcy came close.

For all those who had no "long credit" or much hope of ever achieving it, there was a wealth of fashionable color to be gathered from the gardens and orchards, roadsides and woodlands. The adjurations were against imported finery and did not extend to the colors an imaginative hard-working colonial housewife might achieve in her dye pot.

The necessary pots and kettles were at hand; the larger ones stored in the buttery or lean-to, or sometimes under bedsteads, to be brought out as needed. The supply of long stirring-sticks, whittled smooth after the bark had been stripped off and the wood dried, would be taken down from handy storage pegs set into the kitchen beams or brought from storage baskets in the garret. Only the winter evening hours of the men and boys had been expended to prepare those hard maple, oak, or hickory utensils, and more would be made; for the sticks became frayed from too much time in the boiling kettle and often had to be dicarded after one day's use. The brass and iron skimming-spoons, the long-handled ladles and forks, the long iron stirrers with hooked ends later would be scoured and returned to their hangers, ready again for their more accustomed use in cooking.

The majority of dyes were made by boiling leaves, roots, barks, and hulls. For those ingredients—certain clays and dried roots, for example—which had to be pounded and granulated, the well-equipped kitchen provided a brass mortar and pestle. Women who had not this extra utensil, and did not want to see a prized wooden mortar impregnated with dye, improvised a mortar by placing a small square of fabric on the hearth or the stone doorstep; a stone or hammer served as a pestle.

The scarlet and the black oaks, the white and the live oaks all contributed barks used in tanning and dyeing. The bark of red oak provided shades of brown and deep yellow; the "blackjack" bark of scrub oak, when steeped with that of red maple, produced a black especially good for cottons; the bark of the black oak was brewed into a golden yellow for linens and woolens.

Other shades of yellow, from pale lemon to deep saffron bordering on orange, were boiled up from goldenrod, from woodwaxen, from the flowers and leaves of garden balsam, sweetleaf, or horse laurel, from barberry roots, the petals of St.-John's-wort, the bracts of Jerusalem artichokes, the roots of yellowwood, and the leaves of devil's-bit.

Blue was made from wild indigo (imported indigo later was cultivated in southern colonies) and from imported woad. Violet-colored juice from the petals of the iris, Josselyn's "fleur-de-luce," produced pale purple, while cedar tops and lilac leaves were used for a deeper tone of that royal color. Oak, walnut, and maple barks produced brown, as did the ripe hulls of walnuts and hickory nuts.

Clear reds, vermilions, and crimsons were more difficult to achieve; they were made from dyer's moss, madder root, and sometimes the roots of nightshade and brazil wood. Sumac berries boiled carefully produced a tan-red; pokeberries boiled with alum produced crimson.

Black was perhaps the most difficult of all to manufacture in a simple dye that would resist fading. (Even if the Massachusetts Puritans had wanted to wear the somber color regularly, it would have been an expensive choice.) Two of the most successful black dyes and writing ink made in the colonial home were one from the gallberry, or oak gall, mixed with vitriol and used to dye woolens and leather and one from green walnut hulls. Linen, boiled first in water with the leaves of the common field sorrel, was removed, dried, then boiled again with logwood and copperas to make it jet-black.

Another difficult dye color was true purple. The juice of pokeweed berries could be used to dye paper a deep purple "as fine as any in the world . . . [but] it is a pity no method has yet been discovered of making this color last on woolen or linen: it fades very soon."[26] An especially rich blue was produced for worsteds and linens when the bark of red maple was boiled in water to which copperas (such as that used by hatmakers) was added. The woven fabric then was boiled in the finished dye.

The sassafras tree proved versatile not only for all sorts of medical recipes. The bark also found its way into the dye kettle to provide a "fine lasting orange" color for worsted "which does not fade in the sun." The women "use urine instead of alum in dyeing and boil the dye in a brass boiler because in an iron vessel it does not yield so fine a color."[27]

Not the least of the various dyes the colonists provided for their families were those used as writing inks. Though commercially made inks could be purchased from stationers, the family that dyed its own fabrics, or "stuffs," also usually produced its own ink for keeping household accounts. As with some fabric colors, the problem was to produce ink that would not dim from long exposure to air and light. Simple inks could be made from deep-hued berry juices, but many of these faded quickly. Long-lasting black ink was made from red-maple bark, and the green peel of black-walnut hulls yielded a "black color which could not be gotten off the fingers in two or three weeks time though the hands were washed ever so much."[28]

Sumac berries when boiled with their branches produced a black ink tincture, as did the sap of poison ivy. Such an ink was "so strong that the letters and characters made upon linen with it cannot be removed, but grow blacker the more the cloth is washed. Boys commonly marked their names with this juice."[29]

A 1760 formula for whitener: mixed rain water, pipe clay, soap, and glue, to be stirred while boiling for two hours

Carding and spinning: 1786 carder; clock flax wheels; small wheels; niddy-noddy; swift

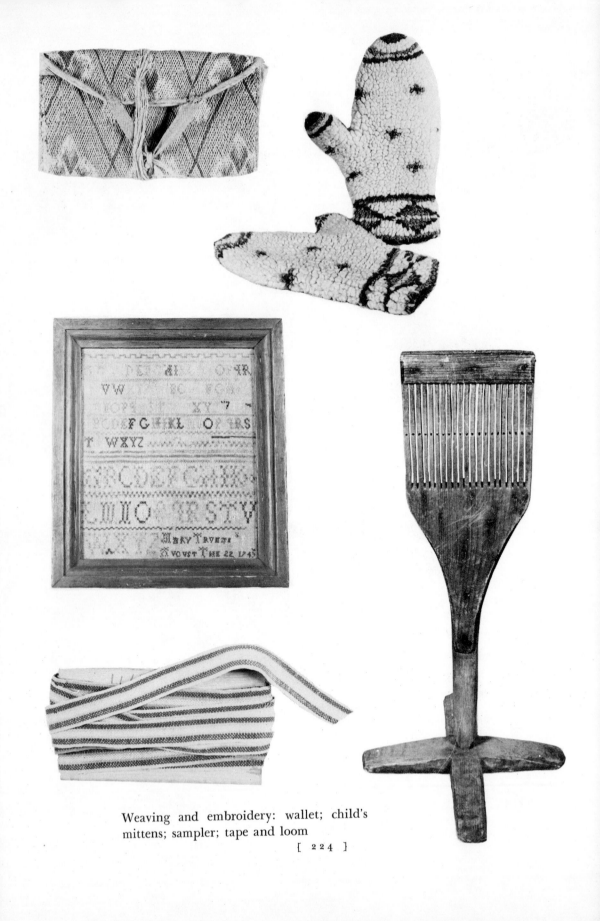

Weaving and embroidery: wallet; child's
mittens; sampler; tape and loom

[224]

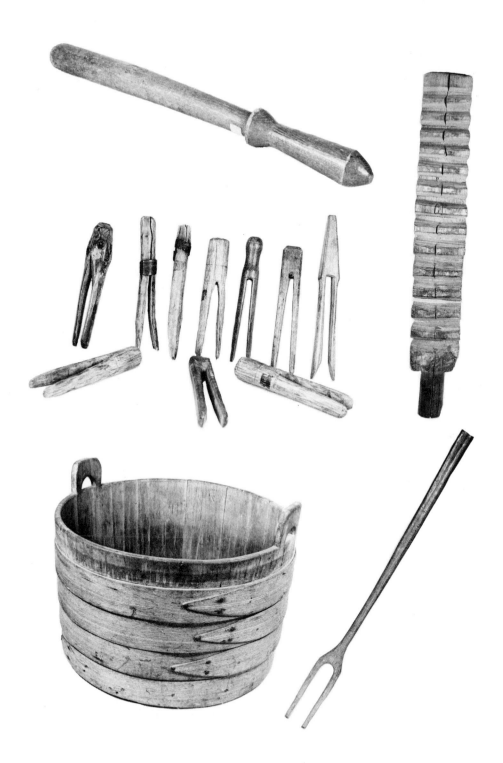

Laundry accessories: clothes stirrer; scrubboard; clothespins; tub; lifting fork

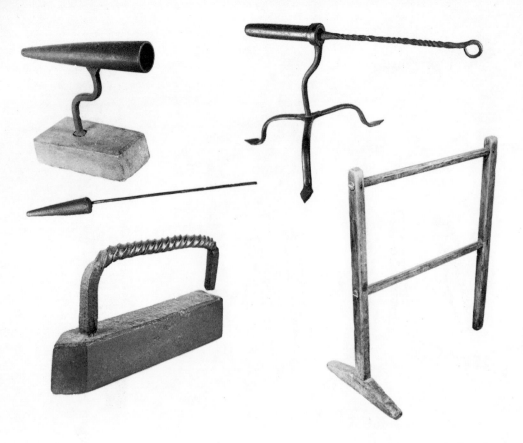

Ironing utensils: goffering irons for ruffles; flat or sad iron; clothes-dryer rack

CHAPTER 4

The Candle Mold

Wife, make thine own candle,
Spare penny to handle;
Provide for thy tallow ere frost cometh in,
And make thine own candle ere winter begin.
THOMAS TUSSER, *Five Hundredth Pointes*

TUSSER INCLUDED THESE VERSES four centuries ago in his popular "Directions to Housewifes," included in *Five Hundredth Pointes,* one of the books most commonly brought here by early settlers. It was the mistress of a rare colonial kitchen who never had reason to ponder the common sense of Tusser's advice, if not the actual need to follow it; throughout the pilgrim century candles were an expensive luxury—and remained so until well after the Peace of Paris ended the Revolution in 1783. So commonly accepted was the old English precept of saving the "lights" that Shakespeare had complimented the good "husbandry" in heaven when on a starless night "their candles are all out," a thrifty sentiment echoed here in America more than 150 years later when Poor Richard remarked on the wisdom and wealth accruing to terrestrial residents who were early to bed and early to rise—at least they saved the twopence a candle cost.[30]

It was more than a generation after settlement before many candles were made in colonial kitchens, and years after the first homes were built before tallow candles became common. Settlers were not apt to slaughter those first few cattle which had survived the Atlantic crossing; however, as the Reverend Higginson noted in 1630, "Though New England has no tallow to make candles of, yet by the abundance of fish thereof it can afford oil for lamps."[31]

The foresighted had brought with them the saucer-shaped wooden, tin, or iron cruses, or pottery grease lamps, which many today refer to as

[227]

betty or phoebe lamps. Those who had not packed old grease lamps for the voyage made new ones here of native "fatt clayes" and hardwoods or traded with the Indians for their hollowed-out stone-bowl lamps.

Many settlers adopted a more pleasantly scented source of light than the smoky flame of the grease-lamp, preferring, as Higginson explained, "such candles as the Indians commonly use . . . and they are nothing else but the wood of the pine-tree, cloven in two slices, something thin, are so full of the moysture of turpentine and pitch that they burne cleere as a torch."

The seventeenth-century housewife's natural objection to candle-wood or lightwood was voiced by William Wood. He said he could not commend the long strip of the pine heartwood for much "singular good, because it droppeth a pitchy kind of substance where it stands."[32] For a longer-lasting light, chunks or knots of pitch pine were burned on the hearth. Later the lightwood was set aflame in a kind of brazier called a cresset—a basket formed of strips of iron suspended from the fireplace lintel or a ceiling beam, or set atop a specially wrought stand.

Strips of pitch pine sometimes were burned (a two-foot sliver lasted an hour) in iron rushlight holders; these dripped tar on tabletops as the baskets did on the floors. The great majority of these pincerlike holders were brought from England or the Continent, where they had been made originally to hold grease-soaked rushes. As soon as there was time to search them out, rushes were gathered from marshy areas here. When dry, the outer skin of the rush was stripped off, and the inner pith dipped in kitchen grease or "scummings" to provide a type of candle that remained popular in village and rural homes for two hundred years.

William Cobbett wrote:

I was brought up by rushlight, and I do not find that I see less clearly than other people. My grandmother who lived to be ninety, never burnt a candle in her house in her life. I know that I never saw one there. She used to get meadow rushes when they had attained their full substance but were still green . . . and [took] off all the green skin except for about a fifth of the way around the pith . . . to hold it together.

The rushes being thus prepared, grease is melted and put into something that is as long as the rushes are. They are put into the grease; soaked in it sufficiently; then are taken out and laid in a piece of bark taken from a young tree.

The rushes are carried about by hand; but to sit by, to work by or to go to bed by, they are fixed in stands made for that purpose. These have an iron part something like a pair of pliers to hold the rush, which is shifted forward as it burns. These rushes give a better light than a common dip candle and they cost next to nothing.[33]

Colonists early discovered the silver-green bayberry growing in abundance along the seaboard, from the berries of which a kind of wax or tallow could be boiled. Swedish colonists called it the tallow shrub, and the English named it the candleberry tree. The bayberries were gathered in the fall, about the time of first frost, and put to boil in huge kettles. After the first skimmings the dark, opaque wax was reboiled to refine out impurities and to achieve the preferred transparent green.[34]

The clean wax was kept in a melted state at the fireside. Sometimes wicks were made from the silky down of milkweed, but more often were spun of flax, hemp, reworked yarns, or twisted cotton threads. The wicks were looped over thin rods of hickory or other hardwood, two, four, or six at a time, then dipped carefully into the wax kettle, drawn out and held until dry, then dipped, and dipped, and dipped again and again until the desired candle circumference had been achieved. The housewife whose budget allowed purchase of an iron, pewter, or tin candlemold, into which wax or tallow might be poured around taut wicks, must have thought that simple utensil a timesaver indeed.

No diary record is found of manufacturing beeswax candles at home, although surely some colonial families attempted the difficult rolling of these wax tapers. If not made here, beeswax candles, required in the Catholic and Anglican churches of the middle and southern colonies, were imported.

As the supply of cattle increased, the sensible wife combined tallow with bayberry wax. This combination saved some of the time spent gathering the berries and skimming the wax, and produced candles which did not bend or melt so easily in warm weather. They retained the slight scent of the berry, which many appreciated. Virginia's Robert Beverley remarked at the turn of the eighteenth century, "If an accident puts a [bayberry] candle out, it yields a pleasant fragrancy to all that are in the room; insomuch," he added, alluding to a common need in close winter houses, "that nice people often put them out on purpose to have the incense of the expiring snuff."[35] Bayberry wax was used as a soap base; Peter Kalm declared it made a most agreeable shaving lather. Because it melted and then hardened again quickly, the wax served as a wound plaster and could be used to seal letters.

By the mid-eighteenth century those who had enough cattle to slaughter and who could afford to keep the suet preferred to make tallow candles rather than expend the many hours needed in bayberry-wax manufacture. Thus the tallow candle, an expensive luxury in the early days, became the least expensive as the colonial era neared its end. True to the proverb that time is money, tapers of tediously gathered and hand-dipped bayberries rose in price in the markets.

Where expense was no problem, the candle preferred above all others was the translucent white spermaceti. "The advantages which the *new* candles have, besides their rarity, are: they hardly ever have to be snuffed . . . they never drip and though it may be warm in the room . . . they do not become soft, nor do they melt in the hand when being carried as tallow candles do."[36] But their cost was almost five times that of tallow. Bayberry "tallow is dearer than common tallow, but cheaper than wax," Kalm reported from Philadelphia in 1748. At that time he found that common tallow candles were sold at one-half shilling per pound, bayberry candles at one shilling per pound, and "wax costs as much again."

True enough, agreed James Clemens, a Boston chandler, his wares did call for greater cash outlay at the time of purchase, but, he assured his customers, they really proved a saving, for "Sperma Ceti Candles" exceeded "all others for Beauty, Sweetness of Scent when extinguished; Duration, being more than double Tallow Candles of equal size; Dimension of Flame, nearly four Times more, emitting a fast easy expanding Light, bringing the Object close to the Sight, rather than causing the Eye to trace after them, as all Tallow Candles do, from a constant Dimness which they produce. One of these Candles serves the Use and Purpose of three Tallow ones, and upon the whole are much pleasanter and cheaper."[37]

Other chandlers continued to appeal to the thrifty householder, taking every opportunity to slight the new lights, as did Edward Langdon, "in Fleet Street near the Old North Meeting House," who in 1750 offered "a Quantity of Hard Soap by the Box, soft Soap by the Barrel, and *good old Candles* both Mould and Dipt . . . also Mould Candles of Bayberry Wax, all by the Box or by Retail."[38]

When the housewife had a choice between being able to pay for one disagreeable job by doing another herself, her inclination was to color fabrics in her own kitchen from home-produced vegetable dyes and hire someone else to make the tallow candles and soap her family needed.

That this was a popular decision can be read between the lines of a paragraph in Benjamin Franklin's *Autobiography*. Franklin's father, Josiah, had been trained in the trade of dyer but had been forced to give up that business in Boston for lack of custom. To maintain his large family, the senior Franklin instead became a "Tallow Chandler and Sope Boiler," apprenticing young Benjamin to himself: "At 10 years old, I was taken home [from school] to assist my Father in his Business. . . . I was employed in cutting Wick for the Candles, filling the Dipping Mold, and the Molds for cast Candles, attending the Shop, Going of Errands, et c."

Lighting accessories: candle dryers, also used for herbs; snuffers; late-seventeenth-century and eighteenth-century adjustable-height candle-stands

It was a trade Franklin, who protested he wanted only to read, loathed. He must have been a most persuasive youngster and to have had a more than ordinarily understanding father, for Josiah in spare moments took Benjamin to visit other tradesmen, attempting to find some kind of work the boy might prefer to candle molding and soap boiling. Finally, although one printer in the family seemed enough, Josiah allowed Benjamin to be apprenticed to an older son, James, in whose shop it was hoped the future diplomat (and a founder of America's first library association) could get "enough of letters."[39]

Lighting accessories: wall candle box; small candle or tinder box; tinder-box with candleholder

Candlestands: early X-base wood stand; adjustable-arm iron stand

Lighting accessories: rachet hanging-style grease lamp; ovoid table-type grease lamp with hanger; work lights in suspension and combination suspension and table style

Lighting accessories: wall candleholders: spike, bracket style; tin sconce

Lighting accessories: seventeenth- and early-eighteenth-century pewter and brass candlestick holders

Lighting accessories: horn and glass lanterns used in the eighteenth century with wood, iron, and tin frames

PART X

"*A Country New and Wonderful*"

Can the mind have a greater pleasure than in contemplating the rise and progress of cities and kingdoms . . . than in perceiving a rich and opulent state arising out of a small settlement or colony? America is formed for happiness.

ANDREW BURNABY,
Travels through the Middle Settlements

ON APRIL 27, 1759, the Reverend Andrew Burnaby, Vicar of Greenwich, embarked from England "with several North-American gentlemen" for Virginia. His ship accompanied "thirty-three sail of trading vessels" also bound for the colonies. On July 3 he noted, "We had fine weather, with a gentle breeze [and] were, according to the commodore's reckoning about sixty leagues from land. The air was richly scented with the fragrance of the pine-trees." Two days later they sailed "through the capes into Chesapeak Bay and at eight in the evening came to an anchor in York river, after a voyage of almost 10 weeks." Thus did the vicar, "going to a country . . . new and wonderful," begin his observations of the "middle settlements in North America," which notes were "the fruit of the most impartial queries and best intelligence that I was able to procure."[1]

On the eve of revolution, beauty, then as now, was in the eye of the beholder, as was pride of home in the heart of the owner. From July 1759 until near the end of October 1760 the Reverend Burnaby traveled leisurely throughout Virginia, Maryland, Delaware, Pennsylvania, the Jerseys,[2] New York, Rhode Island, Massachusetts Bay, and New Hampshire. He concluded there was no town in the colonies that could compare

[237]

favorably with Boston, except perhaps Philadelphia: "If we consider that not eighty years ago the place where it now stands was a wild and uncultivated desert, inhabited by nothing but ravenous beasts and a savage people—[the city] must certainly be the object of every one's wonder and admiration. . . . The streets are laid out with great regularity and are handsomely built."

New York City was "tolerably well built [with] several good houses; the streets are paved and very clean . . . the houses along the Broad-Way have most of them a row of trees before them which form an agreeable shade and produce a pretty effect."

Boston (then larger than New York, having upwards of 20,000 residents) enjoyed buildings that "are in general good; the streets are open and spacious, and well-paved, and the whole has much the air of some of our best counrty towns in England. Most of these buildings are handsome. The arts are more elegant; and there is a more general turn for music, painting and the belles lettres."[3]

The smaller colonial communities could only suffer by comparison. The gentle vicar considered Williamsburg "the capitol of Virginia, [which] consists of about two hundred houses . . . far from being a place of any consequence. At the ends of the dusty, unpaved principal street (one of the most spacious in North America) are two public buildings, the college and the capitol . . . the houses are of wood, covered with shingles, and but indifferently built." Nevertheless, he said, "the whole made a handsome appearance," although "far from being magnificent . . . the governor's palace is tolerably good . . . but the church, prison, and other buildings are all of them extremely indifferent.

"Annapolis . . . is not laid out regularly, but is tolerably well built [up], and has several good brick houses. None of the streets is paved, and the few public buildings are not worth mentioning," while Newcastle "is a place of very little consideration; there are scarcely more than 100 houses in it, and no public buildings that deserve to be taken notice of. The churches, court house and market house are almost equally bad and undeserving of attention."

On his way to Philadelphia, the vicar appreciatively "passed by a very pretty village called Wilmington and rode through two others, Chester and Derby." At Princeton, Burnaby found "a handsome school and college for dissenters. . . . There are about twenty boys in the grammar-school and sixty in the college; at present there are only two professors. The name of the college is Nassau-Hall."

Burnaby proceeded to Brunswick, "a small city of about 100 houses . . . celebrated for the number of its beauties; and, indeed, at this place and Philadelphia were the handsomest women that I saw in America. New

Jersey in its present state can scarcely be called flourishing; for although it is extremely well cultivated, thickly settled and the garden of North America, yet, having no foreign trade, it is kept under."

He arrived at Newport harbor on August 7, 1760, where there were "about 800 or 1,000 houses, chiefly built of wood [but] few buildings in it worth notice, [although] the court-house is indeed handsome, and of brick, and there is a public library, built in the form of a Grecian temple by no means inelegant . . . but the whole is spoilt by two small wings annexed to it." The capital of New Hampshire, Portsmouth, "is situated upon the River [Piscataqua]; it is an inconsiderable place, and chiefly built of wood. The province of New Hampshire, I was informed at Portsmouth, has grown rich during the war, by the loss of its own vessels; they having been commonly insured above value."

Although in general the Reverend Burnaby's opinion of the American colonies in 1759–60 agreed with that of Dr. Alexander Hamilton, who made his own leisurely tour in 1744, the intervening fifteen years had caused a notable difference in the political attitudes of colonists.

> [I] found but little difference [Hamilton wrote] in the manners and character of the people in the different provinces I passed thro', [although] as to constitutions and complexions, air and government, I found some variety. Their forms of government in the northeren provinces I look upon to be much better and happier than ours [Virginia], which is a poor, sickly, convulsed state. Their air and living to the northward is likewise much preferable, and the people of a more gygantick size and make.
>
> In this itineration I compleated, by land and water together, a course of 1624 miles. The northeren parts I found in generall much better settled than the southeren. As to politeness and humanity, they are much alike except in the great towns where the inhabitants are more civilized, especially att Boston.[4]

In 1760, Burnaby echoed the doubts of many in England that the separate colonies could ever be united successfully, for "fire and water are not more heterogeneous than the different colonies in North-America. Nothing can exceed the jealousy . . . which they possess in regard to each other. Such is the difference of character, of manners, of religion, of interest that I think, were they left to themselves there would soon be a civil war, from one end of the continent to the other; while the Indians and Negroes would, with better reason, impatiently watch the opportunity of exterminating them all together."[5]

At the time of Burnaby's visit, whatever their other differences, the colonies did have one unifying passion: resentment over the lack of parliamentary representation and anger over repressive taxes. It was a combination of pride and rebellion that even then was becoming audible; for there was a deep appreciation of the accomplishments of their own generation and those of the six generations that had preceded them. In terms of history, the time was momentary: 130 hard years had been expended to make Boston the "large and flourishing metropolis of Massachusetts-Bay in New England," as Burnaby esteemed it, and only a few more had been needed for Virginians to become, in the vicar's words, "so impatient of restraint [that] many consider the colonies as independent states, not connected with Great Britain otherwise than by having the same common king, and being bound to her with natural affections."[6]

His reading of the times was prophetic. The second half of the eighteenth century was well under way, and the end of the colonial era had been forecast. Each colonist whatever the uniform he later chose, might have subscribed to the passion inherent in Viscount Bolingbroke's words: "I am in my farm, and here I shoot strong and tenacious roots; I have caught hold of the earth, to use a gardener's phrase, and neither my enemies nor my friends will find it an easy matter to transplant me again."[7]

The more some patterns of life changed as Americans moved westward, the more others remained the same. Today, seventeenth-century-style log houses built on the western Virginia frontier at Fincastle have been restored to their 1770 appearance. Basically similar frontier kitchen—common-room houses stand in Wisconsin and Minnesota to mark the first settlements along that cold northern route. French dreams of empire, which once sent settlers poling down the Missouri, are reflected in the restoration of Sainte Genevieve[8] of the 1780s, sixty miles south of St. Louis. Other first

One of several types of enlistment forms signed by volunteers in the army of the newly declared United States of America

homes trace the middle way that led from Kentucky and from Pennsylvania through Ohio, and Indiana into Illinois. There, in Pleasant Grove township, a log house has been restored to the way it looked in the 1840s when a rising young Springfield attorney-politician purchased it for his father and stepmother.[9]

Lora Case, the youngest son of a Granby, Connecticut, family that emigrated by covered wagon to Ohio, recalled his family's first home, built in 1814 in the new settlement at Hudson, as one of "logs hewn inside and outside," where "the first thing my father did was to build a fireplace of cobblehead stones laid up with clay mortar. The hearth was eight feet long, made of clay tamped down. The chimney was built of sticks and clay mortar."[10]

Though he wrote of a time nearly two hundred years after those first fire-rooms had been built along the Atlantic coast, Case described a building method no different from that his English emigrant ancestors might have used in the seventeenth century: "There was a crossbar of wood in the chimney," said Case, describing the lug-pole, "eight feet above the hearth [and] from which was suspended a hook to hang the kettle on for cooking." Thus the trammel chain and hook continued in use.

"Then he laid the puncheon floor of logs split in two and hewed," Case wrote. "Next he replaced the blanket door with one made of boards, hung with wooden hinges, and fastened with a wooden latch on the inside. A string fastened to this latch, running through a hole above, made it possible to unlatch the door from the outside. At night the string was pulled in and the door was locked." Thus the sixteenth-century Elizabethan English and the seventeenth-century colonial American batten door continued to serve in nineteenth-century Ohio.

"Next my father cut holes through the logs for board windows which were made to slide back and forth under cleats," and "last of all stopped the cracks between the logs with chinks and mud mortar and our house was done." Thus was the Case house daubed and shuttered, as had been those earlier homes along the Atlantic coast in the 1650s.

In Ohio, too, the first oven was constructed outdoors, "of brick and clay mortar, set on posts two feet high. It was heated with nice dry wood, burnt almost to ashes, then cleaned with a shovel and broom."[11]

The size of the new prairie houses differed little from those "fashionable homes" that had been required of seventeenth-century Connecticut settlers: "Our cabin was twenty-four by eighteen." A list of furnishings, recalled in the 1840s, compares easily with those of earlier Massachusetts and Virginia kitchens: "The west end was occupied by two beds . . . on the side opposite the window, made of clapboards supported on pins driven into the logs, were our shelves . . . upon these were displayed pewter plates, basins, and dishes, and spoons, scoured and bright. A ladder of five rounds occupied the corner near the window; by this, when we got a floor above, we could ascend." Again, as in the East, the chimney and hearth of the fire-room "occupied most of [one] end; pots and kettles opposite the window under the shelves, a gun on hooks over the north door, four split-bottom chairs, three three-legged stools, and a small eight by ten looking glass. These, with a chimney-shovel and a pair of tongs . . . completed our furniture."[12]

The meal of old English hasty pudding, now commonly called mush by Americans, and of Indian cornmeal bread continued in favor, supplemented by game from the woods, for "my father was a very successful hunter and kept our table, which he made, well supplied [with] deer, bear, raccoon, opossum, squirrels, rabbits, turkeys, quails, partridges and pidgions."[13]

Cooking methods were those that had been handed down generation after generation: "We stuffed, dressed and baked the 'possum as [we would have a pig]. The 'coon we hung before the fire to roast. Squirrels, partridges, pidgions, and quails were cooked in pie or broth with dumplings. My mother baked rye and Indian bread in a bake kettle [Dutch oven] set on coals of fire and with coals on the lid. Potatoes were baked in the ashes and eaten with salt." As it had been in early seventeenth-century settlements, "Butter was a very scarce article. Johnny cake was made of corn meal mixed with salt and water, baked on a board before the fire."[14]

Table settings and manners of early ninteenth-century midwestern America continued to be those of the seventeenth century: "My mother had a set of pewter plates and tumblers, also a pewter teapot and platter" from which adults were served. "We young ones had wooden trenchers for meat and potatoes, and wooden bowls for mush and milk. When we came around the table, spread with so many luxuries, we did not forget the giver of every good and perfect gift; we all stood at our places while our father, or in his absence our mother, asked a blessing . . . at the close of each meal, we stood up while one of them returned thanks."[15]

The ancient Anglo-Saxon beverage, mead, brewed before English history was written, continued to sustain the frontier farmer's family until once again a new generation of apple trees could provide cider. Mead was prepared as it always had been, first straining "the honey by hanging it in a large linen strainer before the fire. When it was strained [Father] put the comb in a kettle of water and boiled it, then he dipped it in small quantities into a small bag, hanging it over the end of a board, and, leaning over on it with a rolling pin in his hand, pressed the beeswax with the water into a tub. Then, letting it stand until it got cold, it could be taken from the top of the water and the water was kept in a barrel for methiglin. After a few days it made a very pleasant drink."[16]

The frontier family of the nineteenth century continued to be a self-sustaining unit not only in its ability to build its own home, farm the land, and plant an orchard and a kitchen garden, but also, Case wrote,

> My sisters spun, I quilled, and my mother wove the wool and linen for our winter and summer clothes. The women colored [and made] their own slips and our pants and vests and coats. I have a small twilled towel made from the flax my father raised, my sisters spun, I quilled and my mother wove. . . . We boys helped braid the straw for the women to sew for our summer hats and our sisters'; for winter hats my mother cut red and brown pieces of woolen and sewed them together with a tassel on top. We sometimes wore buckskin pants to church, tanned by our father. They were nice and soft; I have seen a deacon wear them to church.[17]

So it was that the kitchen, the first room of the early American home to be built, was the last to change. So long as the kitchen remained much as it always had been, the American family's past was always a vital part of its present. Indeed, tangible proof of that history, for as many generations back as could be counted, could be reached out to and touched, for more often than not, at least one treasured brass pot or posnet remained from the chest of furnishings first brought from England.

It was not until industry followed the settlers' trails, until mills were constructed with furnaces to fire new and more powerful forges, that the iron cooking range with its built-in oven supplanted the colonial kitchen hearth. Some considered the innovation a mixed blessing. Harriet Beecher Stowe later asked, "Would our Revolutionary fathers have gone barefooted and bleeding over snows to defend airtight stoves and cooking ranges? I trow not. It was the memory of the great open kitchen fire . . . that called to them through the snows of that dreadful winter."[18] In most homes as the range was installed, the contents of the larder changed from wild game to domestic beef, pork, and poultry.

The last rural and village links with our colonial past were the plants of the kitchen garden. In many of the more sparsely populated sections of New England, the south, the middle west, and the northwest, changes in basic garden inventories were few until rural electrification programs were completed, in most areas about 1940. Only two generations ago, without electricity and the radically improved refrigeration and freezing methods developed during World War II, many rural Americans continued to rely on vegetables and fruits dried or made into conserves just as they had been put up for three hundred years in this country. Beef and pork still were powdered with salt, pickled, or smoked for use over winter.[19]

The narrow kitchen, or fire room—the first part of the Louis Bolduc home to be built at Sainte Genevieve, Missouri, at the end of the Revolutionary War era—has only a "new" tin-reflector oven to distinguish its cooking-hearth furnishings from those used by seventeenth-century settlers at the beginning of the colonial period.

[244]

Vertical-plank interior wall was nogged with clay mixture in the late-eighteenth-century Bolduc House kitchen just as had been the earliest Atlantic coast settlers' homes. French influence is obvious in design of the furniture, particularly the table and dough-box. Seed corn is hung to dry on "corn hands," and herbs are suspended from nails in ceiling beams.

More than one American born after 1900 recalls the excitement of finding an orange in his Christmas stocking or the wonder engendered by a golden banana that somehow had survived the long, hot journey by steamship north to New York, overland by rail to a village general store, and finally by horse and carriage to a prairie farm home.

Today's air-freight transportation, linking continents in a matter of hours, thus has wrought the greatest change of all from the colonial larder, and hence in our use and design of kitchens and gardens. The change is more startling to some in this century than it might have been to those of the seventeenth who foresaw no bounds to man's ingenuity and daring. After all, as Joseph Glanville said in 1665 of those who first ventured across the Atlantic into the New World:

> Should those heroes go on, as they have happily begun, they'll fill the world with wonders, and it may be, some ages hence a voyage to the Southern unknown tracts, yea possibly the moon, will be no more strange than one to America.[20]

PART XI

The Glossaries: "All Things Fitting for Your Use"

GLOSSARY 1*
The Common Utensils

Back. A cast-iron plate standing upright at the back of the fireplace to reflect heat.

Bark. A tanner's tub.

Bass. A stuffed chair-seat; a rush seat. "A cushion made of straw, used in churches to kneel on." (Bailey)

Bed. "A place prepared to stretch and compose the body on, for rest and sleep; made chiefly of feathers in closed in a ticken case. We say feather-bed." (Chambers) Other fillings included dried mosses, seaweed, cornhusks, bits of old cloth.

Bedstead. "A place or frame for the bed." (Johnson)

Berry boxes. "Some had boxes, pails and the like made of the bark of the button-wood tree and little dishes of this bark for gathering whortleberries." (Kalm; see Bibliography)

Board. A plank, a table. "The festive *board*." (Johnson)

Basin. "A small vessel to hold water." (Johnson) "14 May, 1714. Saturd fair. I Recd ½ dozn *Basons* of Mr. Davise on acct of old Pewter." (Hempsted, *Diary*; see Bibliography)

Basinet. A small wooden bowl.

Basket. "A vessel made of twigs, rushes, or other slender bodies interwoven." (Johnson)

Basket-bed. "In the garden, a bed banked by heavy stakes over which basket work is woven." (Johnson)

Basket-spit. A spit made with a basket, formed of wrought-iron strips, in the middle; meat was placed in the basket, and the spit was rested on the andiron hooks and turned to roast the fowl or small game.

Batlings. Twigs and clippings used as kindling.

Beam. A horizontal timber support; also a candle.

---

* The glossaries are drawn from the dictionaries of the period—Messrs. Chambers', Bailey's, Johnson's, and Middleton's lexicographies—exemplified by quotations from travelers' and settlers' journals and books common to colonial libraries.

Becker.   A wooden dish.

Becket.   A rope handle.

Besom.   A broom to sweep with, "of cane, rush, birch, corn." (Johnson)

Bicker.   A small and shallow wooden tub.

Birch broom.   A birch stick, one end of which was shaved to form long slender shreds.

Bird-spit.   A footed pan to catch drippings, with hooks for roasting small birds. "To Roast Quails: Get quails, truss them, stuff their Bellies with Beef-sewet and Sweet-herbs, chopp'd well together; *spit* them on a *small spit*, and when they grow warm, baste first with Water and Salt, but afterwards with Butter, and drudge them with Flour. For sauce, dissolve an Anchovy in Gravy, into which put two or three shalots, slic'd and boil'd; add the juice of two or three Seville oranges and one Lemon; dish them in this sauce and garnish with Lemon peel and grated Manchet; Be sure to serve them up hot." (*The Lady's Companion*, 1753)

Bittlin.   Milk bowl of wood, pewter, glass, or pottery.

Boultel or boulter.   A cloth bag in which meal was shaken as a means of sifting.

Bowl.   A vessel to hold liquids, rather wide than deep.

Box-iron.   "Smoothing iron with an inner chamber to hold hot coals." (Johnson)

Brandreth, brandlethe, or brandlet.   A tripod to support a pot or kettle above embers; a framework, generally of iron.

Brandy-warmer.   Small saucepan to warm spirits; usually of brass, copper, or silver.

Braser.   Also called braising pan, brazero, brazier. Originally, a brass vessel. An open pan on a footed base for braising or broiling; any small portable stove.

Buck-basket.   Laundry hamper. ". . . rammed one in with foul shirts, and smocks, stockings, napkins,—crammed in the basket." (Shakespeare, *The Merry Wives of Windsor.*)

Buffet.   "A kind of cupboard or set of shelves where plate is set out to show in a room of entertainment." (Johnson)

Buret.   A drinking vessel.

Burnt bowl.   A porcelain or pottery vessel or any kind of earthenware which had been fired in a kiln, as opposed to one of wood or metal.

Buttery.   "The room wherein provisions are laid up." (Johnson) "[Plan] all [rooms] that need a cool and fresh temper as cellars, pantries and *butteries* to the north." (Wotton)

Cabbage plane.   Also called sauerkraut machine. "This method of slicing cabbage is much more efficient than with ordinary knives: A tray was made of boards with a flat even bottom about three feet long and seven inches wide and with two-inch sides. In the middle of the tray was a large, square opening about four inches wide. Across this were placed three knives parallel to one another. The width of each knife was one and a half inches. The edges were set aslant [as] in a plane. The cabbage was grated by these knives." (Kalm, *Travels*; see Bibliography)

Caldron. A pot, boiler, or kettle.

Can. "The *can* is the large vessel out of which the cup is filled; a cup made of metal." (Johnson)

Cannister. "An instrument used by coopers in racking off wines." (Bailey)

Carpet. "A sort of covering, worked either with the needle or on a loom; to be spread on a table, trunk, an estrade or even, a passage, or floor. Persian and Turkey *carpets* are the most prized; especially the former." (Chambers)

Cellar. The pit below the house; a cool storage place.

Chaffern or chafing dish. A vessel for heating water. "A vessel to make anything hot in [using] a portable grate for coals." (Johnson)

Chandlery. Any drawer, box, or other container for candle storage. "Jan. [1715/16] Saturd 7th fair. In ye forn I was home. made a Candlebox Contains 29½ lb." (Hempsted, *Diary*; see Bibliography)

Chimney. "A fire-hearth." (Bailey)

Chopping knife. "A knife with which cooks mince their meat." (Johnson)

Cob. Plaster of clay, water, straw, or thatch, whitened with slaked lime. "Wedns 7 (dec. 1720): fair & cold. I was at home al day. I Salted Meat & Plaistered ye Cellar." (Hempsted, *Diary*; see Bibliography)

Cobirons. "Cob" indicates "rounded" or "knobbed." "The irons which support the spit." (Johnson)

Cotterel or cotter pole. A trammel or bar from which to hang a pot over a fire.

Cricket-stool. Perhaps from Saxon *crice* ("crutch"), something on which to rest. A footstool.

Crock. A cup; any earthen vessel.

Crook-chain. A chain with a hook from which to hang a pot, affixed to the chimney.

Crotch. A hook or fork; a long-handled fork usually made from a slender branch terminating in a narrow V, used in place of an iron flesh-fork by poorer families, and also used in laundry and dye work; also the tall V-terminated trunk of a young tree, preferably cedar or chestnut, used to support a wellsweep.

Cruet. "Here also vinegar is placed in a special container on the table to be used on the kale. I must confess this dish tastes very good." (Kalm; see Bibliography)

Cruse. Also called cruskin, crusekyn, cruiskin. A pot-shaped vessel with spout and handle.

Cupboard. A shelf for cups or crockery. "A case with shelves in which victuals or earthenware is placed." (Johnson) "Some trees are best for planchers, as deal; some for tables, *cupboards* and desks, as walnut." (Bacon, *Natural History*)

Dade-strings or dading strings. Lead strings or a kind of cloth-tape harness, used to teach infants to walk.

Delft.   Tin-glazed earthenware; Dutch faïence copied at Lambeth, Liverpool, and other English potteries, whence much was exported to the colonies.

Dibble.   A small spade. "A pointed instrument with which gardeners make holes for planting." (Johnson) "Through cunning, with *dibble*, rake, mattock and spade, / By line and by level trim garden is made." (Tusser, *Husbandry*; see Bibliography) "I'll not put the *dibble* in earth to set off them." (Shakespeare, *A Winter's Tale*)

Dish.   "A broad wide vessel in which food is served up at table; a deep hollow vessel for liquid food." (Johnson)

Dough-tray or dough-box.   A trough, sometimes on its own frame, in which bread dough was mixed and kneaded; also called kneading-box; usually with a lid that served as a kneading table.

Dripping-pan.   "The pan in which the fat of roast meat is caught." (Johnson)

Drudger or dredger.   "The box out of which flour is thrown at roast meat." (Johnson)

Dutch oven.   A heavy iron pot or kettle on feet, used for roasting or baking at the hearth; set above coals and with coals placed on lid to provide more heat.

Earthenware.   Potter's work; clay turned and shaped into bowls, jugs, and other vessels for the kitchen; fired in a kiln and glazed. "New York has hills of fuller's earth and some fine clay such as white, yellow, red and black, suitable for pots, dishes, plates, tobacco pipes and like wares." (Van der Donck, 1653; see Bibliography) "It is thought here is good clay to make Bricke and Tyles and Earthen-Pots as needs to be." (Higginson, *New England's Plantation*; see Bibliography) "Monday 24 [Feb. 1728/29]: In the morn I went to Town & borrowed an Earthen Shugar Jarr of Geo Buttolph." (Hempsted, *Diary*; see Bibliography)

Fagot.   A brand for burning; a bundle of twigs or sticks.

Fat or fatte.   A vat. "Fryday 2 (Nov., 1722) Cloudy. I was att home all day. I finished Caulking 1 *Tanfatt* & Sowed & Fenced in a Nursery on the N.E. side of the garden." (Hempsted, *Diary*; see Bibliography)

Fender.   "An iron plate laid before the fire to hinder coals that fall from rolling forward to the floor." (Johnson)

File.   An instrument to smooth down; also, "a line on which papers are strung to keep them in order." (Johnson)

Filter.   A strainer or searce.

Fire-brush.   "The brush which hangs by the fire to sweep the hearth." (Johnson) "When you are ordered to stir up the fire clean away the ashes from between the bars with the *fire-brush*." (Jonathan Swift, *Collected Works*)

Fire-new.   New from the forge; brand-new. "Upon the wedding day I put myself according to the custom, in another suit, *firenew* with silver buttons to it." (Joseph Addison; *Spectator Papers*)

Fire-pan.   A vessel of metal to carry fire. "April 21, 1631. The house of John

Page of Waterton burnt by carrying a few coals from one house to another. A coal fell by the way and kindled the leaves." (*Annals of New England*)

Fire-pike. A poker.

Fire-shovel. "The instrument with which the hot coals are thrown up in kitchens." (Johnson) "Culinary utensils and irons often feel the force of fire: as tongs, *fireshovels,* prongs and irons." (Brown)

Fish-kettle. A caldron made long for the fish to be boiled without bending. "Trout stewed in the juice of Oranges . . . with boiled rice, afforded me a wholesome and delicious supper." (William Bartram, 1773; see Bibliography)

Flag-broom. A broom for sweeping flags or pavements, "commonly made of birch twigs." (Johnson)

Flagon. "A vessel of drink with a narrow mouth." (Johnson) "His trusty *flagon,* full of potent juice was hanging by, worn thin with age and use." (Roscommon)

Flail. "The instrument with which grain is beaten out of the ear; the tool of the thrasher." (Johnson)

Fleeting-dish. A skimming bowl.

Flesh-fork. An iron prong to lift meat from the pot. "I dive with forks that have but two prongs." (Jonathan Swift)

Flesh-hook. "A hook to draw flesh from the caldron." (Johnson)

Foot-warmers. "Nearly everyone had her little container with the glowing coals, under her skirt to keep her warm. The negroes or their other servants accompany them to church carrying the warming pans. When the minister finished his sermon, and the last hymn had been sung, the same came and removed the warming pans and carried them home." (Kalm; see Bibliography)

Form. A long backless seat. "If a chair be defined a seat for a single person, with a back belonging to it, then a stool is a seat without a back, and a *form* is a seat for several persons, without a back." (Isaac Watts, *Collected Works,* 1753)

Frail. A basket made of rushes; also the rush used.

Frower or frow. A cleaving tool.

Frying pan. "The vessel in which meat is roasted on the fire." (Johnson)

Fuel. "The best wood for *fuel* in everybody's opinion is hickory. The white and black oaks are next in goodness." (Kalm; see Bibliography)

Galley balk. Chimney beam from which pots were suspended.

Gallipot or gillipot. A grease or ointment pot; later often called gleypot and glumpot; a small earthenware jar.

Gantree. A stand for kegs or barrels.

Garret. The loft; the topmost room in a house.

Gib-croke or gib-crook. A pot-hook.

Gimlin. A salting tub.

Gipse. A wooden spice or sugar mortar.

Grate.   "A range of bars within which fires are made." (Johnson)

Griddle.   "Solid iron or earthen flat pan in which food is cooked over the fire." (Johnson)

Gridiron.   "A portable grate on which meat is laid to be broiled upon the fire." (Johnson) "[Sunflower] buds before they be flowered, boyled and eaten with butter, vinegar and pepper, are exceeding pleasant meat or they may be broiled upon a *gridiron* and eaten with oil and vinegar." (Gerard, *Herball*; see Bibliography)

Hamper.   "A large basket for carriage." (Johnson)

Hand-basket.   A portable basket. "You must have woolen yarn to tie grafts with and a small *hand-basket* to carry them in." (Philip Miller, *Gardener's Dictionary*; see Bibliography)

Handle.   A haft. "That part of anything by which it is held." (Johnson) "A beam there was on which a beechen pail Hung by the *handle* on a driven nail . . . of bone the *handles* of my knife are made." (Dryden, *Juvenal*)

Hangers.   Pot-hooks. "That by which anything hangs." (Johnson)

Hook.   "An iron to seize the meat in the caldron." (Johnson)

Hopper.   "The box in which corn is put to be ground. Also a basket for carrying seed." (Johnson)

Hutch.   A corn chest; a storage chest with a lid top. "The best way to keep them after they are threshed is to dry them well and keep them in *hutches,* or in close casks." (Philip Miller; see Bibliography)

Ice-cellars.   "Some of the people of quality make use of *ice cellars* to keep beer cool during the summer and to preserve fresh meat in the great heat. These cellars are commonly built of stone under the house, and the walls covered with boards, because the ice is more easily consumed by stones. In winter they fill them with snow, which is beat down and covered with water. They then open the cellar holes and the door to admit cold." (Kalm; see Bibliography)

Jack.   "The name of instruments which supply the place of a boy; foot boys who had the common name of Jack given them were kept to turn the spit, and when instruments were invented for these services they were called jacks. (2) A cup made of waxed leather. ['Be the jacks fair within, the jills without.' Shakespeare] (3) A support to saw wood on. (4) A tool for removing boots." (Johnson)

Jug.   "A large drinking vessel with a swelling belly." (Johnson)

Keeler.   A shallow cooling tub.

Keelfat.   A tub in which liquor is set to cool.

Keg.   A small barrel commonly used for fish.

Kibble.   A wooden bucket used to draw water from the well.

Kneading-box.   *See* dough-tray.

Knife.   "You need not wipe your *knife* to cut bread, because in cutting a slice or two, it will wipe itself." (Swift, *Works*, 1824) "*July 25, 1718*: Visit Mrs. Denison. She invites me to eat. I give her two Cases with a *knife* and fork in each; one turtle shell tackling, the other long with Ivory handles, Squar'd, cost 4S 6d." (Sewall, *Diary*; see Bibliography)

Lade-gorn. A wooden pail, of which one stave is longer and is used as a handle, for drawing water from a spring or larger vessel.

Lamhog. A wooden cup with solid handles.

Lantern. "A transparent case for a candle." (Johnson) "Tis a dark *lantern* of the spirit which none sees by but those that bear it." (Samuel Butler, *Hudibras*)

Larder. A room for provisions; the room where meat is kept or salted.

Limbeck. An alembic. "A vessel or furnace used in distillation." (Bailey)

Livery. A kind of cupboard; sometimes a room for keeping plates or linens.

Loggerhead. An iron with one lozenge-shaped or knobbed end, which is heated, then plunged into a drink to warm it.

Losset. A wooden trencher.

Lumber. "Old household stuff; also things useless and of small value." (Bailey) Hence, a lumber-room, storage room.

Maeser. Also called maser, mazer, mazur, maselin. A wooden drinking bowl, usually of maple.

Mantel-tree. "A piece of timber laid across the head of a chimney [opening]." (Bailey)

Maselin. *See* maeser.

Match. Anything that readily catches fire; generally a card, rope, or chip of wood dipped in sulfur.

Mattock. A kind of spading fork or pick; later a kind of spade (*see* dibble).

Maulkin. "A swab for the oven hearth." (Johnson)

Maund. A wicker basket.

Medder or meader. A wooden cup with handles and feet.

Mether. A wooden goblet.

Milkwood. The willow.

Mop. "Pieces of cloth or locks of wool fixed to a long handle with which maids clean floors." (Johnson)

Mortar. "A strong vessel in which materials are broken by being pounded with a pestle." (Johnson) "*Wednsd 17 (Feb. 1730–31)*: fixt my Samp *Mortar* made a Pestill &c." (Hempsted, *Diary*; see Bibliography) "In July when the chestnuts and corn are green and full grown, they half boil the former and take off the rind; and having sliced the milky swelled long rows of the latter, the women pound it in a large wooden *mortar* which is wide at the mouth and gradually narrows at the bottom. Then they knead them both together, wrap them up in green corn blades about an inch thick and boil them well. This sort of bread is very tempting." (James Adair, 1775)

Mug.　A cup to drink from. "The *mugs* were large, the drink was wond'rous strong." (John Gay, *Beggar's Opera*)

Noggin.　A small mug.

Oast.　A kiln, usually for hop or malt.
Oven.　"Arched cavity heated with fire to bake bread." (Johnson)

Pail.　"A wooden vessel in which water or milk commonly is carried." (Johnson) "Jack and Jill went up the hill to fetch a *pail* of water." (Nursery rhyme) "*Tuesd. July 1 (1746)* fair. I was at home foren I hoopt 2 *pails*, one with iron hoops." (Hempsted; see Bibliography)
Pale.　"A narrow piece of wood joined above and below to a rail to enclose the grounds." (Johnson) "*Fryd 1 (Aug., 1718)* fair I was at home al day Seting up bord fence." (Hempsted, *Diary*; see Bibliography)
Pallet.　A small bed.
Pan.　"A broad and shallow vessel in which provisions are dressed or kept." (Johnson)
Pannier.　"A wicker basket by which fruit or other things are carried on a horse." (Johnson)
Patch.　A small parcel of land, as a garden patch; "We go to gain a little *patch* of ground, that hath in it no profit but the name." (Shakespeare, *Hamlet*)
Peel.　A broad thin board with a long handle used to put bread in and out of the oven; a slice or thibble.
Pewter.　"The plates and dishes in a house." (Johnson) "The eye of the mistress was wont to make her *pewter* shine." (Joseph Addison, *Spectator Papers*)
Piggin.　A wooden vessel for dipping from a tub, usually with one stave longer than the others; sometimes used with cream pails; also, a bowl-shaped, long-handled drinking ladle.
Pipkin.　A small earthenware boiler; a small earthenware pot. "A Sallet of Rose-Buds and Clove-Gillyflowers. Pick Rose-buds, and put them in an earthen *pipkin*, with White Wine Vinegar and Sugar; so may you use Cowslips, Violets and Rosemary-flowers." (J. Murrel, *Two Bookes of Cookerie and Carving*, 1650)
Platter.　Any large plate or tray or common dish, of wood, pewter, or earthenware. "The servants wash the *platter*, scour the plate, then blow the fire." (Dryden, *Juvenal*) "Jack Sprat could eat no fat, / His wife could eat no lean; / And so between them both you see, / They licked the *platter* clean." (John Clarke, *Paroemiologia Anglo-Latina*, 1639)
Poker.　"The iron bar with which men stir the fire." (Johnson)
Pomander.　"A sweet ball comforting of the heart and provoking of sleep." (Bacon)
Porringer:　"A vessel in which broth is eaten; a small pan or basin." (Johnson) "Went to bed early at Mr. Sparhawk's, pinned my stocking about my neck and drank a *porringer* of sage tea." (Sewall, *Diary*; see Bibliography)

Posnet. A little skillet, though more commonly a little basin or porringer, sometimes on a tripod base.

Pot. "A vessel in which meat is boiled on the fire; also, a vessel to hold liquid." (Johnson) "The people of New England already cast their own cannon, plates, *pots* and cannon balls from native iron." (Van der Donck; see Bibliography)

Pot-brake, pot-crook, pot-hook. A trammel to hold pots; also commonly called a claw or lifter.

Pottinger. A small basin; porringer.

Powdering tub. A large container in which meats were powdered (that is, covered with salt) to preserve them.

Prong. A kind of fork. "The cooks make no more ado, but slicing it into little gobbets, prick it on a *prong* of iron and hang it in a furnace." (George Sandys, *Collected Works*)

Puncheon. A large cask, its capacity depending on what it was to contain; also a split log.

Quaich or quaigh. Originally a wooden-staved cup hooped together and with two ears; later a wood, metal, or ceramic two-eared cup.

Quern. A small mill for grinding grain at home.

Range. A kitchen grate. "The implements of the kitchen are spits, *ranges*, cobirons and pots." (Bacon, *Physical Remains*)

Redware and stoneware. "Made and sold reasonably by Thomas Symmes and Company at Charlestown near the Swing Bridge, blue and white *stone ware* of forty different sorts; also red and yellow ware of divers sorts, either by Wholesale or Retale." (Boston *Gazette*, April 16, 1745)

Roster or roaster. A gridiron.

Rug. Any bed or table cover.

Rundlet. A small barrel; a canteen.

Runge. An oval wooden tub with handles.

Salamander. A browning iron with a long handle used to brown or toast the surface of roasts or pastry. "To make a Welch Rabbit: Toast the Bread on both sides, then toast the Cheese on one side, lay it on the Toast, and with a hot *Iron* brown the other Side. You may rub it over with Mustard." (Mrs. Hannah Glasse; *Art of Cookery*; see Bibliography)

Salver. "A saver to catch the juices" (made of any ware). (Johnson)

Sauce-pan. "A small skillet with a long handle in which sauce or small things are boiled." (Johnson)

Sauerkraut machine. *See* cabbage plane.

Save-all. A small pan inserted into a candlestick to save the ends of candles.

Sconce. "A pensile candlestick, generally with a looking glass to reflect the light." (Johnson)

Scuttle. A wide shallow basket; a hod.

Shopboard.   A bench on which any work is done.

Sideboard.   "The side table on which conveniences are placed for those who eat at the other table." (Johnson)

Skillet.   Originally a deep, footed pan with a cover.

Slice.   "A broad head fixed in a handle; a peel, a spatula." (Johnson)

Spit.   "A long prong on which meat is driven to be turned before the fire." (Johnson)

Stillyards.   Originally, steelyard or yard of steel, indicating the length of the scale; the common scales, usually of iron. "January 7, 1748. I put on iron peices on the poze of both pair of *Stillyards* and Made them Exact, only the Great Sid goes Slow, and ye little Side Quick of the Great *Stillyards*." (Hempsted, *Diary*; see Bibliography)

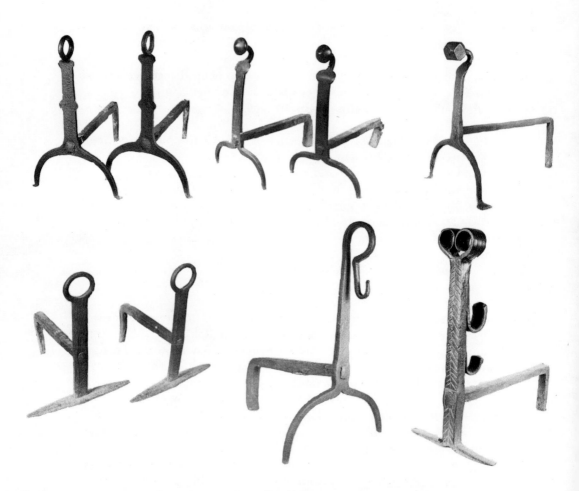

Hearth furnishings: ring-top andirons for spits; standard irons; cobiron; creepers; American andirons made to support spits for roasting

Temse. A sifter or strainer; a sieve.

Thibble or thible. A slice; skimmer; spatula.

Tin reflector oven. Open-faced tin or iron box, sometimes fitted with a spit, for roasting before the fire. "To make an English Rabbit: Toast a Slice of Bread brown on both sides, then lay it on a Plate before the Fire, pour a Glass of red Wine over it, and let it soak the Wine up; then cut dome Cheese very thin, and lay it very thick over the Bread, and put it in a *Tin Oven* before the Fire, and it will be toasted and browned presently. Serve it away hot." (Mrs. Hannah Glasse, *Art of Cookery*; see Bibliography)

Toaster. A wire grid or clamp to hold bread before the fire, with a long handle and a swivel-foot so that the toast could be turned.

Trammel. An adjustable rack from which pots were hung above the fire.

Treen. Wooden; made of wood. "An obsolete word." (Johnson, 1755)

Trencher. A wooden plate.

Trug. A hod or scuttle, as an ash-trug.

Tyg. A communal cup.

Wafer irons. Two-hinged, usually round, small griddles attached to long handles; held over fire to bake wafers, much as waffles were baked later. "Rose *Wafers*. Put the yolks of four eggs, and three spoonfuls of Rose-water to a quart of flower, mingle them well, make them into a batter with cream and double-refined sugar, pour it on very thin, and bake it on Irons." (John Nott, *Recipe Book*, 1723)

Whisk. "Then take a stycke and make it cleane, and then cutte it in the end four sqware, and therewith beate all the aforesayde thynges together." (*A Proper Newe Booke of Cokerye*, 1575)

Worm. "A long spirally winding pewter Pipe placed in a tub of water to cool and thicken the vapours in distilling of Spirits." (Bailey)

Circa 1700 cooking vessels, iron

Circa 1700 cooking vessels, brass

Hearth furnishings: seventeenth-century Dutch ovens; footed iron kettles

Hearth furnishings: seventeenth- and early-eighteenth-century frying pans and skillets

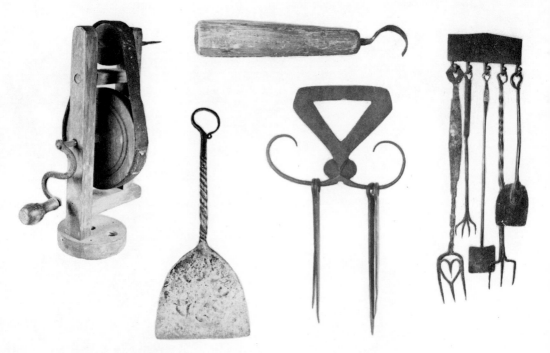

Food-preparation accessories: two apple corers; turner or spatula; skewers and holder; flesh-forks and turners

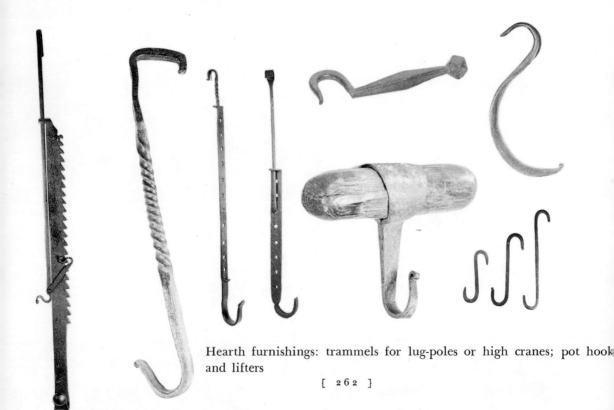

Hearth furnishings: trammels for lug-poles or high cranes; pot hook and lifters

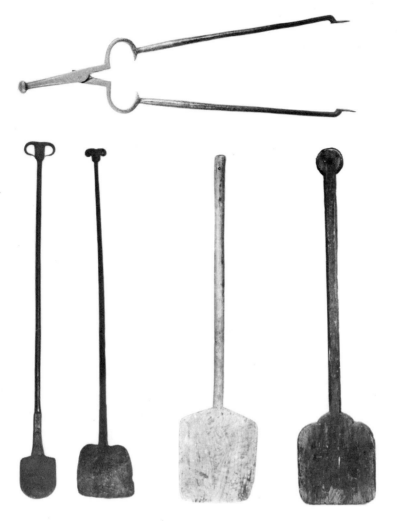

Hearth furnishings: tongs; salamander or browning iron; iron peel or shovel; wooden peels

Hearth furnishings: standing spit-toasters; footed and swivel toasters for bread

[264]

Hearth furnishings: wafer irons; pot pusher; potato rake

Hearth furnishings: hanging griddle; swivel-type hearth gridirons

[265]

Brass teapot; pails; posnet, or saucepan

Iron teakettle with lifters; patty pan; chafing dish; coal carrier; trivet; iron posnet

Delft, or faience, decorated and polychrome seventeenth- and early-eighteenth-century designs for caudle, or posset, cups; sack, or sherry, bottle; punch bowl. At right is gray stoneware jug with incised blue decoration.

Early Delft monochrome and polychrome decorated plates include those with ciphers and dates often purchased at the time of wedding; King William commemorative; floral, bird, and chinoiserie motifs.

Pewter spoons and accessories: circa 1700 wall rack; mold for home-casting; finished set; service basin; service plate; platter

[269]

Small stands and tables: joined; X-base; adjustable screw top; tripod style

Kitchen tables: hutch chair-table shown open and closed; oval work or writing table; two other stretcher-based styles; take-apart board and form

Table boxes and chests: spice chest; carved desk and book boxes; painted desk-box; tooled-leather, paper-lined document box; brass box

Benches and stools: made-at-home wood styles; rush-seat stool; cricket-style stool

Chairs: in order of age from the early seventeenth century through the eighteenth. Dutch-influenced English styles gradually evolved into an obviously American type.

Basic furniture: seventeenth- and early-eighteenth-century clothes boxes; 1689 trunk

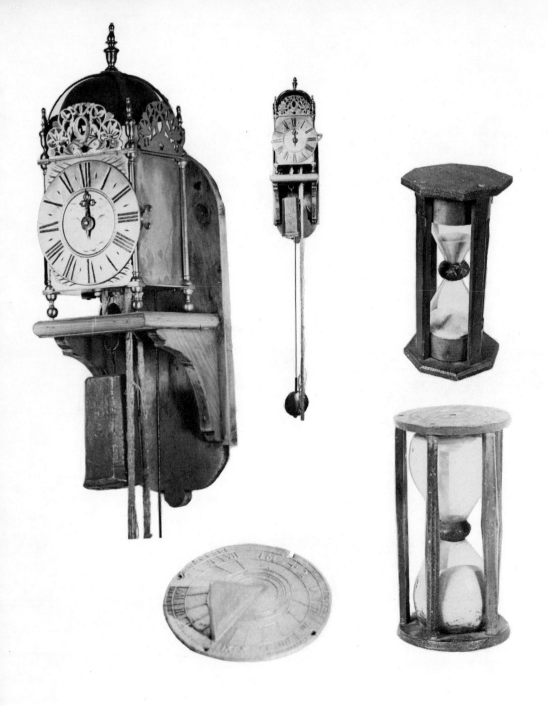

English brass lantern clock; hourglasses; windowsill pewter noonmark, or sundial

Kitchen accessories: polychrome ewer; syrup or cream jug; powder horn; dinner whistle; pewter chamberpot

[277]

Brass and iron bedwarmers; bed rope key; seventeenth-century cradle;
birch floor broom; oven broom

[278]

Table furnishings: salt and sugar containers; sugar nippers

Table furnishings: turned wood bowls and, at lower right, gourd bowl, for service and individual use

Table furnishings: hand-carved wooden porringer forms; pewter porringer

Table utensils: knives and forks; horn and wood spoons

[282]

GLOSSARY 2
Beverages and Brews

Ale, beer. Originally the two were synonymous: alcoholic liquor produced by the fermentation of malt and flavored with hops or some other bitters. In the colonies beer was made by the individual family from whatever was available: corn, pumpkins, nettles, potatoes. For *corn beer*, a mash from fresh corn was covered with sweet water and allowed to ferment; the liquid then was tapped off and drunk as beer. Commercially made beer was stronger and tastier; that imported from England was preferred: "Every Farmers Son, when he goes to the Market-Town, must have money in his purse; and when he meets with his Companions, they goe to the Tavern or Ale-house, and seldome away before Drunk, or well tipled. It is rare to find men that we call Drunkards, but there are abundance of Tiplers in New-England." (Samuel Nowell, *Abraham in Arms*, Boston, 1678)

Persimmon beer. In the middle colonies, after the fruit had been touched by the frost, some colonists brewed persimmons into a "very palatable liquor." To do so, they gathered "a sufficient quantity, which is very easy as each tree is well-stocked. Then these persimmon apples are put into a dough of wheat or other flour, formed into cakes and put into an oven in which they remain until baked and sufficiently dry. To brew the liquor, a pot full of water is put on the fire and some of the cakes are put in. They become soft by degrees as the water grows warm and crumble to pieces. The pot is then taken from the fire and the water well stirred so that the cakes may mix with it. This is then poured into another vessel and they continue to steep and break up as many cakes as are necessary for the brewing. Then malt is added and one proceeds as usual with the brewing. Beer thus prepared is reckoned much preferable to other beer." (Kalm, *Travels*; see Bibliography)

Beer bread. Persimmons and wheat bran baked as a loaf of bread. When it was cut into a bowl of hot water and allowed to cool, each slice provided a cup of "table beer." A bite-size piece of "beer-bread sop" sometimes was given to infants as a pacifier.

Aleberry. Boiled ale to which spices and bread sops were added.

Apple ale. "One who has not tasted it before would not believe that such a palatable drink could be prepared from apples. Mr. Hesselius' daughter's recipe for a pleasant beverage of apples [is to] take some apples, which need not be the best, and apple peelings are taken and dried. Half a peck of this dried fruit is then boiled in ten gallons of water and when removed from the fire the solid part [is] taken out. Then yeast is added to the water, which is allowed to ferment, whereupon it is poured into vessels like any other drink. . . . It is . . . better than that made from persimmons because it retains its quality longer and does not get sour. — I forgot one thing: when the apple ale is made, some bran should be added to the water." (Kalm, *Travels*; see Bibliography)

Apple brandy. "Apples yield a brandy when prepared in the same manner as the peaches. But for this purpose the apples are chiefly taken which fall from the tree before they are ripe." (Kalm, *Travels*; see Bibliography)

Beer. *See* ale.

Beverage. The popular name for "water cyder, made by putting the mure into a fat adding water as you desire it stronger or smaller (weaker, as small beer). The water should stand 48 hours on it before you press it; when it is pressed tun it up immediately." (Manuscript, 1756)

Bishop. A punch of wine or brandy to which roasted oranges and/or lemons were added; a favorite drink of such politically diverse men as Benjamin Franklin and Samuel Johnson. "Fine oranges, well roasted, with sugar and wine in a cup, / They'll make a sweet *bishop* when gentlefolks sup." (Jonathan Swift, *Collected Works*, 1823)

Blackberry wine. "Has a very fine taste [and] is made in the following manner— The juice of the blackberries is pressed out and put into a vessel; with half a gallon of this juice, an equal quantity of water is well mixed. Three pounds of brown sugar are added to this mixture which must then stand for awhile, and after that it is fit for use." (Kalm, *Travels*; see Bibliography)

Blackstrap. Molasses mixed with rum.

Bombo. "A compound of Rum and Water in equal parts, made palatable with Long Sugar [molasses]." (William Byrd, *History of the Dividing Line*; see Bibliography)

Bounce. Fresh fruit juices mixed half and half with rum; bilberry bounce, for example, was blueberry juice and rum.

Bramble wine. "The American brambles are in great abundance . . . on some old land which had long been uncultivated there were so many bushes of this kind that it was very troublesome and dangerous walking among them. A wine is made of the berries [which are] likewise eaten when they are ripe and taste well. No other use is made of them." (Kalm, *Travels*; see Bibliography)

Buttered ale. "Sugar, cinnamon, butter and beer brewed without hops." (Samuel Pepys, *Diary*)

Caudle. A warm, thin gruel to which wine or ale was added, the mixture enhanced when possible with sugar and spices. It had been a favorite medieval English cup to soothe those who were ill or elderly.

Cherry cordial. To make a cherry cordial: "Take Black Cherries, large and full ripe, plucking off their Stalks only, 12 Pounds; put them into a large Stone Bottle, to which put choice Brandy six Quarts, Double Refined Loaf Sugar 3 pounds in Powder, Lime Juice a Pint and a half, Cinamon bruised, Cloves slit, Nutmegs bruised, of each a quarter of an ounce; stop them up close, shaking the Bottle every Day: After three weeks you may use it: Two, three or four spoonfuls, will be an extraordinary *Cordial*, at any time upon any Fainting, or Illness, especially in a Morning fasting." (Dr. Salmon, see Bibliography) "*Oct. 24, 1720*: She gave me a dram of Blackcherry Brandy, and gave me a lump of the Sugar that was in it." (Sewall, *Diary*; see Bibliography)

Cherry wine. "Is made in the same manner [as blackberry wine] but care must be taken that when the juice is pressed out, the stones be not crushed, for they give the wine a bad taste." (Kalm, *Travels*; see Bibliography) "*Mond 1 (July, 1723)* fair. I fell off ye Ladder Climbing to get black Cherrys in ye orchard." (Hempsted, *Diary*; see Bibliography)

"*Cherry Wine*: Take the best Cheeries, pick them, stone them, and strain them; into a Gallon of Juice, put two pound of Sugar, put it into a Tub, and let it work, when done, stop it up for two Months, and then draw and bottle it with a little Sugar, and let it be kept six Weeks for use." (Dr. Salmon; see Bibliography)

Cider. "*Fryd 20 (Oct. 1720)* fair, I was about home al day Triming & fitting of Cask & Stowing away *Cyder*. I filied the Rum hhd I had of Joseph Coit with Cydar made with pairmains and Sweetins that grew back Side the Lot." (Hempsted, *Diary*; see Bibliography)

Cider, sweet or aged to a potent hardness, provided a base for numerous other drinks. *Stewed Quaker* signified a bowl of hard cider served with a hot roasted apple floating on top, while *yard of flannel* was the name given to cider or ale to which a dollop of rum had been added before it was mixed with cream and beaten eggs, then enhanced with whatever spices were available. *Applejack* was made fairly routinely throughout the winter; *apple brandy* was achieved by simply allowing hard cider to stand open in the unheated cellar, or the keg was removed for the occasion to a bench outside the kitchen door, and the cider was allowed to freeze so that the alcohol could be tapped off.

Flip.   A liquor much used aboard ships, made by mixing beer with spirits and sugar. Usually made by warming and spicing ale, to which brandy and eggs were added. The mixture was poured from one mug to another until it frothed and creamed, then poured into the original mixing vessel, where it was reheated by a hot loggerhead thrust into the liquid. "The days are short, the weather's cold, / By tavern fires tales are told. / Some ask for dram when first come in, / Others with *flip* and bounce begin." (*New England Almanac*, 1704)

Gilliflower cordial.   "Take two Ounces of dried Clove Gilliflowers, and put them into a Bottle of Canary; add three Ounces of fine Sugar, and half a Scruple of Ambergrise in Powder; put them into a Stone Bottle, and stop it close, often shaking it; and when it has stood 10 Days, then strain it through a jelly Bag; and putting it up for use, take two or three Spoonfuls of it at a time, and it will greatly strengthen the Heart, and restore Health again, &c." (Salmon; see Bibliography)

Grog.   A mixture of spirits and water; usually rum and water; sometimes used as a synonym for rum. "Sat. Apr. 16, 1774: This evening drank our Sweethearts in a large Can of *Grog*. It is a custom at Sea on Saturday nights. Very sick indeed." (Nicholas Cresswell; see Bibliography)

Hungary water.   Distilled water made from rosemary flowers infused in rectified spirits of wine. Also flavored with thyme or sage, according to taste.

Lamb's wool.   Ale mixed with the pulp of roasted apples, to which sugar and spices sometimes were added. "A cup of *lamb's wool* they drank to him there." (*Song of the King and the Miller*)

Love potion.   A drink made of various herbs added to spirits, although the most important ingredient was hope. A willing partaker was necessary. "*Saturd 5 (Oct., 1723)* fair. most of ye day getting a Nurse for Eliz Fox Widow of Cuz John Fox. She is aged about 42 years & hath been a Widow near 12 years & yet it is feared She is distracted for Love of Jno Richards although he protests he never toucht her lips but once. itt is hardly Credable yet no other Reason prevails. I got Widow Mosier again to look after her." (Joshua Hempsted, *Diary*; see Bibliography) "I once took notice of a wanton Womans compounding the solid roots of (Orchis) with Wine, for an Amorous Cup, which wrought the desired effect." (John Josselyn; see Bibliography)

Mead.   From the Saxon *meeth*, the Dutch *meth* ("meadow"). A mixture of honey and water allowed to ferment to form an alcoholic liquor.

Metheglin.   From the Welsh *meddyglynn*: *medd* ("mead") and *glyyn* ("to glue"), or *medclyg* ("physician") and *llyn* ("drink")—thus a medicinal drink. Metheglin was an ancient English drink popular throughout each of the colonies, and was still enjoyed in many rural areas in the nineteenth century. Made in the south, especially, by grinding honey-locust beans, which then were mixed with honey, water, and flavoring herbs and allowed to ferment.

Negus. Wine and water; usually port or sherry to which was added hot water, sugar, lemon juice, and spices. A punch invented by or named for Colonel Francis Negus in the early eighteenth century.

Peach brandy. "The fruit is cut asunder and the stones are taken out. The pieces of fruit are then put into a vessel, where they are left for three weeks or a month till they are quite putrid. They are then put into the distilling vessel and the brandy is made and afterward distilled over again. This product is not good for people who have a more refined taste, but it is only for the common people such as workmen and the like." (Kalm, *Travels*; see Bibliography)

Perry. "The next liquor in esteem after cyder, in the ordering of which let not your pears be over-ripe before you grind them, and with some sorts of pears the mixing of a few crabs [apples] in the grinding is of great advantage, making *perry* equal to the redstreak cyder." (Philip Miller, *Gardener's Dictionary*; see Bibliography)

Persimmon brandy. "Having collected a sufficient quantity . . . [persimmons] are put into a vessel where they lie for a week till they are quite soft. Then . . . pour water on them and . . . leave to ferment of themselves. The brandy is then made in the ordinary way and is very good, especially if grapes (of the sweet sort) which are wild in the woods, be mixed with the persimmon fruit." (Kalm, *Travels*; see Bibliography)

Posset. "Take a fair scoured Skellet, put in some milk and marygold petals, after boyling, strain out the marygolds, add ale *or* beer and some sugar, *or* leave out the sugar." (Robert May, 1671)

Punch. Spirits mixed with water, sugar, and the juice of lemons, and often spiced.

Quincy. Hot rum to which quince jelly was added.

Rambooze or rambuse. "A drink made of wine, ale, eggs, and sugar in the winter time; or of wine, milk, sugar and rosewater in the summertime." (Bailey)

Sampson. Hot cider laced with rum.

Sangaree. Wine to which water, sugar, nutmeg, and bayleaf were added.

Sillabub. "Fill your Sillabub Pot with Syder (for that is best for a Sillabub) and good store of Sugar and a little Nutmeg, stir it wel together, put in as much thick Cream by two or three spoonfuls at a time, as hard *as you* *can as though you milke it in,* then stir it together exceeding softly once about and let it stand two hours." (Samuel Sewall, *Diary*; see Bibliography)

Snapdragon.   "A kind of play in which brandy is set on fire, and raisins thrown into it, which those who are unused to the sport are afraid to take out; but which may be safely snatched by a quick motion, and set blazing into the mouth, which being closed, the fire is extinguished." (Johnson)

Strong water.   Any form of alcoholic spirits used as a beverage.

Toddy.   Hot rum and water mixed, spiced, buttered, or otherwise flavored.

GLOSSARY 3
Common Foods and Prepared Dishes

Bait. Food. To bait: "To stop for refreshment." (Johnson)

Batter. A mixture of several ingredients, beaten together with some liquor; so called from being beaten.

Brackle. To break bread or cake into milk, tea, soup, coffee, or chocolate.

Brasyll. Fish sauce.

Breakfast. The meal which breaks the night's fast; food at sunrise. "Hope is a good breakfast, but it is a bad supper." (Francis Bacon, *Apothegms*)

Bride-cake. Richer than ordinary cake, of milk, eggs, wheat flour, spices, raisins, and other fruit, the variety depending on budget and season. "It is Customary and Commendable to begin with a marriage feast." (Thomas Thatcher, *Boston Sermons*) "*May 8th, 1712.* At night, Dr. Increase Mather married Mr. Sam Gerrish and Mrs. Sarah Coney; Dr. Cotton Mather pray'd last. . . . [Had] Sack-posset and Cake." (Sewall, *Diary*; see Bibliography)

Bustard. A wild turkey.

Caper. An acid pickle. "To pickle Nasturtiums for capers: Gather your little knobs quickly after your Blossoms are off, put them in cold Water and Salt for three Days, shifting them once a day; then make a Pickle but do not boil it at all of some White-wine, some White-Wine Vinegar, Eschalot, Horse-Radish, Pepper, Salt, Cloves and Mace Whole and Nutmeg quartered; then put in your Seeds and stop them Close; they are to be eaten as Capers." (Mrs. E. Smith, *Compleat Housewife*, London, 1739) The true caper is the pickled flower bud or berry of a Mediterranean plant not hardy in North America.

Carlings. Peas steeped in water and fried in butter.

Cates. Food; specifically purchased food as opposed to that prepared in one's own kitchen.

Catsup. A kind of pickle.

Shrimp catsup, 1760 manuscript recipe

Cheesecake. A cake made of soft curds, sugar, and butter.

Chine. "A part of the back in which the spine is found." (Johnson)

Chocolate. A late-seventeenth-century luxury import, milled in the colonies after 1765. "I was very civilly Received, and courteously entertained, in a clean comfortable House, and the Good woman was very active in helping off my Riding clothes, and then ask't what I would eat. I told her I had some *Chocolett*, if shee would prepare it; which with the help of some milk, and a little clean brass kettle, she soon effected to my satisfaction." (Mme. Knight, *Journal*; see Bibliography)

Coddling cream. Peas cooked in rosewater and served cold with cream.

Coddlings. Green peas.

Cod fish. "Saturday, July 21, 1744; Boston: I was invited to dine with Captain Irvin upon salt cod fish, which here is a common Saturday's dinner, being elegantly dressed with a sauce of butter and eggs." (Hamilton, *Itinerarium*; see Bibliography)

Coffee. Any beans or corns roasted and then boiled in water. Real coffee was a late-seventeenth-century luxury imported from Arabia via England to the colonies and was rivaled in popularity only by tea. "At Nine we met over a Pot of *Coffee* which was not quite strong enough to give us the Palsy." (William Byrd, *Dividing Line*; see Bibliography)

Cole sla. "My landlady prepared an unusual salad which I never remember having seen or eaten. She took the inner leaves of a head of cabbage and cut them in long, thin strips about ½ to ⅙ of an inch wide. She put them upon a platter, poured oil and vinegar upon them, added salt and some pepper while mixing. In place of oil, melted butter is frequently used. This is kept in a warm pot or crock and poured over the salad after it has been served. This dish tastes better than one can imagine. She told me many strangers who had eaten at her house like this so much . . . they said they were going to have it prepared for them when they reached home." (Kalm, *Travels*; see Bibliography)

Collop. "A morsel of food." (Johnson)

Comfit. Correctly, "confect." A dry sweetmeat; a fruit or root preserved with sugar and dried. "There were *comfits* in the cabin and apples in the hold." (Nursery rhyme)

Cordial. A medicine that increases the force of the heart, or any medicine that increases strength, or anything that comforts, gladdens, and exhilarates.

Coriander. The fruits or seeds of an herb in the parsley family. "Israel called the name thereof manna; and it was like *coriander* seed, white." (Exodus XIII, 31)

Cream. "When it is cold [it] floats on milk and is changed by the agitation of the churn into butter; the flower of milk." (Johnson) "To make Clouted *Cream*. Take a Gill of New Milk and set it on the Fire and take six Spoonfulls of Rose-water; four or five pieces of large Mace, put the Mace on a Thread; when it boils, put to them the Yolks of two Eggs very well beaten; stir these very well together; then take a Quart of very good *Cream*; put it to the Rest; and stir it together, but let it not boil after *Cream* is in. Pour it out of the Pan you boil it in and let it stand all Night; the next day take the Top off it and serve it up." (Mrs. Hannah Glasse, *Art of Cookery*; see Bibliography) "*Satterday, June 5th, 1686.* I rode to Newbury to see my little Hull, and to keep out of the way of the Artillery Election, on which day eat Strawberries and *Cream* with Sister Longfellow at the Falls." (Sewall, *Diary*; see Bibliography)

Cream-posset. A rich posset, a kind of syllabub.

Crust. "The case of a pie, made of meal and baked." (Johnson)

Crustade. "A pie of eggs and milk with flavoring." (Johnson)

Cucumber pickle. "Cucumbers are pickled with [guinea pepper], or the pods are pounded while yet tender, and being mixed with salt are preserved in a bottle. This spice is served on roasted or boiled meat or fried fish and gives them a fine taste." (Kalm, *Travels*; see Bibliography)

Curds. Day-old milk cheese. "June 17, 1718. She gave me very good *curds*." (Sewall, *Diary*; see Bibliography)

Custard. "A kind of sweetmeat made by boiling eggs with milk and sugar, till the whole thickens in a mass." (Johnson)

Dainty. An out-of-the-ordinary dish; also, one specially prepared. "Their corne they rost in the eare greene, and bruise it in a mortar of wood with a Polt, lapp it in rowles in the leaves of their corne and so boyle it for a *daintie*." (John Smith, *Virginia*, 1612; see Bibliography)

Daryels or dariels. "Take creme of cowe milk. Do thereto ayren [eggs] with sugar, safron, and salt. Medle it afere [together]. Do it in a coffyn [pan] of two ynche depe; bake it well and serve it forth." (*The Forme of Cury*, 1780 reproduction of a manuscript cookbook)

Dinner. The nooning meal; the main meal of the day. "Bad dinners go hand in hand with total depravity, while a man properly fed is already half-saved." (Anon.)

Dried peaches. "To preserve peaches for winter use, they are cut into four parts, put up on a thread on which they are exposed to the sunshine till they are sufficiently dry. They are then put into a vessel." (Kalm, *Travels*; see Bibliography)

Entertainment. To be served with food. "We went slay-riding out to the Bowery to Madame Dowes, a Gentlewoman that lived at a farm House, who gave us a handsome *Entertainment* of five or six Dishes and choice Beer and metheglin, Cyder, et c. all which she said was the produce of her farm." (Mme. Knight, *Journal*; see Bibliography) "*Thursd 4 (Nov., 1731)* fair & moderate. I was at Madam Winthrops at an *Entertainment,* or treat of Colln Samll Brownes, a Barbaqued." (Hempsted, *Diary*; see Bibliography)

Entremets. From the French word. Small plates set between the main dishes. "Chards of beets are plants of white beet transplanted producing great tops which, in the midst, have a large white main sheet which is the true chard used in pottages and *entremets.*" (Philip Miller, *Gardener's Dictionary*; see Bibliography)

Fish soup. "*Sunday, May 7, 1775; Muddy Creek*: One of the Company cought a large Catfish, which made a most delicious pot of Soup." (Nicholas Cresswell, *Journal*; see Bibliography)

Flitch. The side of a hog salted and cured. "But heretofore 'twas thought a sumptuous feast on birthdays, festivals or days of state, A salt dry *flitch* of bacon to prepare." (John Dryden, *Juvenal*)

Flounder. A small flat fish. "Like the flounder, out of the frying pan into the fire." (William Camden, *Britannia*, 1607)

Flower. "The edible part of corn; the meal." (Johnson)

Flummery. A kind of food made by coagulation of wheat flour or oatmeal.

Fricasee. "A dish made by cutting chickens or other small things in pieces and dressing them with strong sauce." (Johnson)

Fritters. Fragments or cut pieces of food fried in batter. "Elder Flower and Vine Leaf *Fritures*: Those of Elder Flowers are made while they are in bloom; and those of Vine Leaves, by breaking off the tops of the small tender shoots in little branches; both are to be marinated. . . . When drained, dip them in good thick Batter to fry, and serve with rasped Sugar as most usual." (B. Clermont, *The Professed Cook*, 1776)

Frog's legs. "Some people eat the thighs and hind legs [of bullfrogs] and say that they are very palatable." (Kalm, *Travels*; see Bibliography)

Froise. "A kind of food made by frying bacon enclosed in a pancake." (Johnson)

Frumenty. Hulled wheat, boiled in milk, seasoned with cinnamon, sugar or other sweetening. "Here a custard, there a pie, and here all tempting *frumenty.*" (Robert Herrick, *Hesperides*)

Fry. A dish of things fried, as a fish-fry.

Furmenty. *See* frumenty. "Remember, wife, therefore if I do not, the seed-cake, the pasties and *furmenty* pot." (Tusser, *Advice to Housewives*; see Bibliography)

Gammen or gammon. The buttock of a hog salted and dried; the lower end of the flitch. "Gammons that give a relish to the taste." (Dryden)

Garbage. "That part of the inwards which is separated and thrown away. To pull and *garbage*: to cut apart and dress for cooking." (Johnson)

Gingerbread. "Bread or biscuit sweetened with treacle and flavored with ginger and some other aromatick seeds." (Johnson) Hence, a thin, hard pastry until about 1800. "Her currants there, and gooseberries were spread With the enticing gold of *gingerbread*." (King, *Art of Cookery*; see Bibliography) "An' I had but one penny in the world, thou shouldst have it to buy *gingerbread*." (Shakespeare, *Taming of the Shrew*) "Oct. 6, 1720. Gave her a piece of Mr. Belcher's Cake and *Ginger Bread* wrapped up in a clean sheet of Paper." (Sewall, *Diary*; see Bibliography)

Gobbet. A mouthful; as much as can be swallowed at once.

Gravy. "Juice that runs from meat not [too] much dried by fire." (Johnson)

Gravies. "The spirit of each dish, and ZEST of all / Is what ingenious cooks the relish call; / For though the market sends in loads of food / They are all tasteless 'til that makes them good." (King, *Art of Cookery*; see Bibliography)

Grocery. A grocer's wares; derived from "gross" or large quantity. "A grocer is a man who buys and sells tea, sugar and plumbs, and spices for gain." (Isaac Watts, *Collected Works*, 1753)

Gruel. Any kind of food made by boiling oatmeal in water or boiling other ingredients. "Essence of oatmeal makes a noble and exhilirating meal." (Thomas Tryon)

Guinea pepper. "Capsicum annum is likewise planted in gardens. When the fruit is ripe it is almost red; it is added to a roasted or boiled piece of meat, a little of it being strewed on it or mixed with the broth. The fruit itself is as sharp as common pepper." (Kalm, *Travels*; see Bibliography)

Ham. The thigh of a hog salted.

Hastings. Peas that come early.

Hodgepodge or hotchpotch. "A medley of ingredients boiled together (in slang, a mishmash)." (Johnson)

Hops. The catkins of a coarse vine used as bitters in the manufacture of beer. "Have the poles without forks, otherwise it will be troublesome to part the *hop* vines and the poles." (Philip Miller, *Gardener's Dictionary*; see Bibliography)

Jam. A conserve of fruits boiled with sugar and water.

Jelly or gelly. Sweetmeats made by boiling sugar and the juice of fruits containing pectin; to bring to a gelatinous state.

Juncate or junket.   Cheesecake; a kind of sweetmeat of curds and sugar.

Kell or kale.   A form of pottage; a soup made from greens.

Lard.   "Grease of swine." (Johnson)
Larden.   A bit of bacon.

Merry-thought.   The wishbone. "A forked bone of fowls which boys and girls pull in play, the longest part broken betokening marriage." (Johnson) "Let him not be breaking *merrythoughts* under the table with my cousin." (Echard)
Mess.   A dish of food, as a "mess of greens"; supper. "Herbs and other country *messes* / Which the neat-handed Phillis dresses." (John Milton, *L'Allegro*) To mess: to eat together.
Milk pottage.   "For breakfast, milk, *milk pottage*, watergruel, and flummery are very fit for children." (John Locke, *Essay Concerning Human Understanding*, 1776)
Minced meat pie.   "Beef, mutton and pork; Shred pies of the best Pig, veal, goose and capon and Turkey well drest." (Thomas Tusser, *Advice to Housewives*; see Bibliography)
Misickquatash.   Succotash. A stew of corn, beans, and sometimes peas, made by "boyling them all to pieces into a broth, or boyling them whole untill they bee soft." (Thomas Hariot; see Bibliography)
Mortress.   A dish of meats of various kinds beaten together. "A *mortress* made with the brawn of capons strained and mingled with like quantity of almond butter is excellent to nourish the weak." (Francis Bacon, *Natural History*)

Pancake.   "A thin pudding baked in a frying pan." (Johnson) "Farmers sow considerable buckwheat . . . used in preparing . . . *pancakes*. As these come from the pan they are covered with butter which is allowed to soak into them. These cakes are eaten in the morning while they are still warm with tea or coffee." (Kalm, *Travels*; see Bibliography)
Paste.   Anything mixed up, such as flour and water, for bread and pies.
Pasty.   Pastry, pie or tart. "A pie of crust." (Johnson) "We supped with a good venison *pasty* and good beer." (John Winthrop, *History of New England*; see Bibliography)
Peason.   Plural of "peas." "Sow *peason* and beans in the wane of the moon, / Who soweth them sooner he soweth too soon." (Thomas Tusser, *Advice to Housewives*; see Bibliography)
Porridge.   "Food made by boiling meat in water." (Johnson)
Pot-herb.   An herb fit for the pot. "Leaves eaten raw are termed sallad; if boiled, they become *potherbs*; and some of these plants which are *potherbs* in one family are sallads in another." (Isaac Watts, *Collected Works*, 1753)

Pottage. Pot foods, soup or stew. "Best Ordinary *Pottage*: [to oatmeal add] violet leaves, Succory, Strawberry leaves, Spinage, Langdebeef [bugloss], Marygold Flowers, Scallions, and a little Parsley." (Gervase Markham, *The English Housewife*; see Bibliography)

Poupicks. "A mess of victuals made of veal steaks and slices of bacon." (Bailey)

Pudding. A kind of food usually boiled, sometimes baked, but generally made of meal, milk, and eggs.

Pudding pie. "A pudding with meat baked in it." (Johnson)

Quiddany. A marmalade; a confection of quinces made with sugar.

Quince-cream. A delicacy of boiled, pulped quinces and cream whipped with wine and sugar; a kind of pudding used also to fill tart shells and meringues. "They call for dates and quinces in the pastry." (Shakespeare)

Redbud. "By some called the 'sallad tree' because its flowers are eaten in salads and the buds pickled." (Kalm, *Travels*; see Bibliography)

Roasted warden. A baked winter pear. "There powder'd beef & *warden*-pies were found, / And pudding smok'd within her spacious bound." (Mary Leaper, *Crumble Hall*, 1748)

Salad. Pronounced formerly sallet. "You have to rectify your palate on olives, capers, or some better *salad* ushering the mutton." (Ben Jonson) "Many herbes in the Spring time are commonly dispersed throughout the woods —good for broths and *sallets*, as Violets, Purslins, Sorrel &c." (John Smith, *A True Declaration*; see Bibliography) "Sea tears grow upon the sea banks in abundance [and are] boiled & eaten as a *Sallade* & the broth drunk with it." (John Josselyn, *New England's Rarities*; see Bibliography)

Sauce. Something eaten with food to improve its taste. "A *Sauce* for Roast Venison. Jelly of Currants melted and serv'd hot, with a lemon squeezed into it." (Mrs. E. Smith, *Compleat Housewife*, 1739; see Bibliography) "What is *Sauce* for the Gander is *Sauce* for the Goose." (Traditional English proverb)

Shrive. A slice of bread.

Sippets. Slender pieces or wedges of toasted bread on which food was served, or which were used as "pushers" in lieu of forks. "Stew a Quart of Shrimps in Half a Pint of white-wine, a Nutmeg grated, and a Good Piece of Butter; when the Butter is melted, and they are not through, beat the Yolks of Four Eggs with a little White-wine, and pour it in; and shake it well, till it is of the Thickness you like; then dish it on *sippets*." (Mrs. E. Smith, *Compleat Housewife*, 1739; see Bibliography)

Sops. Pieces of bread dropped into broths or beverages as a kind of instant dumpling.

Sorrel greens in pot liquor. "They prepare greens of a kind of sorrel that grows at the edge of cultivated fields. Green leaves are gathered in April by everyone everywhere [and] used in the same way Swedes prepare

Spinach [as a salad]. But they generally boil the leaves in the water in which they had cooked meat. Then they eat it alone with meat. It is served on a platter and eaten with a knife." (Peter Kalm, *Travels*; see Bibliography)

Spoonmeat.   A broth prepared with barley. "Water gruel is a kind of *spoon meats*; the queen of soups and gratifies nature beyond all others." (Tryon)

Tansy.   The aromatic plant, and also a kind of omelet. "How to make a *Tansy*: Take a little tansy, featherfew, parsley and violets, and stampe them altogether and straine them with thee yolkes of eight or tenne eggs and three or foure whites, and some vinegar and put thereto sugar or salt and frie it." (*The Good Housewife's Handmaid*, 1588)

Tea.   The luxury from China. "We have one far-fetched and dear-bought plant . . . believe the medicinal and balsamick Virtues of it; it revives the Heart, and it refreshes the Spirits, and is a Remedy against a World of Distempers." (Cotton Mather)

Temsed bread.   Bread made from flour more finely sifted than common flour.

Vegetable stew. A 1760 manuscript recipe used cabbage, lettuce, cucumbers, butter, salt, pepper, peas, and veal or mutton.

Food-preparation accessories: eighteenth-century iron vegetable choppers

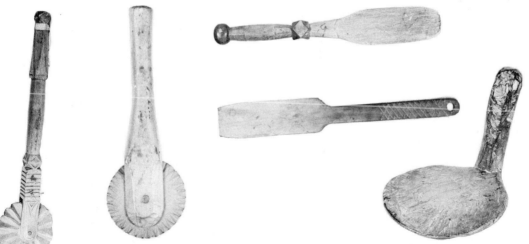

Carved dough-trimmers or wheels; stirrers or scrapers; skimmer

Table mortars: spice mortar; lignum vitae; plain style; painted; turned burl; handle style

Long-handled cooking ladles; serving spoons or ladles

Tall samp or corn mortars; flour or meat storage barrels

Wooden tray; milk basins or tubs; covered butter or cheese tub; dough-box; powdering trough

Herb and corn dryers; herb baskets; multipurpose shears

Wooden pails for milk and water; dippers or ladles

Dairy-room furnishings: cheese press; basket; cradle for strainer; strainer basket; scales; churn; shaper

CHAPTER NOTES

Part I: The Wilderness Rim

1. John Smith, 1579–1631, *The Generall Historie of Virginia, New England and the Summer Isles; Travels and Works of Captain John Smith,* see Bibliography.

2. Smith, *The Generall Historie.* "Captain Smith, who next to Sir Walter Raleigh, may be considered the founder of our Colony, has written its history. . . . He was honest, sensible, and well-informed, but his style is barbarous, and uncouth. His history, however, is almost the only source from which we derive any knowledge of the infancy of our state." Thomas Jefferson, *Notes on Virginia* (see Bibliography).

3. Smith, *The Generall Historie.* "The President [Edward Maria Wingfield] had felt neither Want nor sickness because he had embezzled the Publick [food] and had lived in great Plenty and Elegance. . . . It raised such indignation that they deposed him and elected Captain John Ratcliffe in his Room," according to William Stith, *History of the First Discovery and Settlement of Virginia* (see Bibliography).

4. Smith, *The Generall Historie.*

5. *Ibid.*

6. *Ibid.* "Tuftaffety" was a slang term for an unskilled gentleman, a dude, fop, dilettante.

7. *Ibid.* "Some cut down and clear away the trees to make a place to pitch their Tents. . . . The President's [Wingfield's] Jealousy would not admit any other Fortification but the boughs of Trees cast together in the Form of a Half-Moon," according to Stith (see 3. above).

8. *Ibid.*

9. *Ibid.* "Last" referred generally to any great weight, load, or burden, the exact quantity varying with the goods measured; by the late eighteenth century it usually referred to two tons' weight, occasionally just one. "Trial": an experiment or sample to prove possibility.

10. *Ibid.*

11. *Ibid.* The pigs and chickens were turned out into the woods to forage for acorns, nuts, seeds.

12. *Ibid.* "Clapboard" referred to rough-sawed narrow boards, "wainscot" to rough wide boards.

13. *Ibid.* Wild tales circulated in England that one starving Jamestown colonist killed his wife and, after slaking immediate hunger, powdered or salted the remains for later use; when found out, he was said to have been hanged. Smith denied the tale, remarking "whether she was better roasted, boyled or carbonado'd [barbecued] I know not, but such a dish as powdered wife I never heard of."

14, 15. *Ibid.* Smith used as his armorial motto, *Vincere est vivere,* "To overcome is to live."

16. Cotton Mather, *The Christian Philosopher: A Collection of the Best Discoveries in Nature, with Religious Improvements* (London, 1721).

17. "Salt horse" was the British seaman's euphemism for any kind of pickled meat, hopefully beef.

18. Brownism, so called for its founder, Robert Brown, who in 1581 advocated a new system of church government; his followers chose to establish an independent or separate church. The term "Pilgrim" did not become popular until after 1856, when it first began to appear in print. Bradford's manuscript, handed down from father to son and stored for years in the library of Boston's Old South Church, was taken to England—perhaps as a soldier's souvenir—just prior to the Revolution. Here it remained until an historian learned by chance of its existence. When Charles Deane of the Massachusetts Historical Society copied the old papers, he found Bradford's stirring account of the Saints' leavetaking from Leyden: "The time being come that they must departe . . . they lefte that goodly & pleasante citie, which had been their resting place near 12 years; *but they knew they were pilgrimes,* & looked not much on those things, but lift[ed] up their eyes to ye heavens, their dearest cuntrie, and quieted their spirits." Deane and others thought the name fitting, though the word "pilgrims" was mentioned just once in Bradford's *History of Plimouth Plantation.*

19. Henry Wadsworth Longfellow, *The Courtship of Miles Standish.*

20. William Bradford (1590–1657), with William Brewster, James Robinson, and others, organized the Separatist church at Scrooby, England, 1606; went into exile in Amersterdam and Leyden, where he worked as a weaver and say maker. One of the leaders of the migration to Plymouth, he became the second governor on John Carver's death, 1621. Began writing his *History of Plimouth Plantation* in 1630, working on the text until 1650 (see Bibliography).

21. *Ibid.* Bradford called it a "combination . . . being the first foundation of their governmente in this place."

22. "Mourt's" *Relation* (see Bibliography). "Cast" meant to throw, and "scour" was, in this instance, to scour out the stomach.

23. *Travels and Works of Captain John Smith* (see Bibliography).

24. Bradford, *History*. Captain Myles Standish (1584?–1656), professional soldier, led First Discovery, 1620; organized settlers' militia; served as colony's agent; as its purchaser, 1626; as its undertaker or agent, 1627–41; settled in Duxbury, 1632; was assistant governor, 1633, and treasurer, 1652–55; believed in principle of religious toleration, never became a member of the colonists' church.

25. *Ibid.*

26. *Ibid.*

27. *Ibid.*

28. *Ibid.* Squanto, or Tisquantum, served as interpreter between colonists and Indians.

29. Edward Johnson (1598–1672), Canterbury joiner, emigrated to Boston in 1630, returned to England for his family, and in 1636 settled at Charlestown; helped found Woburn in 1640; was selectman, captain, deputy to the General Court; served as speaker, House of Deputies, 1655; began writing *Wonder Working Providence* in 1650 (see Bibliography).

30. Edward Winslow (1595–1655), *Good Newes from New England* (see Bibliography). Worcestershire printer, he served as colonial agent, 1623; member of the General Court, 1624–46; returned to England, 1646; served in Cromwell's government.

31. *Ibid.*

Part II: The Kitchen Common Room

1. Edward Johnson, *Wonder Working Providence*. See Note 29. Part I.

2. *Ibid.*

3. William Bradford, *History of Plimouth Plantation*. See Note 20, Part I.

4. John Smith, *Advertisements for the unexperienced Planters of New-England* (see Bibliography).

5. Thomas Hooker (1586–1657), *The Christian's Two Chiefe Lessons* (see Bibliography). Surrey rector; a Puritan leader in England forced to retire in 1626 because of his religious beliefs; self-exiled to Holland, 1630; emigrated to Massachusetts in 1634, as pastor for Newtown; in 1636 led his congregation to Hartford, establishing that new colony.

6. Mattatuck is now Waterbury, Connecticut.

7. Joshua Hempsted, *Diary* (see Bibliography). "July 1, 1738: Adam began to mow before ye Door"; "Oct. 16, 1748: The violent wind in ye morn blew down the locust tree before the door which hath been an excellent shade for me to work under in ye summer above thirty years."

8. Robert Cushman (1578–1625), sermon; *Danger of Self-Love* (London, 1622).

Canterbury wool comber, joined exiles in Leyden; deacon; emigrated to Plymouth aboard the *Fortune*.

9. The New Amsterdam report agrees with Edward Johnson's "Casting the earth aloft upon timber."

10. Thomas Dudley (1576–1653) came with Massachusetts Bay Colony as deputy governor; reelected deputy thirteen times; governor four terms; one of the founders and first overseers, Harvard College. The law was followed only if convenient, however, no matter how much assented to verbally. Records are many of such fires as that reported in Winthrop's *Journal* (see Bibliography) in May 1646: "A barn at Salem was set on fire with lightning and all the corn and hay consumed suddenly. It fell upon the thatch." Dudley's own house burnt in 1632, "the hearth of the Hall chimney burning all night upon the principal beam. River sedge and rye straw were used to thatch the roofs, the bundles being fastened to slats, not boards."—Peter Force, (see Bibliography).

11. Peter Kalm, Swedish scientist, *Travels in North America* (see Bibliography).

12. *Ibid.*

13. Samuel Maverick (1602?–1676?), *Brief Description of New England and the Severall Townes Therein* (see Bibliography). A staunch Anglican and critic of the Separatists, Maverick is believed to have been associated with Sir Ferdinando Gorges, colonial proprietor. Appointed a Royal Commissioner by Charles II in 1664.

14. The custom of building a home for the pastor, often to his specifications, continued throughout the colonial period. The Reverend James Lockwood house, Main Street, Wethersfield, Connecticut, was built by public subscription of $1,500 in 1767, in gratitude to the clergyman because he consistently refused calls to more lucrative pastorates.

15. John Hammond, *Leah and Rachel* (see Bibliography).

16. Jasper Danckaerts, *Journal* (see Bibliography).

17. Samuel Sewall (1652–1730) was graduated from Harvard, 1671; became wealthy through marriage to Hannah Hull; managed Bay Colony's printing press, 1681–84; General Court deputy, 1683; Council member, 1684–86; judge at Salem witchcraft trials; superior court justice, 1692; probate judge, Suffolk County, 1715; chief justice, 1718–28. In addition to his *Diary* (see Bibliography), Sewall wrote the first American protest against the slavery system, *The Selling of Joseph* (1700), and many pamphlets.

18. Sewall, *Diary*.

19. Benjamin Franklin, *An Account of the New Invented Pennsylvanian Fireplaces* (Philadelphia, 1744). The Swedish traveler Peter Kalm wrote in December 1749 that "Mr. Franklin lent me one of the stoves for the winter. It kept the house quite warm although one had to use short wood in it. It proved often unecessary to have a fire in the kitchen and one could prepare chocolate and other food in the little stove. Also, by suspending a cord from above in front of the fire-box, it proved possible to roast meat

or fowl attached to it and turned" (*Travels in North America*, see Bibliography).

20. Alexander Hamilton, *Itinerarium* (see Bibliography).

21. John Josselyn, *Two Voyages* (see Bibliography).

22. John Winthrop, *Journal* (see Bibliography).

23. Hempsted, *Diary*.

24. Sarah Kemble Knight (1666–1727), *Journal* (see Bibliography). Wife of a Boston merchant, Mrs. Knight traveled alone from that city to New York in 1704, an extraordinary and hazardous undertaking at the time. Starting out in October 1704, she rode through Rhode Island and Connecticut and returned by the same route. The house described here was twelve miles beyond Dedham. The adjective "sad" meant "heavy" when applied as in sad-iron and "gray" when used to describe a color, as pewter sometimes was called sad-ware.

25. Such kitchen extensions as listed in other houses sometimes were situated in the cellar.

26. Mme. Knight, *Journal*. The house described was about twenty miles from Kingston, Rhode Island.

27. Hempsted, *Diary*. The phrase "moderately visited" referred, of course, to the degree of illness, not to the number of guests. The widow Miner was Molly's mother-in-law.

28. The Webb House is maintained as a museum by the Society of Colonial Dames of America in the State of Connecticut and is open daily to visitors.

29. Enoch Hale, *Diary*. Original in Connecticut Historical Society collections. The Nathan Hale Homestead is maintained as a museum by the Antiquarian and Landmarks Society, Inc., of Connecticut and is open May through October 15 to visitors.

30. Deacon Hale's newly wed second wife apparently approved the continued use of the thirty-year-old kitchen facilities.

31. By the nineteenth century, the term "necessary house" generally had given way to "privy."

32. Hempsted, *Diary*. From his notes on a journey to Maryland in 1749: "very well entertained after the Country fashion in Cribb houses, a dozen or more. . . . Sunday I went to meeting to Notingham . . . the minister and people here are very modest in their apparel and in their houses, mostly Log houses, cribb fashion." At Ogletown "are mostly wooden houses cribb fashion & old; those that are newly built the logs are hewed & framed handsomely."

33. Danckaerts, *Journal*.

34. William Byrd II, *History of the Dividing Line* (see Bibliography).

35. Hamilton, *Itinerarium*.

36. Kalm, *Travels*.

37. Nicholas Cresswell, *Journal* (see Bibliography). A visitor to Virginia just

prior to the outbreak of war, Cresswell wanted to emigrate there permanently but was forced to return to England because of his Loyalist sympathies. During his year in America he helped survey the Virginia frontier while looking for a possible homesite.

38. John Josselyn, *New England's Rarities Discovered* (see Bibliography).

39. Cresswell, *Journal*.

40. Some have held the bacon strip instead was a rack for utensils. This seems improbable, since the heat from embers and flames would make the tools too hot to handle easily, as well as smoke-grimed and grease-encrusted.

Part III: The Seventeenth-Century Kitchen

1. John Smith, *The Generall Historie of Virginia, New England and the Summer Isles* (see Bibliography). "Twenty thousand pounds would have hired good laborers and mechanical men, and furnished them with cattle and all necessaries, and 100 of them would have done more than a thousand of those that went."

2. Francis Higginson (1586–1630), *New England Plantation* (see Bibliography). "Fowles of the Aire are plentifull here, and all sorts as we have in England. . . . Here are likewise abundance of Turkies, exceeding fat, sweet and fleshy . . . in Summer all places are full of [strawberries] and all maner of berries and fruits. This Country doth abound with Wild Geese, wild Duckes and other Sea Fowle. . . . Here is good living."

3. John Smith, *Description of New England* (see Bibliography).

4. William Bradford, *History of Plimouth Plantation* (see Bibliography). "What crosses, trouble, fears, wants, and sorrowes they had been lyable unto is easy to conjecture . . . they were in journyings often, in perils of waters, of robers, of their owne nation, in perils among the heathen, in perills of the wildernes, in perills of the sea, in perills of false brethern; in wearines and painfulnes, in watching often, in hunger and thirst, in fasting often, in could and nakednes." Ref. 2 Corinthians: 11, 26, 27.

5. Edward Johnson, *Wonder-Working Providence* (see Bibliography).

6. *Ibid.*

7. Higginson, *New England Plantation*.

8. *Ibid.*

9. *Ibid.*

10. William Wood, *New England's Prospect* (see Bibliography).

11. *Ibid.*

12. *Ibid.*

13. William Stith, *The History of the First Discovery and Settlement of Virginia* (see Bibliography). In 1619 the Governor proposed "there should be sent over 100 maids, young and uncorrupt, to make wives for the Inhabi-

tants . . . and that such as were married to the publick Farmers should be transporte at the Company's Expense . . . . 90 maids were sent the following Spring." In 1621 "the Company's Treasury was so reduced that it could not pay for . . . necessary Provisions and Utensils [or for] the Maids to make Wives. The price was an hundred and twenty Pounds of Tobacco [each]," and the settlers were enjoined to buy them outright. "I find that the Governor was obliged [in 1624] to issue a Proclamation forbidding Women to Contract themselves to several Men at one time. For Women being yet scarce and much in Request this Offence was become very common . . . and no small trouble to the Government. For such offense [they should] undergoe corporal Correction [usually flogging], or be punished by Fine, or otherwise according to the Quality of the Person so offending."

14. John Josselyn, *Two Voyages* (see Bibliography).

15. *Ibid.*

16. Stith, *History*: In Jamestown "our houses, for the most part, are rather built for Use than Ornament. . . . Henrico was quitted in Sir Thomas Smith's time, only the Church and one house remaining. Charles-City never had but six houses."

17. Josselyn, *Two Voyages*.

18. Samuel Johnson, *Dictionary* (see Bibliography).

19. The Buttolph-Williams Mansion House, designated a National Historic Landmark by the Department of the Interior in 1969, is maintained as a museum by the Antiquarian and Landmarks Society, Inc., of Connecticut and is open to visitors from May to October 15.

Part IV: The Eighteenth-Century Kitchen

1. Gervase Markham, *Farewell to Husbandry* (see Bibliography).

2. As in the biblical sense: "My children are gone forth of me: there is none to stretch forth my tent any more, and to set up my curtains" (Jeremiah X: 20). So Markham says, "Now it may be intended," that is, it is God's will, "that there may be in the household more servants than one."

3. "Cattell" or "cattle" was used to mean not only milch cows, but any domestic beast of burden, including oxen, steers, and horses.

4. Markham, *The English Huswife* (see Bibliography).

5. Pennsylvania *Packet*, September 23, 1780.

6. Corner stakes were set, usually carved or painted with the landowner's name and sometimes with directional indications N, S, E, W, at the outer bounds of a homestead. These were removed when he left the lot or claim to denote his quitting, and for economical reuse. The phrase still is used as a colloquialism in some parts of the country.

7. Benjamin Franklin, *Letters* (see Bibliography).

8. The Hartford (Connecticut) *Courant*, August 18, 1788.

9. Thomas Hooker, *A Survey of the Summe of Church Discipline* (see Bibliography).

10. Edward Johnson, *Wonder Working Providence* (see Bibliography).

11. John Josselyn, *Two Voyages* (see Bibliography).

12. Jasper Danckaerts, *Journal* (see Bibliography). Even so, smiths had to work hard for a good living and use their skills as custom required. "Whereas many persons are so unfortunate as to lose their Fore-Teeth by accident, and otherways, to their great Detriment, not only in Looks, but speaking both in Public and Private—This is to inform all such, that they may have them replaced with artificial ones, that look as well as Natural, & answer the End of speaking to all Intents, by Paul Revere, Goldsmith, near the head of Dr. Clarke's Wharf, Boston."—Boston *Gazette*, September 19, 1768.

13. Joshua Hempsted, *Diary* (see Bibliography).

14. Israel Acrelius, *History of New Sweden* (see Bibliography).

15. Danckaerts, *Journal*.

16. Samuel Sewall, *Diary* (see Bibliography).

17. As quoted by James Boswell, *The Life of Samuel Johnson*, 1791.

18. Sarah Kemble Knight, *Journal* (see Bibliography). Norwalk, Connecticut named as Mme. Knight noted, from North-walk, "its half-Indian-name."

19. Alexander Hamilton, *Itinerarium* (see Bibliography).

20. Joseph Green (1675–1715), pastor at Danvers, Massachusetts, 1698. *Essex Institute Historical Collections*, Vol. X (1869).

21. Sir William Berkeley (1606–77), Virginia governor, 1641–77, successfully defended colony against Indians and Dutch; persecuted Quakers and Puritans. His tyrannical administration resulted in the uprising generally called Bacon's Rebellion. The schools Berkeley referred to were no doubt the type of free Sunday schools known in England; on nonworking days children of tradesmen, artisans, and farmers were taught in Sabbath classes to read, write, and cipher.

22. Peter Kalm, *Travels* (see Bibliography).

23. *Ibid.*

24. Hempsted, *Diary*.

25. A calloused hand was the best recommendation. As Dietrich Heinrich von Bulow reported in *Der Freistat von Nordamerika in seinen neusten Zustand* (Berlin, 1797), "It is easy to sell the farmers, but there often are men it is not easy to dispose of as officers and scholars. I have seen a Russian captain offered for sale eight days, and not one bid ·made [even when] his owner [offered] fifty per cent discount."

26. During the same period, however, London importuned New Jersey and New York to better support the Royal African Company (1702).

27. From the Massachusetts General Court records. Reference is to enemies

captured in the frequent border wars with the French and the Indians, and to emigrants who sought work, that is, were sold to pay for their passage here.

28. John Williams, *The Redeemed Captive Returning to Zion* (Boston, 1707). Williams, a pastor in Deerfield, Massachusetts, was one of numerous white slaves who returned to write of captivity by the French and Indians. (The Revolutionary War hero John Stark was one such redeemed or ransomed by negotiation, almost fifty years after Williams.) On February 29, 1704, Williams wrote, "the enemy came like a Flood upon us. . . . I was seized by Three Indians who disarmed me and bound me Naked . . . they would carry me to Qebeck. . . . They carried to the door two of my children and murder[ed] them . . . many of the houses of my neighbours in Flames." During the forced march of three hundred miles, Mrs. Williams was drowned. In October 1706, Williams was returned to Massachusetts, as were his other children save one daughter, Eunice, who remained with the Indians.

29. Hempsted, *Diary*. If so, she was the "lost" daughter, Eunice Williams, cited above.

30. *Ibid.*

31. Kalm, *Travels.*

32. Lora Case, *Reminiscences* (see Bibliography).

33. Hempsted, *Diary.*

34. Kalm, *Travels.*

35. Sewall, *Diary.*

36. Hempsted, *Diary.*

37. As shown in inventories cited in Part IV, Chapter 1.

38. Hempsted, *Diary*. The justice stayed longer to help than he had anticipated; it was not until Thursday, January 5, that he "came away," stopping en route "at Ms. Denisons to warm my Self." He recovered sufficiently from his chill by Tuesday, January 10, to spend the "evening at Brother Starrs who had Many of his Neighbours & friends to gather to Rejoyce with him bringing home his wife 23 years & 15 days younger than he. he 70 Next April and She 47 in May next."

Part V: The Wild Plenty

1. Peter Kalm, *Travels in North America* (see Bibliography). A cure for dysentery would have been a boon indeed during those centuries when many suffered after drinking water from shallow wells or which had been stored too long in cisterns. Various barks were experimented with to find a substitute for the South American Jesuit's bark. Alexander Hamilton, who learned pharmacy and received his degree in 1737 in Edinburgh, joined his brother in Annapolis in 1739. He advertised regularly in the

Maryland *Gazette* that there was "To be sold at the subscriber's shop in Annapolis, JESUIT'S BARK, at Twelve Shillings, currency, the Pound; where sundry other Medicines may be had, at reasonable Prices. ALEXANDER HAMILTON."

2. John Smith, *The Generall Historie of Virginia, New England and the Summer Isles* (see Bibliography).

3. *Ibid.* There was great English interest in the possibility of establishing silk plantations in the colonies.

4. *Ibid.* "Vines" referred to grapes, "crabs" to crabapples.

5. Roger Williams, *A Key into the Language* (see Bibliography).

6. Thomas Tusser, *Five Hundreth Points* (see Bibliography).

7. John Josselyn, *New England's Rarities Discovered* (see Bibliography).

8. Kalm, *Travels.*

9. Josselyn, *New England's Rarities.*

10. Kalm, *Travels.*

11. Josselyn, *New England's Rarities.*

12. As quoted by James Boswell in his biography of Johnson (London, 1791).

13. Smith, *Generall Historie.*

Part VI: The Standing Dishes

1. Joshua Hempsted, *Diary* (see Bibliography).

2. Edward Johnson, *Wonder Working Providence* (see Bibliography).

3. John Josselyn, *New England's Rarities Discovered* (see Bibliography).

4. *Ibid.*

5. "This grosse watry pompion," or pumpkin-head.

6. Robert Boyle (1627–91), British natural philosopher and chemist.

7. Peter Kalm, *Travels in North America* (see Bibliography).

8. *Ibid.*

9. Josselyn, *New England's Rarities.*

10. Adrien Van der Donck, *Description of the New Netherlands* (see Bibliography).

11. Sarah Kemble Knight, *Journal* (see Bibliography). Reference is to Stonington, Connecticut.

12. Kalm, *Travels.*

13. Knight, *Journal.*

14. Kalm, *Travels.*

15. Mme. Knight at one time kept a writing school in Boston. Obviously a critic of inns and lodgings, she is said to have herself conducted an inn

late in life near New London, Connecticut. Her journal first was published by Theodore Dwight, one of the Connecticut Wits.

16. Kalm, *Travels.*

17. Van der Donck, *Description.*

18. *Ibid.* The reference is to young Indian women.

19. Josselyn, *New England's Rarities.*

20. Van der Donck, *Description.*

21. Kalm, *Travels.*

22. Benjamin Tompson (1642–1714). *New England's Crisis. Or a Brief Narrative of New-Englands Lamentable Estate at present, compar'd with the former (but few) years of Prosperity . . . by a Well wisher to his Countrey* (London, 1676). Tompson was the first colonial poet born in America; he taught school briefly and practiced medicine.

23. Amelia Simmons, *American Cookery* (see Bibliography).

24. One of many sets of verses set to an old English drinking tune, better known today as "Yankee Doodle."

25. Thomas Hariot, *A Briefe and True Report on the New found land of Virginia,* (see Bibliography). Roanoke Island is off the coast of North Carolina. Hariot (1560–1621), a mathematician and astronomer, was sent by Raleigh to Virginia as a surveyor. Two exploring parties were sent in 1584–85 and a request for assistance sent back to England in 1586. Those who managed to survive were returned to England in June, 1586. Another expedition shortly afterward left eighteen men to protect English rights. These were killed by the natives.

26. *Ibid.*

27. John Gerard, *The Herball or General Historie of Plantes* (see Bibliography).

28. Roger Williams, *Key into the Language* (see Bibliography).

29. Josselyn, *New England's Rarities.*

30. *Ibid.*

31. Simmons, *American Cookery.*

32. William Strachey, *The Historie of Traveile into Virginia Britannica* (see Bibliography). Strachey was first secretary of the colony.

33. Williams, *Key into the Language. Sukquttahhash* became, obviously "succotash," but the dish was minus today's familiar lima beans.

34. Josselyn, *New England's Rarities.*

35. *A Journal of Josiah Atkins, Waterbury in ye State of Connecticut, N. England written by himself, 1781.* Mattatuck Historical Society, Waterbury, Connecticut, 1954. "June 15: 18 miles from Alexandria [Virginia]. This evening we had our general's applause for our fortitude to bear hardships with patience, especially our want of provisions. Our bread was made chiefly of coarse Indian meal, which we wet & bake on barks on stones. This is what people live on chiefly in these parts & what they call Hoe cakes. However,

we not being used to such bread nor such country . . . all these together make my trials unsupportable." Atkins had been a teacher in 1770–72, and at one time owned a blacksmith's shop. He enlisted in 1781, when he was either thirty-one or thirty-two, and died in service in Virginia in October of that year.

36. W. C. Sims, Shelbyville, Illinois.

37. William Wood, *New England's Prospect* (see Bibliography).

38. Van der Donck, *Description*.

39. William Byrd II, *History of the Dividing Line*. Byrd's diary, kept when he served as a member of the commission to survey the boundary between North Carolina and Virginia, was first published, along with his *Journey to the Land of Eden* and *Progress to the Mines*, in 1841 as *Westover Manuscripts* (see Bibliography). Byrd (1674–1744), a wealthy landowner on whose lands Richmond was laid out, had in 1737 what is believed to have been the largest—4,000 volumes—library of any early eighteenth-century colonist.

40. The earlier English belief that corn was fit only for the poorer classes, as Gerard had indicated, was revived as political squabbles with the colonies increased. Benjamin Franklin, writing under the pseudonym Homespun to the London *Gazeteer* on January 2, 1766, thus was constrained to defend cornbread cakes: "Johnny or hoe-cake hot from the fire is better than a Yorkshire muffin." Others indicated hoe cakes or johnnycakes were considered trailbreads, to be baked before an open fire. Henry David Thoreau in *Walden Pond* said, "Bread I at first made of pure Indian meal and salt, genuine hoe-cakes, which I baked before my fire out of doors on a shingle at the end of a stick of timber . . . but it was wont to get smoked."

41. Simmons, *American Cookery*.

42. As quoted by James Boswell in *Life of Samuel Johnson*, London, 1791. Boswell and Johnson met in 1763; both were members of The [Literary] Club.

43. Josselyn, *New England's Rarities*.

44. David Pietersze de Vries, *Voyage of D. P. de Vries* (see Bibliography). De Vries's garden included also "different kinds of sweet smelling herbs, such as rosemary, sage, marjoram and thyme . . . around the house were plenty of peach trees."

45. William Fitzhugh, *Letters*. Virginia Historical Society, Manuscript Collection.

46. Kalm, *Travels*.

47. Samuel Sewall, *Diary* (see Bibliography).

48. Kalm, *Travels*.

49. Israel Acrelius, *A History of New Sweden* (see Bibliography). The Swedish clergyman wrote of Delaware, New Jersey, and Pennsylvania following his stay here between 1749 and 1756.

50. Simmons, *American Cookery*.

51. John Parkinson, *Theatrum Botanicum* (see Bibliography).

52. Gerard, *The Herball or General Historie of Plants . . . Very much Enlarged and Amended by Thomas Johnson, Citizen and Apothecarye of London* (see Bibliography). It was a copy of this edition which Josselyn apparently used in helping to identify plants found during his two voyages here.

53. Joseph Pitton de Tournefort (1656–1708), French naturalist, professor of botany and medicine. Scotland went so far as to make potato production illegal in 1728, believing the potato a form of truly deadly nightshade, because there was no mention of it in the Bible. Not quite a century later, however, in 1775, no such fears lingered with Nicholas Cresswell on the western Virginia frontier: "Got to one Doctor Briscoe's plantation about a mile from the river. Found the house deserted. We all went into the Garden, dark as it was. . . . Found a Potato bed and I ate about a dozen of them raw and thought them the most delicious food I ever ate in my life." (*Journal*, see Bibliography).

54. Kalm, *Travels*.

55. *Ibid.*

56. Hempsted, *Diary*.

57. Simmons, *American Cookery*.

58. Kalm, *Travels*.

Part VII: The Seventeenth-Century Garden

1. Francis Higginson, *New England Plantation* (see Bibliography). Higginson said he did not exaggerate, for "it becometh not a Preacher of Truth to be a Writer of Falsehood; and therefore I have beene carefull to eport nothing of New-England but what I have partly seen with mine owne yes, and partly heard and enquired from the mouths of very honest and religious persons, who by living in the Country a good space of time have had experience and knowledge."

2. Anne Bradstreet (1612–1672), *The Tenth Muse Lately sprung up in America* (see Bibliography). She wrote, "I am obnoxious to each carping tongue who says my hand a needle better fits."

3. Daughter of Bay Colony governor Thomas Dudley, wife of Governor Simon Bradstreet. The poet's home in America was on a frontier farm on the Merrimac River. The verses quoted all are from *The Four Seasons of the Year* ("Spring").

4. John Smith, *Travels and Works of Captain John Smith* and *A Description of New England* (see Bibliography).

5. Edward Johnson, *Wonder-Working Providence* (see Bibliography).

6. Alexander Whitaker, *Good News from Virginia*. Whitaker was a Puritan minister. Stith (*History of Virginia*) said that in 1610–11, "Mr. Whitaker . . . empaled a fair parsonage, with an hundred acres of land, calling it

Rock-Hall," and that Whitaker was "very careful and assiduous in instructing Pocohantas in the Christian Religion."

7. William Wood, *New England's Prospect* (see Bibliography).

8. *A Relation of the Successful Beginning of Lord Baltimore's Plantation in Virginia*, London, 1634.

9. Thomas Glover, *An Account of Virginia &c*, printed in (Samuel) *Purchas His Pilgrimage*, London, 1619, 1625; Glasgow, 1905–07.

10. Smith, *True Relation* (see Bibliography); *Works*, Birmingham, 1884.

11. *Ibid.*

12. "E. W. Gent., London," *Virginia, more especially the south part thereof Richly and truly valued.*

13. Israel Acrelius, *History of New Sweden* (see Bibliography).

14. *Ibid.*

15. De Rasieres.

16. William Bradford, *History of Plimouth Plantation* (see Bibliography).

17. Bradford, *A Description and Historical Account of New England* (see Bibliography).

18. *Ibid.*

19. John Winthrop, *Life and Letters* (see Bibliography). John Davenport (1597–1670) was the founder of New Haven colony; he concealed regicides Whalley and Goffe.

20. John Josselyn, *New England's Rarities Discovered* (see Bibliography).

21. *Ibid.*

22. *The Belcher Papers*, Collections of the Massachusetts Historical Society, Sixth Series, 1893–94.

23. Thomas Morton, *New English Canaan* (see Bibliography). Morton was expelled from Plymouth, and also from the Massachusetts Bay Colony, for what was considered scandalously immoral conduct. Wrote Bradford in his *History*, "Morton they brought away . . . he was kepte till a ship came for England."

24. Josselyn, *New England's Rarities*. Josselyn was the son of Sir Thomas Josselyn, who was especially interested in the Province of Maine. Josselyn's brother, Henry, whom he visited, owned land at Black Point and served as magistrate and deputy governor of the colony.

25. *Ibid.*

26. *Ibid.* Josselyn used Johnson's edition of Gerard as his guide. All quotations following are from *New England's Rarities*.

27. "What various ways has Nature for Scattering and sowing of the Seed! It is a little surprizing that seeds found in the Gizzards of wild fowl have afterwards sprouted in the Earth; and seeds left in the Dung of the Cattel. The Seeds of Marjoram and Strammomium, carelessly kept, have grown after seven years." Cotton Mather, *The Christian Philosopher*, London, 1721.

28. Checking Josselyn's descriptions and labels against records of other travelers and settlers of the time, and against the Gerard-Johnson *Herball* on which he relied, there still must be doubt today as to exact identification of some of the plants he lists.

29. Winthrop, *Journal* (see Bibliography).

30–33. *Ibid.* Time and circumstance had much to do with belief in witchery, as Winthrop makes clear also in his *Journal or History of New England* when he reported on a sea storm that same year: "The Master, and other Seamen, made a strange construction of the sore storme they met withall, saying their ship was bewitched, and therefore made use of the common charme ignorant people use, nailing two red hot horseshoes to their maine, mast." Iron was believed anathema to witches, who were thought to have no power against its strength. Numerous reports of executions in England tell of accused witches being burned at the stake; those hanged there, and in this country, sometimes had iron poles driven through their bodies before burial.

34. George Herbert, *Country Parson*, printed in *Remains* (1652), and in *Complete Works*, edited by Grossart (1874). Izaak Walton called Herbert's text "plain, prudent, useful rules for the country parson." Other Herbert admonitions included: "By suppers more have been killed than Galen cured"; "Go not for every grief to the physician, nor for every quarrel to the lawyer, nor for every thirst to the pot."

35. William Coles, *The Art of Simpling* (see Bibliography).

36. *Ibid.*

37. *Ibid.*

38. Adrien Van der Donck, *Description of the New Netherlands* (see Bibliography).

39. The Dutch were the first to settle what now is New York, establishing Fort Nassau, near Albany, and New Amsterdam, now New York City. Separate English and French settlements were made shortly thereafter in other parts of the colony.

40. Van der Donck, *Description*. Hereafter, all quotations within this chapter are from this source.

41. Galen, in this instance, is a slang term for "physician." Galen (c. 130–c. 200) was a Greek physician and surgeon, a follower of Hippocrates, and eventually court physician to Marcus Aurelius. He urged the use of vegetable remedies; these, as a result, were called Galenicals.

Part VIII: The Eighteenth-Century Garden

1. Peter Kalm, *Travels in North America* (see Bibliography).

2. *Ibid.*

3. Charleston (South Carolina) *Gazette.*

4. Francis Higginson, *New England Plantation* (see Bibliography).

5. Thomas Morton, *New English Canaan* (see Bibliography).

6. John Gerard, *The Herball or General Historie of Plants* (see Bibliography).

7. *Ibid.*

8. John Parkinson, *Theatrum Botanicum* (see Bibliography).

9. John Winthrop, *Life and Letters* (see Bibliography). Governor Endecott of Salem sent Governor John Winthrop, Jr., a recipe to cure a "fit of the mother." He recommended a mixture of "syrop of Violets, sirrup of Roses, Spirit of Mints, Spirit of Annis, mugwort and organie, also galingall root" and suggested snuff would be of more help than hellebore.

10. Philip Miller, *The Gardener's Dictionary* (see Bibliography).

11. Gerard, *Herball.*

12. Robert May, *The Accomplish't Cook* (see Bibliography).

13. William Coles, *The Art of Simpling* (see Bibliography).

14. Quotations throughout are from Thomas Jefferson, *Notes on the State of Virginia* (see Bibliography). Virginia was then the largest colony in British America, claiming as its territory approximately one-third of the continent. Jefferson was thirty-seven during the year 1780–81, when he completed the book, which was achieved under stress: It was the year Benedict Arnold invaded Virginia, and Jefferson knew the tragedy of the death of an infant daughter, Elizabeth, and worry over his wife's lingering illness. Despite these difficulties, which were added to by rumors that his conduct in office might be inquired into by the Virginia legislature, Jefferson finished his *Notes* during Christmas week, 1781. During the following three years he revised the text. While he was in Paris in 1785 the first edition of 200 copies was printed; this was followed by a second Paris edition, and one in London in 1787 of 1,000 copies. The book was reprinted in Philadelphia in 1788. Jefferson worried over the accuracy of his data, checking his work with correspondents throughout the colony who, like himself, were amateur botanists, and others who were physicians and naturalists.

15. Amelia Simmons, *American Cookery* (see Bibliography).

16. Kalm, *Travels.*

17. *Ibid.*

18. Andrew Burnaby, *Travels through the Middle Settlements* (see Bibliography).

19. John Josselyn, *New England's Rarities Discovered* (see Bibliography).

20. The Reverend Erasmus Middleton *et al. The New Complete Dictionary of Arts and Sciences* (see Bibliography).

21. Samuel Sewall, *Diary* (see Bibliography).

22. *Ibid.* The seventeenth-century porch was an integral part of the house. See photographs of the Hempsted house. The entry would be equivalent to a

modern foyer. Obviously on a hot July day, the Sewall's front door had been left open.

23. Joshua Hempsted, *Diary* (see Bibliography).

24. Sewall, *Diary*. Fruit trees were customarily pruned high to avoid such damage. (see page 33).

25. Hempsted, *Diary*.

26. Thomas Tusser, *Five Hundreth Points of Good Husbandry* (see Bibliography).

27. Middleton *et al. The New Complete Dictionary*.

28. Manuscript receipt and note book, 1774; author's collection.

29. *Ibid.*

30. *Ibid.*

31. Jasper Danckaerts, *Journal* (see Bibliography).

32. Robert Beverley, *The History and Present State of Virginia* (see Bibliography). Beverley (1673?–1722) was born on his father's Middlesex County plantation; he served on the Virginia General Court, and in Council and Assembly. He sought to write a correct history. Jefferson, however, said of him in *Notes on Virginia*, "He has comprised our history from the first propositions of Sir Walter Raleigh to the year 1700 in the hundredth part of the space which Stith [see Bibliography] employs for the fourth part of the period."

33. William Byrd II, *History of the Dividing Line* (see Bibliography).

34. Anne McVickar Grant (1755–1838), *Memoirs of an American Lady*. Published anonymously in 1808, this is a collection of reminiscences of her girlhood near Albany, New York, where her father was stationed at a British army post.

35. Chic Sale (pseud. Charles Partlow; 1885–1936), *The Specialist*, 1929. Sale, an actor and humorist, wrote of a subject never before published, the proper construction of an outhouse.

36. One of New England's handsomest eighteenth-century restored museum houses, the Webb House was the site of the so-called Yorktown Conference, at which Washington met with Rochambeau and other colonial and French leaders to plan the decisive battle of the Revolutionary War. The house, on Main Street, Wethersfield, Connecticut, is maintained by the Society of Colonial Dames of America in the State of Connecticut and is open daily to visitors.

Part IX: The Kitchen Manufactory

1. William Wood, *New England's Prospect* (see Bibliography).

2. John Cotton (1584–1652) was a dominant leader in the Church of England for two decades, but gradually became nonconformist and emigrated to

Massachusetts in 1633. More than any other writer's, his essays on New England religion were looked to, on both sides of the Atlantic, as the clearest explanations of Congregationalism. He was Increase Mather's father-in-law and Cotton Mather's grandfather.

3. Sarah Kemble Knight, *Journal* (see Bibliography).

4. Peter Kalm, *Travels in North America* (see Bibliography).

5. Samuel Sewall, *Diary* (see Bibliography).

6. Caudled apples were fruit cooked with sugar, spices, and perhaps wine, similar to what would be called apple sauce today. Hurtleberries (*Vaccinium Myrtillus*) was an English name applied to whortleberries, bilberries, blueberries, and huckleberries.

7. Kalm, *Travels*.

8. Joshua Hempsted, *Diary* (see Bibliography). Hempsted made coffins and engraved headstones for many in the New London, Connecticut, area.

9. Kalm, *Travels*.

10. *Ibid.*

11. Stiegel referred to the opening of a new shop in New York City.

12. Thomas Tusser, *Advice to the Huswife* (see Bibliography).

13. "Thursd 2 March, 1720. fair. I Whet a Saw to Cut Samll Foxes wifes arm"— Hempsted, *Diary*.

14. Bradford, *History*.

15. *Ibid.*

16. Dorothy Bradford, the governor's wife, was lost overboard while the *Mayflower* was still in harbor; no explanation was made by Bradford in his records.

17. Edward Johnson, *Wonder-Working Providence* (see Bibliography).

18. David Neal, *The History of New England* (London, 1720): "The Conversation of this Town is as polite as in most Cities and Towns of England; many of their merchants having travell'd to Europe; and those that stay at home, having the Advantage of a free Education with Travellers; *so that a gentleman from London could almost think himself at home in Boston*, when he observes the numbers of People, their Houses, their Furniture, their Tables, their Dress and Conversation, which perhaps is as splendid and showy, as that of the most considerable Tradesman in London."

19. Urian Oakes (1631–1681), *New-England Pleaded with* (Cambridge, 1673). Oakes was graduated from Harvard in 1649; returned to England to preach, but was expelled from his ministry there; was called to the church at Cambridge in 1671; was acting president of Harvard, 1676–81.

20. Benjamin Franklin, *Letters*, Vol. I. A. H. Smyth, ed. (New York, 1907).

21. Craftsmen and their apprentices usually wore leather aprons and breeches; leather was cheaper than cloth. Those who seemed to dress above their

income and social status might be asked to prove themselves not in danger of overspending on luxuries, as was Mrs. Nicholas Mays of Newbury, who in September 1653 "was presented for wearing a silk cloak and scarf, but cleared on proving her husband was worth more than £200." Such caution aimed to keep towns and colonies free of paupers and bankrupts.

22. Ebenezer Pemberton, *Sermons and Discourses on Several Occasions* (London, 1727).

23. John Cotton, *A Meet Help: Or, a Wedding Sermon, Preached at New-Castle in New-England, June 19, 1694* (Boston, 1699).

24. *Ibid.*

25. John Winthrop, *Journal* (see Bibliography). "Her husband," said Governor Winthrop of his colleague, "saw his error when it was too late . . . being very loving and tender of her [he] was loath to grieve her." According to Winthrop, Mrs. Hopkins spent too many hours reading and writing instead of "honorably in the place God had set her."

26. Kalm, *Travels.*

27. *Ibid.*

28. *Ibid.*

29. *Ibid.*

30. Franklin, *Poor Richard's Almanack.* Franklin established his own printing business in Philadelphia in 1728 and in 1729 bought the *Pennsylvania Gazette.* He wrote and published the *Almanack* from 1732 to 1757.

31. Francis Higginson, *New England Plantation* (see Bibliography).

32. Wood, *New England's Prospect.*

33. William Cobbett (1763–1835), *The Rushlight* magazine, 1799. Cobbett, a controversial British journalist, lived here between 1792 and 1800 and again in 1817–19. At one time he owned a Philadelphia bookstore and later settled as a farmer on Long Island. He wrote *Grammar of the English Language; Journal of a Year's Residence in the United States; Rural Rides; Cottage Economy; The English Gardener;* and numerous other books.

34. Kalm, *Travels.*

35. Robert Beverley, *History and Present State of Virginia* (see Bibliography).

36. Kalm, *Travels.*

37. Boston *News-Letter*, March 30, 1748. Founded in 1704, the *News-Letter* was the first newspaper in America. Publication ceased in February 1776.

38. Boston *Gazette*, July 24, 1750. Believed to be the second colonial paper, it had been printed by James Franklin before he formed the *Courant.*

39. Franklin, *Autobiography* (see Bibliography). At his shop in Boston, James, a half-brother, published the *New-England Courant* (1721). The brothers soon quarreled, however—although not until Benjamin's first essays, *The Dogood Papers* (1722), had been published in the *Courant.*

Part X: "A Country New and Wonderful"

1. Andrew Burnaby, *Travels through the Middle Settlements* (see Bibliography).

2. New Jersey became one province in 1702, but the area customarily still was referred to as "the Jerseys."

3. Almost 100 years earlier, John Josselyn in *New England's Rarities Discovered* described Boston in 1663 as a city where "the buildings are handsome, joining one to the other as in London, with many large streets, most of them paved with pebblestones, in the High street toward the Common there are fair Buildings, some of stone."

4. Alexander Hamilton, *Itinerarium* (see Bibliography). From May 30 to September 26, 1744, Dr. Hamilton and his slave, Dromo, traveled to Philadelphia, Manhattan, up the Hudson to Albany, thence to New England by way of Long Island, to Boston by way of Newport, as far as Portsmouth, New Hampshire, and York, Maine, before returning to Alexandria.

5. There were, of course, more specific reasons for "misery acquainting such strange bedfellows" as the leaders of the Revolutionary movement. Hard money was short in the South, where planters had continued to import necessities as well as luxuries from England, charging them against future tobacco profits. Nicholas Cresswell noted in June 1774: "It appears to me that there is a scarcity of Cash amongst the people, of all ranks here. They Game high, Spend freely, and Dress exceedingly gay, but I observe they seldom show any money, it is all Tobacco Notes." John Hancock, who had inherited a thriving mercantile business, increased his warehouse inventories by smuggling. Franklin, when he said at the signing of the Declaration in July 1776 that "we must all hang together, or assuredly, we shall all hang separately," may have been enjoying a rather grim joke.

6. The young English traveler, Nicholas Cresswell, who had earlier hoped to buy his own plantation in Virginia, wrote during a visit to Nanjemoy, Maryland, while awaiting ship back to England in February 1775: "The Committee . . . give [those suspected of British sympathies] over to the mobility to punish and it is seldom they come off without tarring and feathering. The people are arming and training in every place. They are liberty-mad."

7. Alexander Pope, "Bolingbroke in a Letter to Swift," in *Works*.

8. Specifically, the Louis Bolduc home, maintained by the National Society of Colonial Dames of America in the State of Missouri.

9. Contrary to general belief, Abraham Lincoln did own property other than the house in Springfield, Illinois, where he lived with his own family prior to leaving for Washington. He had purchased a roughly built one-room log cabin with attached shed in Coles County near what is now Lerna, for

the use of his father, Thomas, and his stepmother. In recent years the farm has been landscaped and the cabin rebuilt, and is now maintained as a public area, known as the Lincoln Log Cabin State Park.

10. Lora Case, *Reminiscences* (see Bibliography). The Case family left Connecticut "in a two-horse covered wagon, with a cow hitched on behind to supply us on the road with milk. . . . When we moved in the house had neither floor, doors, windows, nor chimney . . . I was only about two-and-a-half years old at that time, but I remember distinctly how it looked."

11. *Ibid.* This is the same type of exterior oven described by Peter Kalm in Pennsylvania in 1749.

12. *American Pioneer*, October 1843.

13. Case, *Reminiscences*.

14. *Ibid.*

15. *Ibid.*

16. *Ibid.*

17. *Ibid.*

18. Better known as the author of *Uncle Tom's Cabin*, Mrs. Stowe collaborated with her elder sister, Catherine Esther Beecher, on *The American Woman's Home; or, The Principles of Domestic Science* (New York, 1869).

19. Sealed glass containers for food were in some use in New England after 1815; the first "tin case" patent was awarded in 1825, and the stamped-out can was invented in 1847 and was used to preserve army rations during the Civil War. A machine for manufacturing tin cans was exhibited at the Centennial Exposition at Philadelphia in 1876. The 1858 Mason glass canning-jar did the most to revolutionize home preserving methods for those who could afford the cost.

20. Joseph Glanville, *Scepsis Scientifica*. Glanville foresaw also air flight, telephones, cosmetic surgery, organ transplantation, and modern irrigation methods: "To them that come after us it may be as ordinary to buy a pair of wings to fly into remotest regions as now a pair of boots to ride a journey. And to confer at the distance of the Indies by sympathetic conveyances may be as usual to future times as to us in a literary correspondence. The restoration of grey hairs to juvenility, and renewing the exhausted marrow may at length be affected without a miracle; and the turning of the now comparative desert world into a paradise may not improbably be expected from late agriculture."

BIBLIOGRAPHY

THE LIST that follows includes only those texts from which lengthy quotations have been made. These books were turned to again and again because they provided differing viewpoints of colonization and daily life in early America as the average family knew it. Other books, newspapers, almanacs, and manuscripts are identified in the text as they are quoted from, and in chapter notes. It seems unreasonable to repeat their titles here.

Nor is it feasible to list the titles of the several thousand books and periodicals imported here during the colonial period by the literate well-to-do. That there was a greater general interest in owning and reading books than we sometimes assume is obvious from a perusal of the inventories of kitchen furnishings. Only the truly poor did not own at least a few books, even if they could not afford to have them bound. Indeed, if London bookseller John Dunton is to be believed, many colonists had such an appetite for the latest best-sellers that he was forced to travel here to collect his back bills. As did so many transcontinental travelers of the time, he kept notes for his own book describing the New World. It is hoped that its publication repaid the costs of his sojourn through New England.

As Others Saw Us: Writings of Explorers and Travelers

Acrelius, Israel. *A History of New Sweden, or the Settlements on the River Delaware.* Stockholm, 1759.

Blanchard, Claude. *The Journal of Claude Blanchard, Commissary of the French Auxiliary Army Sent to the United States during the American Revolution, 1780–1783.* Thomas Balch, ed., Albany, 1876.

Brickell, John. *Natural History of North Carolina.* Dublin, 1737.

Burnaby, Andrew. *Travels through the Middle Settlements in North-America in the Years 1759 and 1760.* London, 1775. Virginia Historical Register, V.

Cresswell, Nicholas. *The Journal of Nicholas Cresswell, 1774–1777.* New York, 1924.

Danckaerts, Jaspar. *Journal of Jaspar Danckaerts* (and Peter Sluyter), 1679–80. Long Island Historical Society, 1867.

deVries, David Pietersze. *Voyage of D. P., 1633.* Translated from the Dutch by Henry C. Murphy. New York Historical Society, Second Series, III.

Dunton, John. *Letters from New England,* London, 1686, 1705. Prince Society, Boston, 1867.

Hakluyt, Richard. *Divers Voyages Touching the Discovery of America and the Islands Adjacant.* Hakluyt Society, London, 1850.

———. *Hakluytus Posthumous, or Purchas, His Pilgrims.* London, 1625; reprinted Glasgow, 1905–06.

Hammond, John. *Leah and Rachel, or, the Two Fruitful Sisters, Virginia and Maryland: Their Present Condition Impartially Stated and Related.* London, 1656.

Hariot, Thomas. *A Brief and True Report of the New found land of Virginia.* Diligentlye Collected and Drawne by John White. Frankfort, 1590.

Jones, Hugh. *The Present State of Virginia.* London, 1724. Joseph Sabin, ed., New York, 1868.

Josselyn, John. *New England's Rarities Discovered.* London, 1672.

———. *An Account of Two Voyages to New England.* London, 1674, 1675; reprinted Boston, 1865.

Kalm, Peter. *En Resa til Norra Amerika.* Stockholm, 1753–61.

———. *Pehr Kalms Resa till Norra Amerika.* Helsingfors, 1904, 1910, 1915, 1929.

——— translations: *Travels in North America.* Warrington, England, 1770, 1812, 1892. *Voyage de Kalm in Amerique.* Montreal, 1880.

Lawson, John. *A New Voyage to Carolina, Containing the Exact Description and Natural History of that Country.* London, 1709–18.

Lechford, Thomas. *Notebook kept by Thomas Lechford, Esq., Lawyer in Boston, Massachusetts Bay from June 27, 1638 to July 29, 1641.* Transactions and Collections of the American Antiquarian Society, VII. 1885.

———. *Plain Dealing; Or, News from New England.* London, 1642; reprinted Boston, 1867.

Morton, Thomas. *New English Canaan.* Amsterdam, 1637; Prince Society, Boston, 1883.

Smith, John. *Advertisements for the unexperienced Planters of New-England, or anywhere; Or, the Pathway to experience to Erect a Plantation:* London, 1631. Massachusetts Historical Society Collections, Third Series, III, 1833.

———. *A Description of New England, or the Observations and Discoveries of Capt. John Smith.* London, 1616. Massachusetts Historical Society Collections, Third Series, VI, 1837.

———. *The Generall Historie of Virginia, New England and the Summer Isles with the Names of the Adventurers, Planters and Governours from their First Beginning in 1584 to the Present 1624 . . . Also the Maps and*

Descripions of All those Countreys their Commodities, People, Government, Customs and Religion yet Knowne. Divided into Six Bookes by Captain John Smith sometymes Governour in These Countries & Admirall of New England. London, 1624. Reprinted in *Travels and Works of Captain John Smith,* Edward Arber, ed., Edinburgh, 1910.

———. *A True Relation of Such Occurances and Accidents of Note as Hath Happened in Virginia.* London, 1608; reprinted Edinburgh, 1910.

Smith, Samuel. *The History of Nova Caesarea or New Jersey.* London, 1765.

Smith, William. *The History of New York.* London, 1757. Collections of the New York Historical Society, IV-V.

Strachey, William. *The History of Traveile into Virginia Britannica.* London, 1615. R. H. Major, ed., London, 1849.

Thomas, Gabriel. *An Historical and Geographical Account of Pennsylvania and West New Jersey.* London, 1698.

Van der Donck, Adrien. *Description of the New Netherlands by Adriaen Van der Donck, J.U.D.* Translated from the Dutch by Jeremiah Johnson. Collections of the New York Historical Society, Second Series, I. New York, 1841.

Wingfield, Edward Maria. *A Discourse of Virginia.* London, 1608. Charles Deane, ed., American Antiquarian Society, Boston, 1860.

As We Saw Ourselves: *Writings of Emigrants and Permanent Settlers*

Bartram, William. *Travels [1773–75] through North and South Carolina, Georgia, East and West Florida, the Cherokee Country, the Extensive Territories of the Muscolgulgas or Creek Confederacy and the Country of the Choctaws.* Philadelphia, 1791.

Beverley, Robert. *The History and Present State of Virginia, In Four Parts. The History of the First Settlements of Virginia, and the Government thereof, to the present Time. The Natural Productions and Conveniences of the Country suited to Trade and Improvement. The Native Indians, their Religion, Laws and Customs in War and Peace. The Present State of the Country as to the Polity of the Government and the Improvement of the Land. By a Native and Inhabitant of the Place.* London, 1705; revised 1722. Reprinted by Charles Campbell, Richmond, Va., 1855.

Bradford, William. *History of Plimouth Plantation (1606–1646).* Massachusetts Historical Society Collections, Fourth Series, III, 1856.

———. *A Description and Historical Account of New England in Verse.* Massachusetts Historical Society Collections, First Series, III, 1794. Facsimile, London, 1896.

———. *Letter-Book.* Massachusetts Historical Society Collections, First Series, III, 1794.

Bradstreet, Anne. *The Tenth Muse Lately sprung up in America. Or Severall*

Poems, compiled with great Variety of Wit and Learning full of delight . . . By a Gentlewoman in those parts. London, 1650. Revised as *Several Poems*, Boston, 1678 and 1758. Reprinted in *The Works of Anne Bradstreet in Prose and Verse*, John Harvard Ellis, ed., Cambridge, 1867.

Byrd II, William. *The History of the Dividing Line betwixt Virginia and North Carolina run in the year of our Lord, 1728.* First published in *Westover Manuscripts: History of the Dividing Line Run in the Year 1728* together with *A Journey to the Land of Eden* and *A Progress to the Mines*, Edmund Ruffin, ed., Petersburg, 1841. Reprinted as *History of the Dividing Line and Other Tracts*, Thomas H. Wynne, ed., Richmond, 1866; and as *Works of Colonel William Byrd of Westover, Esq.*, John Spencer Bassett, ed., New York, 1901.

Case, Lora. *Personal Reminiscences of an Aged Pioneer.* The Hudson (Ohio) *Independent*, February-August, 1897. Reprinted under title *Hudson of Long Ago*, Hudson Library and Historical Society, 1963.

Cotton, John. *Spiritual Milk for Boston Babes.* Cambridge, 1656.

———. *A Practical Commentary, or an Exposition with Observations, Reasons and Uses upon the First Epistles Generall of John.* London, 1656.

———. *The Way of the Church of Christ in New England.* London, 1645.

Force, Peter. *Tracts and Other Papers Relating Principally to the Origin, Settlement and Progress of the Colonies in North America.* Washington, D.C., 1836–46.

Franklin, Benjamin. *The Works of the late Dr. Benjamin Franklin; Consisting of His Life, Written by Himself; Together with Essays, Humorous, Moral, and Literary, Chiefly in the Manner of the Spectator.* New York, 1798.

———. *Writings of Benjamin Franklin.* John Bigelow, ed. New York, 1868.

———. *The Writings of Benjamin Franklin.* Albert Henry Smyth, ed. New York, 1907.

Green, Joseph. *Diary.* Essex Institute Historical Collections, 1868–1900.

Hamilton, Alexander. *Itinerarium: Being a Narrative of a Journey From Annapolis, Maryland, Through Delaware, Pennsylvania, New York, New Jersey, Connecticut, Rhode Island, Massachusetts, and New Hampshire from May to September, 1744. By Dr. Alexander Hamilton.* Originally printed for private distribution by W. K. Bixby; Albert Bushnell Hart, ed., St. Louis, 1907.

Hempsted, Joshua. *Diary.* New London, Connecticut, Historical Society Collections, I, 1900.

Higginson, Francis. *A True Relation of the Last Voyage to New England Written from New England July 24, 1629.* Manuscript printed in a *Collection of Papers* (Hutchinson), Boston, 1769.

———. *New England Plantation; Or, a Short and True Description of the Commodities and Discommodities of that Countrey.* London, 1630. Reprinted in Force's *Tracts*, Vol. I, No. 12; and in Massachusetts Historical Society Proceedings, LXII, 1930.

Hooker, Thomas. *A Survey of the Summe of Church Discipline.* London, 1648.

————. *The Christian's Two Chiefe Lessons.* London, 1640.

————. *The Soules Exaltation.* London, 1638.

Jefferson, Thomas. *Notes on the State of Virginia illustrated with a Map, including the States of Virginia, Maryland, Delaware and Pennsylvania.* London, 1787.

Johnson, Edward. *Wonder Working Providence of Sions Saviour in New England: A History of New England From the English Planting in the Yeere 1628, until the Yeere 1652.* London, 1654. Reprinted, Andover, Massachusetts, 1867, and New York, 1910.

Knight, Sarah Kemble. *The Journal of Madam Knight.* New York, 1825.

Mather, Cotton. *Diary.* Massachusetts Historical Society Collections, Seventh Series, VII and VIII, 1911, 1912.

————. *Magnalia Christi Americana, or The Ecclesiastical History of New England.* London, 1702. Reprinted, Hartford, 1853–1855.

Mather, Increase. *A Relation of the Troubles which have happened in New-England, by Reason of the Indians there.* Boston, 1667. Reprinted under title *The Early History of New England.* Albany, 1864.

Maverick, Samuel. *A Briefe Description of New England and the Severall Townes Therein together with the Present Government thereof.* Massachusetts Historical Society Proceedings, Second Series, I.

Morton, Nathaniel. *New England's Memoriall.* Cambridge, 1669.

"Mourt, G." *A Relation or Journall of the beginning and proceedings of the English Plantation setled at Plimouth.* London, 1622. Reprinted in Collections of the Massachusetts Historical Society, First Series, VIII, 1802; Second Series, LX. Regarded as a collaboration of William Bradford and Edward Winslow. Added to by Winslow in *Good Newes from New England.* London, 1624.

Prince, Thomas. *Chronological History of New England in the Form of Annals.* Boston, 1736.

————. *The Vade Mecum for America; or, a Companion for Traders and Travellers.* Boston, 1732.

Rowlandson, Mary White. *The Soveraignty & Goodness of God, Together, with the Faithfulness of His Promises Displayed.* Cambridge, 1682; Lancaster, Mass., 1903. (Often reprinted as *The Narrative of the Captivity of Mrs. Mary Rowlandson.*)

Sewall, Samuel. *Diary* (1674–1729). Massachusetts Historical Society Collections, Fifth Series, V–VII, 1878–1882.

————. *Letter-Book.* Massachusetts Historical Society Collections, Sixth Series, I–II, 1882.

Stith, William. *The History of the First Discovery and Settlement of Virginia: Being an Essay towards a General History of this Colony.* Williamsburg, 1747.

Trumbull, Benjamin. *A Complete History of Connecticut, Civil and Ecclesiastical, From the Emigration of Its First Planters from England.* Hartford, 1797.

Walker, Thomas. *Journal of an Exploration in the Spring of the Year 1750.* Boston, 1888.

Williams, Roger. *Key into the Language of the Indians of New England.* London, 1643. Massachusetts Historical Society Collections, III, 1794.

———. *The Bloody Tenet of Persecution for Cause of Conscience.* London, 1644. Publications of the Narragansett Club, 1867.

Winslow, Edward. (See listing under "Mourt, G.") *Good Newes From New England.* London, 1624. Massachusetts Historical Society Collections, First Series, VIII, 1802.

Winthrop, John. *Journal or History of New England* (March 29, 1630—January 11, 1649). Boston, 1825–26, 1853.

———. *Life and Letters of John Winthrop.* Robert C. Winthrop, ed., Boston, 1869.

———. *Papers.* Massachusetts Historical Society Proceedings, 1929.

Wood, William. *New England's Prospect.* London, 1634, 1635, 1639; Boston, 1865, 1898.

Writings of the Cooks, Housekeepers, and Other Instructors

Adam's Luxury and Eve's Cookery. London, 1744.

Allde, Edward. *The Good Hous-wives Treasurie.* London, 1588.

Boorde, Andrew. *Dyetary of Health.* London, 1542.

Bradley, Martha. *The British Housewife.* London, 1770.

Carter, Susannah. *The Frugal Housewife or Complete Woman Cook.* Boston, 1772.

Cleland, Elizabeth. *A New and Easy Method of Cooking.* Edinburgh, 1755.

Clermont, B. *The Professed Cook.* London, 1776.

Digby, Sir Kenelm. *The Closet of the Eminently Learned Sir K. Digby.* London, 1669.

Eales, Mary. *Mrs. Eales's Receipts.* London, 1718.

———. *The Compleat Confectioner.* London, 1742.

Evelyn, John. *Acetaria: A Discourse of Sallets.* London, 1699

Glasse, Hannah. *The Art of Cookery Made Plain and Easy.* London, 1747.

King, William. *The Art of Cookery.* London, 1709.

Markham, Gervase. *Countrey Contentments, in two Bookes: the Second Intituled, The English Huswife: Containing the Inward and Outward Vertues which ought to be in a Compleate Woman: as her Physicke, Cookery, Banqueting-Stuffe, Distillation, Perfumes, Wool, Hemp, Flaxe, Dairies, Brewing, Baking and all other Things Belonging to an Household.* London, 1615.

———. *Farewell to Husbandry.* London, 1620.

———. *The Pleasures of Princes.* London, 1635.

May, Robert. *The Accomplish't Cook.* London, 1685.

Moody, Eleazer. *The School of Good Manners.* Boston, 1715.

Murrell, John. *Two Bookes of Cookerie and Carving.* London, 1631.

Nott, John. *The Recipe Book.* London, 1723.

Plat, Sir Hugh. *Delightes for Ladies.* London, 1594.

Raffald, Elizabeth. *The Experienced English Housekeeper.* London, 1769.

Simmons, Amelia. *American Cookery or the Art of Dressing Viands, Fish, Poultry and Vegetables, and the Best Modes of Making Pastes, Puffs, Pies, Tarts, Puddings, Custards and Preserves, and All Kinds of Cakes, from the Imperial Plumb to Plain Cake, Adapted to this Country, and all Grades of Life* by *An American Orphan.* Hartford, 1796; Albany, 1800; Boston, 1819; Woodstock, Vermont, 1831.

Smith, Eliza. *The Compleat Housewife or Accomplish't Gentlewoman's Companion.* London, 1727; Williamsburg, 1742.

Tusser, Thomas. *Five Hundreth Pointes of Good Husbandrie; Also a Table of Husbandrie and Another of Huswiferie.* London, 1593.

The Herbalists, Physicians, and Gardeners

Boorde, Andrew. *The Brevarie of Health.* London, 1546.

Clayton, John. *See* Gronovius.

Coles, William. *The Art of Simpling. An Introduction to the Knowledge and Gathering of Plants . . . whereunto is added, A Discovery of the Lesser World.* London, 1657; Reprinted Clarkson, Milford, 1938.

Culpepper, Nicholas. *The English Physician Enlarged, or an Astrologo-Physical Discourse of the Vulgar Herbs of This Nation.* London, 1652.

————. *Culpepper's English Physician and Complete Herbal.* London, 1798.

————. *English Physician Enlarged.* London, 1788.

————. *Pharmacopoeia Londonensis of The London Dispensatory.* London, 1683.

Dioscorides. *De Medica Materia.* Venice, 1558. *The Greek Herbal of Dioscorides English'd by John Goodyer.* London, 1652.

Evelyn, John. *Sylva, or a Discourse on Forest Trees.* London, 1664.

————. *Kalendarium Hortense: or, The Gardner's Almanac.* London, 1665, through numerous editions.

Gerard, John. *The Herball or General Historie of Plantes, Gathered by John Gerarde of London, Master in Chirurgie.* London, 1597. *And Very Much Enlarged and Amended by Thomas Johnson, Citizen and Apothecarye.* London, 1633.

Gronovius, Johannes Fredericus. *Flora Virginica, Exhibens Plantas Quas Johannes Clayton in Virginia Observit atque Collegit.* Leyden, 1739–43. (In correspondence with European botanists, John Clayton sent seeds and specimens overseas; these were classified by Gronovius, assisted by Linnaeus, and the list thus published in Holland.)

Hyll, Thomas. *The Gardeners Labyrinth.* London, 1577.

Lawson, William. *A New Orchard and New Garden.* London, 1638.

————. *The Country Housewifes Garden for Herbs of Common Use.* London, 1648.

Meagher, Leonard. *The English Gardener*. London, 1670, 1682.

Miller, Philip. *The Gardener's Dictionary*. London, 1739–1759. First published as *The Gardener's and Florist's Dictionary*, or *A Complete System of Horticulture*. London, 1724. The 1759 seventh edition used the Linnaean system of nomenclature.

Parkinson, John. *Paradisi in Sole Paradisus Terrestis, Or a Garden of All Sorts of Pleasant Flowers, with a Kitchen Garden of All Manner of Herbes, Rootes, & Fruites, for Meate or Sause Used with Us*. London, 1629.

———. *Theatrum Botanicum, The Theater of Plantes*. London, 1640. Title page drawings include American corn and sunflowers with other exotic plants and fruits such as palm trees, pineapples and mulberries.

Rose, John. *The English Vineyard Vindicated*. London, 1675.

Salmon, William. *The Family Dictionary or Household Companion*. London, 1695 through 1792.

The Lexicographers

Bailey, Nathaniel. *Dictionarium Britannicum: Compleat Universal Etymological English Dictionary*. London, 1730.

———. *An Universal Etymological English Dictionary with Considerable Improvements*. London, 1773.

Chambers, Ephraim. *Cyclopedia or an Universal Dictionary of Arts and Sciences*. London, 1751.

Johnson, Samuel. *A Dictionary of the English Language*. London, 1755.

Middleton, Erasmus (with William Turnbull, Thomas Ellis, John Davison). *The New Complete Dictionary of Arts and Sciences*. London, 1778.

Public Records and Lists

Colonial Laws of Massachusetts, The. Reprinted from the editions of 1672, William H. Whitmore, ed. Boston, 1890.

Colonial Records of Virginia, The. Richmond, 1874.

Documentary History of New York, The. New York, 1850.

Original Lists of Persons of Quality, Emigrants, Religious Exiles, Political Rebels, Serving Men Sold for a Term of Years, Apprentices, etc., Who Went from Great Britain to the American Plantations, 1600–1700, The. Compiled by John Camden Hotten, London, 1874.

Probate Records of Essex County, Massachusetts, The. Salem, 1916–20.

Public Records of the Colony of Connecticut, The. J. Hammond Trumbull and Charles J. Hoadley, eds. Hartford, 1850–90.

Records of the Colony or Jurisdiction of New Haven, The. Charles J. Hoadley, ed. Hartford, 1858.

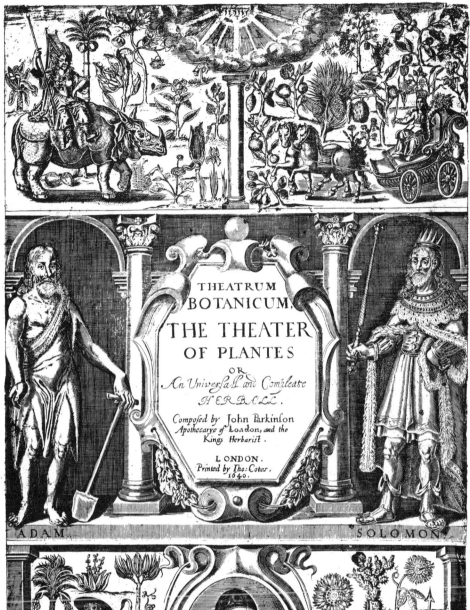

THEATRUM
BOTANICUM.
THE THEATER
OF PLANTES
OR
An Universall and Compleate
HERBALL.

Composed by John Parkinson
Apothecarye of London, and the
Kings Herbarist.

LONDON.
Printed by Tho: Cotes.
1640.

ADAM.
SOLOMON.

W. Marshall sculpsit

Records of the Colony of New Plymouth in New England, The. David Pulsifer, ed. Boston, 1855–61.

Records of the Colony of Rhode Island and Providence Plantation, The. J. R. Bartlett, ed. Providence, 1856–65.

Records and Files of the Quarterly Courts of Essex County, Massachusetts, The. George F. Dow, ed. Salem, 1911–21.

Records of the Governor and Company of Massachusetts Bay in New England, The. Nathaniel B. Shurtleff, ed. Boston, 1853–54.

See also histories by Robert Beverley, William Stith, Thomas Jefferson, and John Smith for lists and laws.

INDEX